SIMON FRASER UNIVERSITY
W.A.C. BENNETT LIBRARY

C8

B 2138 M3 M37 2005

D1603033

Perfection and Disharmony in the Thought of Jean-Jacques Rousseau

In *Perfection and Disharmony in the Thought of Jean-Jacques Rousseau*, Jonathan Marks offers a new interpretation of the philosopher's thought and its place in the contemporary debate between liberals and communitarians. Against prevailing views, Marks argues that Rousseau's thought revolves around the natural perfection of a naturally disharmonious being. At the foundation of Rousseau's thought Marks finds a natural teleology that takes account of and seeks to harmonize conflicting ends. The Rousseau who emerges from this interpretation is a radical critic of liberalism who is nonetheless more cautious about protecting individual freedom than his milder communitarian successors. Marks elaborates on the challenge that Rousseau poses to liberals and communitarians alike by setting up a dialogue between him and Charles Taylor, one of the most distinguished ethical and political theorists at work today.

Jonathan Marks is assistant professor of political science and philosophy at Carthage College. He has contributed to *Polity*, the *American Journal of Political Science*, and *Responsive Community*.

To My Parents, Rebecca and Joseph Marks

Perfection and Disharmony in the Thought of Jean-Jacques Rousseau

JONATHAN MARKS

Carthage College

CAMBRIDGE UNIVERSITY PRESS
Cambridge, New York, Melbourne, Madrid, Cape Town, Singapore, São Paulo

Cambridge University Press
40 West 20th Street, New York, NY 10011-4211, USA

www.cambridge.org
Information on this title: www.cambridge.org/9780521850698

© Jonathan Marks 2005

This book is in copyright. Subject to statutory exception
and to the provisions of relevant collective licensing agreements,
no reproduction of any part may take place without
the written permission of Cambridge University Press.

First published 2005

Printed in the United States of America

A catalog record for this publication is available from the British Library.

Library of Congress Cataloging in Publication Data
Marks, Jonathan, 1969–
Perfection and disharmony in the thought of Jean-Jacques Rousseau /
Jonathan Marks.
p. cm.
ISBN 0-521-85069-x (hardcover)
1. Rousseau, Jean-Jacques, 1712–1778. 2. Philosophical anthropology.
3. Perfection. I. Title.
B2138.M3M37 2005
194–dc22 2004026

ISBN-13 978-0-521-85069-8 hardback
ISBN-10 0-521-85069-x hardback

Cambridge University Press has no responsibility for
the persistence or accuracy of URLs for external or
third-party Internet Web sites referred to in this book
and does not guarantee that any content on such
Web sites is, or will remain, accurate or appropriate.

Contents

v

Acknowledgments

Among my teachers, I am most indebted to the late Allan Bloom for bringing me into the company of books and friends who have pleased and instructed me since. Along with Joseph Cropsey, Ralph Lerner, and Nathan Tarcov, he inspired my interest in political philosophy. Along with Clifford Orwin, he inspired my interest in Rousseau.

It is a pleasure to thank Nathan Tarcov for guiding the graduate study out of which this book eventually emerged. He has been generous with his time and extraordinarily kind. Robert Pippin served on my dissertation committee and made many helpful comments.

From the beginning of this project, I had the great good fortune to get help from one of Rousseau's most insightful and rigorous interpreters. I am grateful to Arthur Melzer for his detailed comments on and encouragement of my work. My book was inspired by his unsurpassed interpretation of Rousseau, *The Natural Goodness of Man: On the System of Rousseau's Thought.*

Since my book is about Rousseau, it is no surprise that one of my anonymous reviewers revealed himself and the other confessed. I thank both reviewers for their thoughtful comments, which I have done my best to address. It was a particular pleasure to learn the identity of one of the reviewers, whose work I have long admired.

I would also like to thank those who have been good enough to comment on different stages and parts of the manuscript, including Ruth Abbey, Aditya Adarkar, Laurence Cooper, Werner Dannhauser, Wendy Gunther-Canada, Leon Kass, Ronald Lee, Dan Magurshak, Roger Masters, Clifford Orwin, Joseph Reisert, Jeffrey Smith, Paul Ulrich, David Williams, Richard Zinman, and Rachel Zuckert. I am especially grateful to two of my friends. Steven Kautz applied his formidable skills as an editor and strategist to the many problems I consulted him about. Christopher Lynch showed great patience and mocked me only a little in discussions that helped clarify the ideas in this book.

Thanks to the editors at Cambridge University Press for taking on and taking good care of this book. My copy editor, Elise M. Oranges, saved me from numerous embarrassments.

Thanks, also, to the Bradley, Earhart, and Olin foundations, and the Symposum on Science, Reason, and Modern Democracy at Michigan State University for supporting my research.

A version of Chapter 1 appeared in "Who Lost Nature? Rousseau and Rousseauism," *Polity* 34:4 (Summer 2002). A version of Chapter 2 appeared in "The Savage Pattern: The Unity of Rousseau's Thought Revisited," *Polity* 31:1 (Fall 1998). I thank the publishers of *Polity* for permission to use material from those articles. Parts of Chapter 4 appeared in "Misreading One's Sources: Charles Taylor's Rousseau," *American Journal of Political Science* 49:1 (January 2005). I thank the publishers of *AJPS* for permission to use material from that article.

My parents, among many other things, took great care and made sacrifices to make sure of my education. This book is dedicated to them.

Because my marriage and dissertation proposals were accepted around the same time, this book has been written under the most fortunate circumstances. I am thankful to my beautiful wife, Anna Marks, whose critical judgment improved this book and whose wit and support made writing it less of a burden. My son, Samuel, was born when much of the book had already been written, but the thought of him as an adult and potential reader made me try to do better.

Introduction

The Natural Perfection of a Naturally Disharmonious Being

The argument of this book is that Jean-Jacques Rousseau's thought is a reflection on the natural perfection of a naturally disharmonious being. The Rousseau who emerges in the pages that follow, though he is anti-liberal, is more moderate than the Rousseaus to whom one has grown accustomed. This Rousseau has more to contribute to contemporary debates and to our understanding of enduring human problems than those other Rousseaus who are too frequently understood, even by friends, as childlike and fanatical. In order to unearth him, however, it is necessary to dig beneath the centuries of interpretation under which he has been buried and to oppose near unanimities of opinion about his understanding of nature and of human happiness or perfection.

Of course, as the footnotes will confirm, I owe a great deal to other interpreters. Although Rousseau's political and philosophical influence, both real and imagined, has caused him to be even more frequently misinterpreted, I think, than most, he has nonetheless drawn the interest of an extraordinary group of interpreters, from, to speak of the fairly recent past, Leo Strauss to Jean Starobinski to Jacques Derrida.[1] Such interpreters, however much their understanding of Rousseau and how to read him may differ, have read his works with rare insight and painstaking attention to detail. While I will deal in this introduction mainly with how my interpretation differs from the ones I know, and consequently emphasize what I think other interpretations have missed, I know full well that some of my predecessors have forgotten more than I know about Rousseau, and that my own attempt is bound to have missed much. I am confident, however, that this book opens up areas of inquiry and proposes

1

answers that, when they have been explored at all, have been too rarely explored by Rousseau's interpreters.

Readers will find detailed remarks on the relationship between my thesis and the existing literature in each chapter. However, a few preliminary remarks are in order. I have said that Rousseau's thought concerns the natural perfection of a naturally disharmonious being. Yet few commentators take seriously the idea that Rousseau is interested in natural perfection at all. Those who think that Rousseau is interested in a kind of perfection point him in Kant's nonnaturalistic direction. The perfection to which human beings are destined is a moral perfection rooted in the spontaneity of the will, or in freedom. Insofar as nature has anything to do with this perfection, it is not because it guides human beings but because it leaves them free to renounce its guidance.[2] Those who take Rousseau to be a naturalist of some kind, whether they understand his conception of nature to be scientific or romantic, find that conception above all in the *Second Discourse*, in which nature appears to exclude not only perfection but the impact of perfectibility, the faculty responsible for taking man beyond the "purely animal functions" with which he begins (*Second Discourse, SD* hereafter, III, 143; I, 18). While human beings may look to the simplicity, unity, or independence of nature as, loosely speaking, a model for their own personal and political lives, the more fundamental meaning of the understanding of nature presented in the *Second Discourse* is that nature has left us to our own devices. However much human beings may flourish once they have left the state of nature, that flourishing cannot be properly called natural. Perhaps it would be better not to speak of flourishing at all, inasmuch as that may imply a natural direction of growth.[3]

The Kantian interpretation of Rousseau's thought, though perhaps the most influential, sacrifices Rousseau's coherence. Ernst Cassirer, the most important of Rousseau's Kantian interpreters, aside from Kant himself, recognizes that neither Rousseau's overwhelming emphasis on happiness nor his conception of reason is consistent with Kant's system. He attributes these inconsistencies to Rousseau's yearnings and to his failure to discover Kant's methodology (Cassirer, 1963, 42, 50–51). I will make the premises of my disagreement with Cassirer clear later, but my conclusion can be given away now: One does not need to dismiss salient aspects of Rousseau's thought to save his coherence. If my interpretation succeeds in showing that Rousseau's thought is coherent on Rousseau's own terms, it will give us good reason to reject Eric Weil's arresting but condescending claim that "it took Kant to think Rousseau's thoughts."[4]

The naturalistic interpretations emphasize the account of nature Rousseau presents in the Preface and First Part of the *Second Discourse* almost to the exclusion of the one he presents in *Emile*. While the *Second Discourse* seems strictly to divide nature from history, so that none of man's historical attainments are natural, *Emile* suggests that certain historical attainments are natural. For example:

> As soon as we have, so to speak, consciousness of our sensations, we are disposed to seek or avoid the objects which produce them, at first according to whether they are pleasant or unpleasant to us, then according to the conformity or lack of it that we find between us and these objects, and finally according to the judgements we make about them on the basis of the idea of happiness or of perfection given us by reason. These dispositions are extended and strengthened as we become more capable of using our senses and more enlightened; but constrained by our habits, they are more or less corrupted by our opinions. Before this corruption they are what I call in us *nature*. (*Emile, E* hereafter, IV, 248; 39)[5]

Now, it is true that having a natural disposition toward something does not mean that attaining it is more natural than not attaining it. All I wish to note here is that *Emile* admits what the *Second Discourse* does not at first seem to admit, that our natural dispositions not only do not exclude historical development but unfold, are extended and strengthened, in history. Indeed, just prior to the passage in question and in other passages in *Emile*, Rousseau compares human development to the growth of plants, which might incline us further, though of course it does not compel us, to think that nature points toward certain outcomes, as we often do when we think of acorns and oak trees. In my view, *Emile* contains good evidence that Rousseau finally does urge us to think in this teleological way.

But again, my claim for now is only that the conception of nature advanced in *Emile* opens up the *possibility* that there is a natural end or perfection for human beings, toward which his constitution, his faculties, and his passions point. The *Second Discourse*, which asserts that human nature is only to be found at the beginning, in original man, prior to the impact of "circumstances and . . . progress" (*SD*, III, 122; Preface, 1), forecloses that possibility – one could say that the whole point of the First Part of the *Second Discourse* is to show that human faculties and passions, such as they are at the beginning, do not point beyond themselves to some idea of happiness or perfection given by reason and consequently do not propel us into a social and civilized life. Some of Rousseau's interpreters have noted this apparent contradiction between *Emile* and the *Second Discourse* and asked which understanding of nature is Rousseau's primary or real understanding. Almost unanimously, they have opted for the conception of nature found in the *Second Discourse*.[6] But this choice is not easy to explain. Rousseau, after all, called *Emile* his "greatest and best book" (*Dialogues, D* hereafter, I, 687; 23).

Some commentators think that the *Second Discourse* contains Rousseau's primary understanding of nature because it seems to be more scientific than *Emile*, and Rousseau, they think, was an exponent of "modern scientific naturalism" (Cooper, 1999, xiv).[7] But, since the *Second Discourse*'s conception of nature is itself the main proof that Rousseau was an exponent of modern scientific naturalism, we cannot use Rousseau's scientific naturalism as a reason to insist on the primacy of the *Second Discourse*. Besides, the *Second Discourse* is not by any means obviously a work of modern natural science. Even if it is anti-teleological like modern physics, there is nothing scientific in Rousseau's time or ours about insisting that the original is the only thing natural. To understand today's human beings as having developed from a primitive predecessor may be a nod in the direction of one of the most important foundations of modern biology – the theory of evolution – but it is hard to imagine anything more contrary to the evolutionary spirit than Rousseau's distinction between nature on the one hand and circumstances and progress, or history, on the other.[8] It is surely a central claim of evolutionism that biological nature is historical through and through.

Indeed, this distinction is not only unscientific but also extremely implausible. Participants in the debate among Rousseau scholars over whether Rousseau intended his depiction of the original state to be scientifically accurate have almost always neglected how ridiculous it is to take a man who by Rousseau's own admission is the product of circumstances and progress and treat him as if he were untouched by circumstances and progress.[9] The distinction between nature as it is described in the Preface of the *Second Discourse* and history breaks down on even a cursory examination.[10] That the conception of nature advanced in the Preface of the *Second Discourse* is incoherent, while it is not a decisive reason for rejecting it as Rousseau's primary understanding of nature, is a pretty good reason. I will offer additional reasons in Chapter 1.

NATURAL DISHARMONY

I have said that Rousseau thinks that human beings are naturally disharmonious beings. But few commentators take seriously the idea that

Rousseau thinks nature itself a source of disharmony.[11] True enough, the modern bourgeois is famously in "contradiction with himself" (*E*, IV, 249; 40), but it is to be expected that the bourgeois is here, as in so many other places, opposed to the natural man, who is above all not in contradiction with himself. Whether the interpreter understands Rousseau's search for unity to be driven essentially by psychological needs, as Jean Starobinski does, or by philosophic considerations, as Arthur Melzer does, or more or less equally by both, as Ernst Cassirer does, he or she tends to understand Rousseau as in search of a lost wholeness that he locates at least at first in nature (Cassirer, 1989, 41, 48–51; Melzer, 1990, 21; Starobinski, 1988, 25–29, 45–47).[12] While estimates of the real importance of nature to Rousseau vary a great deal, the general pattern of natural wholeness–civilized dividedness–restored wholeness pervades the literature devoted to understanding Rousseau's thought even when, as in Cassirer's case, the final objective of the thought turns out to be a kind of freedom.

But if, as I have already suggested, the distinction between nature and history cannot be maintained, then it seems improbable, to say the least, that nature can be cleared of responsibility for the loss of wholeness Rousseau often seems to blame on history. To limit myself to a single portion of a single text and reserve the main argument for Chapter 1, it is obvious as early as the First Part of the *Second Discourse* that at least some kinds of disunity are perfectly natural. That fact is obscured by a passage that occurs toward the beginning of the *Discourse*, which paints an idyllic portrait of the most primitive human beings: "I see him sating his hunger beneath an oak, slaking his thirst at the first Stream, finding his bed at the foot of the same tree that supplied his meal, and with that his needs are satisfied" (*SD*, III, 135; I, 2). The verisimilitude of this portrait is guaranteed only by the assumption of such a natural abundance as to demand no toil, or any adaptation, from human beings. Human beings, in turn, need alter external nature but little for their own advantage. Human nature and external nature are in harmony, so that human beings are not alienated from external nature, let alone their own natures.

But this idyllic portrait is in tension with another, harsher account of the lot of primitive human beings. This account, which follows on the heels of the idyll, is introduced without fanfare: "The Earth, abandoned to its natural fertility and covered by immense forests which no Axe ever mutilated, at every step offers Storage and shelter to the animals of every species" (*SD*, III, 135; I, 3). At first glance, this passage sounds as idyllic as the first, but it reveals that the Earth is not so fertile that it does not require even animals to store up food for later consumption. Nor is it so hospitable that it does not require even animals sometimes to seek shelter. That storage is necessary, incidentally, implies that even animals need foresight or its equivalent. Foresight, however, introduces a potential conflict between present desires (say the desire not to work) and future-oriented desires (say the desire not to starve when nature fails us). The idyll in which human needs are provided for spontaneously, and in which each human being is in harmony with nature and at peace with himself, is immediately exposed as an exaggeration; even animals are not granted so harmonious a relationship to nature. Animals have to work, and human beings "imitate their industry" (Ibid.). Yet the Lockean virtue of industry was hardly needed in the paradise world human beings inhabited but a paragraph ago. It was taken up, presumably without pleasure, by human beings who are said by Rousseau to have a "mortal hatred . . . of sustained work" (*SD*, III, 145; I, 22). Returning to the question of storage, it looks as if human beings are grasshoppers by nature, but external nature, as the fable confirms, compels grasshoppers to be more like ants.

Things get worse. Human beings are altered in body by difficult conditions. They are hardened by bad weather, fatigue, and the need to defend their lives and prey against ferocious animals (*SD*, III, 135; I, 4). These same dangers and nuisances, in addition, frustrate the desires of primitive human beings. Though they like to sleep, for example, the dangers with which they are surrounded compel them to be light sleepers (*SD*, III, 140; I, 13). Rousseau does not add, though one cannot help imagining, that they are often grumpy. They are altered in mind, too. Man must compare himself with the other animals to determine which he should attack and which he should flee: "Savage man, living dispersed amongst the animals and early finding himself in the position of having to measure himself against them, soon makes the comparison" (*SD*, III, 136; I, 6).

This is a remarkable change, though it is not announced as such, for at least two reasons. First, man, Rousseau does not doubt, is naturally frightened of what he does not know (*SD*, III, 136; I, 6). This fear is conquered in him with respect to the other animals only by the ability to make comparisons, which develops in man what Rousseau will later call "mechanical prudence" (*SD*, III, 165; II, 5). A division is introduced in man between a natural and spontaneous passion and an evidently natural but less spontaneous primitive reflection. Second, natural man, in order to compare himself to others, must stand outside of himself for the first time. In order to measure himself, he must look at himself, which requires a part of him to be detached or self-conscious. To this extent, natural man lives outside of himself before he even encounters other human beings, and while this is not as bad as living in the opinion of others, it is not unrelated. Rousseau suggests as much in the Second Part of the *Discourse*, when he admits that when human beings compare themselves to other animals, they begin to experience pride (*SD*, III, 166; II, 6).

I admit, of course, that civilized man in Rousseau's account is more radically divided than natural man. Natural man is, nonetheless, already divided – between present and future, subject and object – from the very beginning. I also think and will show that, for Rousseau, self-consciousness and immediacy, activity and indolence, and solitude and sociality are natural requirements of human happiness that are, at the same time, a source of psychic disharmony. Even in successful attempts to manage this disharmony, the result is not so much a seamlessly unified whole as a life that oscillates between the different goods.[13] While my focus will be on solitude and sociality, since so much of Rousseau's legacy and the questions surrounding it concern individualism and collectivism, I believe I will be able to say enough about the other two oppositions to make this proposition plausible: Rousseau finds the fundamental cause of our disharmony in human nature itself, not in what society or other external forces have done to it.

PERFECTION AND DISHARMONY

If Rousseau's thought is a reflection on the natural perfection of naturally disharmonious beings, what will that perfection look like? Two main approaches to the problem of natural disharmony present themselves: suppress it, or seek to arrange for human flourishing in spite of it. I think that Rousseau takes the second approach and that for him human flourishing requires a difficult and delicate arrangement of conflicting goods.

But commentators have long been struck by Rousseau's presentation of two radically opposed models, the solitary natural man of the *Second Discourse* and of the autobiographical works, and the Spartan or Roman citizen of the *Social Contract* and of other political works. Indeed, this is one of the oldest questions about Rousseau: How can his praise of the asocial and lazy natural man, who lacks self-consciousness, be reconciled with his praise of the utterly socialized and active citizen who, far from lacking self-consciousness, is constrained by a self-made and self-imposed law? Note that what both models seem to have in common is the suppression of disharmony: Human beings are either utterly socialized or utterly asocial, but not both.

Commentators who seek to defend Rousseau's consistency usually do so without mitigating the apparent polar opposition between natural man and citizen in his thought. As I have already noted, natural wholeness–civilized dividedness–restored wholeness is the typical pattern by means of which Rousseau's thought is understood, where at least one form of restored wholeness is to be found in the Spartan or Roman citizen. And so it is easy enough to claim that the apparently opposed models Rousseau praises have in common that they eliminate the tearing contradictions and complications that beset the bourgeois, whose soul is divided between, among other things, his natural inclinations and his civil duties (*E*, IV, 249–50; 40). This understanding of Rousseau, of course, emphatically denies that Rousseau seeks to preserve rather than suppress the oppositions that lead in the direction of bourgeois misery.

However, there is an obvious sense in which, once the unity of natural man's soul comes into question, Rousseau's demand for unity comes into question, too. Rousseau's psychologistic interpreters find themselves in the most difficulty here, for they have generally insisted, to use Michael Sandel's phrase, that Rousseau is "unable to abide disharmony" (1996, 320). If it can be shown that Rousseau understands that the happiness of "original man" himself depends on a fortunate balance between conflicting goods, there will be much less reason to suppose that Rousseau was pathologically attached to unity. More broadly, there will be much less reason to suppose that Rousseau's favored models are those that decisively choose the goods on one side of the conflict between natural man and citizen to the exclusion of the other – those models found at the extreme ends of Rousseau's supposedly bipolar system.

Emphasis on the Spartan and natural man poles has also been encouraged by the other apparent polarity in Rousseau's thought that I have been discussing, between nature and history. The assertion that natural man is radically solitary seems to depend on the assertion that the historical developments that put an end to that solitude are unnatural. But in the framework of the *Second Discourse*, that claim is maintained mainly as a corollary of the broader claim that all historical developments are unnatural.[14] This claim, which amounts to the claim that natural man is, strictly speaking, original man and only original man, exacerbates the tension between nature and society by making it appear that any development in the direction of society, let alone society itself, let alone a society on the order of Sparta or Rome, negates nature. Nature and society, on this account of Rousseau's thought, are like matter and anti-matter – to seek to put them together is to destroy both. That is likely, it seems to me, one reason that commentators have so often homed in on the Spartan, who is, as much as possible, all society, and the natural man, who is, as much as possible, all nature. The numerous states Rousseau praises between these two possibilities have received less attention because it is difficult to account for these hybrids in terms of the presumed and connected bipolarities of Rousseau's thought.[15]

Certainly, some explanation is needed for the relative neglect on the part of Rousseau's interpreters of one of Rousseau's most striking statements. In the *Second Discourse*, Rousseau praises what I will call the savage nation as "best for man" (*SD*, III, 171; II, 18). The savage nation succeeds the stage in which human beings first form settled families; in this new stage, human beings form troops and finally nations united by a common way of life and by its requirements and consequences. What is striking about the savage in the savage nation is that he, like the unfortunate bourgeois, is "in between."[16] Savages in the savage nation are between laziness and activity and between solitude and sociality, among other things.[17] Rousseau's high praise of this state, the highest praise he gives any historical state, suggests that disharmony is not only a feature of our nature understood as it is in the First Part of the *Second Discourse*, but also a feature of our nature understood as an end or perfection. The savage is not torn apart by the presence of conflicting goods in his life, but such goods, being present, must be arranged by fortune or art so as not to tear him apart. If, as I think I can show, this pattern of savage life is replicated in Rousseau's other and more constructive (as opposed to critical) works, we will have further reason to believe that Rousseau's understanding of human perfection allows and even requires the presence of goods that threaten to destroy each other. The savage is not Rousseau's dream of unity to counter the nightmare of bourgeois disunity, but rather a model that captures Rousseau's perfectly realistic understanding that a disunity natural to human beings should be artfully managed, not suppressed, for the sake of human flourishing.

ROUSSEAU'S LEGACY

Rousseau is often read as one of the great extremists in the history of political thought. So radical is Rousseau that he is at least two extremists in one. The two extremists in question are connected with the natural man and the Spartan that Rousseau praises. The Rousseau who praises natural man is a radical individualist who goes so far as to see even speech and reason, once thought to mark out humanity, as agents of the deformation by society of naturally asocial man. This Rousseau is implicated in the most irresponsible romanticism, a childish but dangerous refusal to meet the most reasonable demands of civilized life. The Rousseau who praises the Spartan is a radical communalist or collectivist. This Rousseau argues that human beings are nothing but dumb, amoral brutes outside of society and that our humanity is ultimately salvaged only by means of the complete transformation of naturally independent individuals into parts of a communal whole, into human beings who are nothing without all the others. He is implicated in totalitarianism, however democratic.

Although these Rousseaus have been decried over and over again, almost no one denies that Rousseau also stands at the beginning of a more or less respectable tradition of individualistic criticisms of classical liberalism, the liberalism of Locke and Montesquieu.[18] Classical liberalism, at best, provides liberty understood as the absence of restraint without providing the autonomy sought after by Rawlsian liberals or the authenticity sought after by romantic individualists. More broadly, even those who complain of Rousseau's extremism are by and large willing to acknowledge that he drew our attention to the way in which dependence on others, not only political but also economic and psychological, may leave us unfree and dissatisfied, and that this concern is not by itself the concern of an extremist.

At the same time, Rousseau stands at the beginning of an equally respectable and sometimes closely related tradition of communitarian criticisms of classical liberalism. Communitarian thinkers like Charles Taylor and Michael Sandel, whatever their difficulties with Rousseau, are willing to concede that he helped initiate, or was at least among the first to articulate, modern concern with the psychological, social, and political consequences of modern individualism. Liberal modernity, which purports to unite human beings through rational self-interest, actually leaves them lonely, favors relationships of hypocrisy and exploitation, and turns them away from politics.

Steven Kautz has observed that, whatever the nominal separation between these two traditions of criticism, both exert a pull on the modern heart, so that Rousseau can be said to stand at the beginning of a single bipolar tradition:

Rousseau stands at the beginning of an enduring tradition of thought whose aim is to restore the "respectable extremes" – natural privacy and moral community – that have been destroyed by the rise of the bourgeois. Such thinkers (and artists, and sometimes even politicians) seek to radicalize our love of privacy or our love of community, in Rousseau's spirit if not always in his manner. (Kautz, 1997, 254)

Kautz suggests that Rousseau has had some influence on the bourgeois whom he criticized. But the unintended effect is that the division of the bourgeois has deepened. For the bourgeois Rousseau knew, though he was torn between self and society, had not had the benefit of Rousseau's teaching and the teachings of his successors to refine and exacerbate his crisis. The bourgeois Rousseau knew did not yet despise the bourgeois.

I am far from denying that Rousseau drew attention to "respectable extremes." But this understanding of Rousseau's influence, of course, goes along with one of the accounts of Rousseau I wish to criticize, one according to which he is a bipolar thinker who prefers the extremes to the middle. I understand Rousseau to be engaged not only in recovering the alternatives of natural man and citizen but also in the attempt to describe and perpetuate ways of life in which elements of both alternatives are present. Consequently, while I agree that Rousseau has helped to radicalize the split between the demands of the individual and the demands of the community, I also think that he has much to say, not all of it discouraging, to those who concentrate on liberalism's defects with respect to individualism and with respect to community equally. Many contemporary communitarians, for whom community is in part a means to "thicker" individuality, are in this camp but fail to notice that Rousseau is, too. As they congratulate themselves on finding a middle ground that Rousseau missed, they neglect the challenges he poses to them from, of all things, a moderate's perspective. Of course, I do not wish to make the implausible claim that Rousseau was a moderate. He was a radical. But there are respects in which he was more moderate than his seemingly moderate successors.[19]

It is perhaps an understatement to say that Rousseau seems to be two extremists in one, since he is often implicated in a third kind of extremism. Here is Kautz again on one source of what he calls the "prevailing moral extremism":

> Rousseau was among the first to teach that human beings are by nature homeless; that nature teaches very few moral lessons; that the human being is almost infinitely malleable . . . ; that the history of the human species . . . so distances us from our original natures that it is hard to see any longer what guidance our speculations about nature or human nature can provide for our various pursuits of happiness. (Kautz, 1997, 267)

On this reading, Rousseau returned to nature only to destroy it, since original man is so like an animal that he offers no moral guidance to human beings. Rousseau empties nature of normative content and, intentionally or unintentionally, becomes the first anti-foundationalist or anti-essentialist. He can thus be tied to the extremisms that at least sometimes follow from those attitudes.[20] Indeed, some friends and some enemies of postmodernism regard Rousseau as at least a distant source of it.

But this understanding of Rousseau's legacy, as Kautz's reference to original natures makes clear, derives from an account of Rousseau's thought I wish to criticize, one according to which Rousseau's primary understanding of nature is to be found in the First Part of the *Second Discourse*, instantiated in original man. If the primary understanding of nature is instead to be found in *Emile*, instantiated in that book's eponymous hero, then Rousseau is no friend of anti-essentialism or anti-foundationalism, for *Emile*'s understanding of nature leaves its normative content intact. In this sense, Rousseau can be turned against the Rousseauian tendencies he is said to have inspired.

PLAN OF THE BOOK

I open with the question of nature in Rousseau's thought. Chapter 1 shows that Rousseau conceives of natural man not as the first man, or even as the man whose native endowments are left free to develop without interference, but as the *perfected* man. Commentators have been misled by Rousseau's physiodicy, or justification of nature, which depends upon the equation of the natural with the prehistoric or original. This equation allows Rousseau to declare nature innocent of the ills human beings suffer in society and of the causes that drive us into societies in the first place. But Rousseau undermines it, even in the *Second Discourse*, in which it is initially proposed. Rousseau, as *Emile* suggests, ultimately conceives of nature not as a prehistoric beginning but as an end or perfection. With this in mind, one can begin to reconsider Rousseau's legacy, since some of the most important political consequences for which his thought is usually credited or blamed rest on his justification and understanding of nature. In particular, Rousseau did not, as some commentators suppose, return to nature only to slay it and liberate man's creative powers.

In Chapter 2, I defend my claim that Rousseau views human perfection not as a natural or imposed unity but as a delicate arrangement of disharmonious elements. This chapter introduces the "savage pattern" of "independent commerce," which falls between the asociality of original man and the apparently complete socialization of citizens. I show that Rousseau seeks to replicate this pattern in his constructive projects, even in the works that are usually cited to prove his extreme collectivism. I also consider, briefly, other examples of Rousseau proposing to balance or arrange conflicting but good tendencies in human nature, rather than choosing one side or the other of the conflict.

The first two chapters play down some of the most striking features of Rousseau's thought, even the thesis of the natural goodness of man as that thesis is usually understood. I must therefore face the problem: Why does my interpretation elevate some things that Rousseau says over others that I also concede he says? Of course, all interpretations face this problem to one degree or another. I take it up in Chapter 3, on the rhetorical considerations that lead Rousseau to exaggerate nature's innocence and to make it appear, at times, as if there is no middle ground between being a human being and being a citizen. Let me emphasize, even here, that my interpretation does not depend on asserting that Rousseau secretly means just the opposite of what he says – there is direct and plentiful textual evidence to back up the assertions I make about Rousseau's thought. Nonetheless, interpretations that contradict mine rely on direct textual evidence as well, and so the interpreter who does not take Rousseau to be mixed up must explain why evidence for such different interpretations can be found in his works. Chapter 3 attempts such an explanation, at least with respect to the specific issues my interpretation raises.

My fourth and last chapter considers Rousseau's legacy by directly comparing him to a single but singularly important contemporary communitarian thinker, Charles Taylor. Taylor offers a not unsympathetic reading of Rousseau as a forerunner of the recent emphasis on authenticity and recognition in today's politics. But like many contemporary defenders of community, he takes Rousseau, for all the important things he had to say in favor of the individual, to have ultimately settled on a kind of tyranny. Consequently, he does not notice that his own project of reconciling authenticity and community, which seeks a middle ground between man and citizen, is closely related to Rousseau's project and can be profitably compared to it. Such a comparison, I argue, reveals that Rousseau, for all his supposed totalitarian tendencies, leaves the individual a good deal less dependent on the community and limits the community's power a good deal more strictly than Taylor does. Although it would be foolish to deny that Rousseau's preferred political outcome is, practically speaking, farther from liberalism than Taylor's, it would be a mistake not to notice that Rousseau's political philosophy provides points of resistance to a community's demands that Taylor's political philosophy ultimately does not. Moreover, insofar as Rousseau considers the individual to be dependent on the community, he notices aspects of that dependence that Taylor misses or at least chooses to leave out; specifically, he acknowledges as Taylor does not the extent to which even relatively good and well-educated people remain dependent on prejudices; the cultural critic ignores this observation not so much to the critic's peril as to the peril of those to whom the critic ministers.

It is worth noting that the argument of the chapter proceeds, in part, by criticizing Taylor's reading of Rousseau. That is part and parcel of the approach of this book, which assumes that it is worthwhile to get Rousseau right. But that approach is questionable and is especially questionable when applied to Charles Taylor, whose aim of diagnosing our culture's ills depends on understanding the forces a thinker and his followers helped set in motion, not on understanding what the thinker meant or intended (Taylor, 1989, 536n.2). On the other hand, Taylor does think the exercise of retrieving the philosophic past is worthwhile insofar as it enables us to get beyond recent attacks on and defenses of modern life, which share a narrow understanding of what modernity is, and to overcome the "cramped formulations of mainstream philosophy" (Ibid., x–xi, 107). The study of the history of ideas is, for Taylor, at least one means of becoming acquainted with richer sources of argument and inspiration than the ones we know. This book is animated by the conviction that we have more of philosophical interest to learn from the study of Rousseau's works than we do from a study of the assorted "mentalities" to which he may or may not have contributed. Taylor himself thinks that Rousseau did no more than articulate "something that was already happening in the culture" (1991, 27). While I do not in the space of this book seek to defend my conviction of Rousseau's originality, I do, in Chapter 4, aim to show that a careful reading of Rousseau that separates him from the broad cultural movements of which his work becomes a part reveals important observations and arguments that merit consideration and might otherwise be missed.

1

Natural Perfection

This chapter takes up Rousseau's justification of nature, as it is widely understood. That justification entails an account of nature so implausible and even strange that it is hard to believe anyone, let alone one of the most influential political philosophers of all time, would seriously advance it. I argue that Rousseau did not seriously advance it. Yet some of the most profound political consequences for which his thought is credited or blamed rest on this very account, according to which human nature and human origins are one and the same.

In the first part of this chapter, I survey some of the prevailing understandings of Rousseau's theodicy.[1] This point of departure is suspect, since justifying nature and justifying God are different undertakings. But it is warranted because these undertakings often overlap in Rousseau's thought and almost always in commentaries on it. The great innovation of Rousseau's theodicy, as it has come to be understood, is to make society the only villain in the story of man's corruption. Nature and God are thereby freed of responsibility for our ills. I follow other commentators in supposing that this innovation has important political consequences. But it depends on a radical distinction between nature and society, and ultimately between nature and history or circumstances. In the second part, I prove that the *Second Discourse* undermines this dubious distinction, although it initially proposes it. That work's "original" man is already the outcome of a certain history. The provisional distinction between nature and history fails because natural man is already historical. In the third part, I look to *Emile* to show that Rousseau conceives nature as not a beginning but an end or perfection; there is a teleological element in his conception of nature.[2] Since the political conseq⌐ ⌐ces of Rousseau's physiodicy, as it is usually understood, spring f⌐m the depreciation of nature that occurs when it is equated with p⌐ original, my argument that Rousseau did not intend such an equa⌐n and depreciation implies that he did not intend such conseque⌐es either. In the conclusion, I argue that Rousseau can be turned a⌐ainst the excesses of Rousseauism.

ROUSSEAU'S THEODICY AND ITS PRESUMED CONSEQUENCES

The Distinction Between Nature and Society

Commentators who agree on little else agree that Rousseau anticipated and perhaps even invented our understanding of the salient source of evil. Rousseau was the first to blame evil not on our conflicted nature or on God but on human inventions, above all society. He advanced the "great principle that nature made man happy and good, but that society depraves him and makes him miserable" (*D*, I, 934; 213). Ernst Cassirer describes the apparent consequences of Rousseau's great principle:

> God is condoned and guilt for all evil is attributed to man.... Rousseau's ethical theory places responsibility where it had never been looked for.... Its historical significance lies in the fact that it creates a new subject of "imputability." This subject is ... society. (1979, 157)[3]

Arthur Melzer, who opposes Cassirer in most matters, agrees that, according to Rousseau's argument, "man's present evil derives wholly from ... society" (1990, 17). Rousseau exculpates God and nature by showing that our most significant ills come from society and its offshoots, the sciences and arts; material, psychological, and political dependence; and a crowd of related causes.

Melzer and Cassirer agree, too, that Rousseau's theodicy offers a radical hope. When we blame original sin or a flawed nature for evil, it seems ineradicable. When we blame it instead on our own artifice or on society, there is hope that by a new application of human creativity or by a transformation of society, evil can be wholly eradicated. Rousseau's theodicy, Melzer says, is "a revolutionary simplification of the human problem" into "a merely social or historical issue where before it had been a natural or divine one"; it raises "energetic but dangerous new hopes that through political action, one might transform the human condition" (Ibid., 84,

82). And here is Cassirer on the heroic task to which Rousseau's theodicy urges human beings:

Man must...become his own savior and, in the ethical sense, his own creator. In its present form, society has inflicted the greatest wounds on humanity; but society alone can and should heal those wounds. (1989, 76; cf. 1979, 158)

At first, nature itself, as Rousseau describes it, seems to support this hope. For Hobbes and Locke, it had been a negative standard; describing the state of nature clarified the problems, such as bellicosity, scarcity, and inflamed passions, that civil society solved. But Rousseau, by showing that these problems are not natural but social, rehabilitates nature as a positive standard, a condition of unity, harmony, and peace that, if it can be recovered, promises an end to alienation, anxiety, and oppression. John Scott gives this description of the consequences of Rousseau's theodicy:

The core of Rousseau's theodicy is the conception that we are by nature physical beings embedded unproblematically in the physical whole of nature. By nature, we are good, or ordered, beings in a good, or ordered, whole. Rousseau's portrait of our original position as good beings in a good natural whole serves (especially in contrast with Hobbes and Locke) as a positive formal model to enable us to remake our corrupted existence. (1992, 697)

Leo Strauss, who, as we will see, also draws attention to a contrary tendency in Rousseau's thought, observes that "the state of nature tended to become for Rousseau a positive standard," so that the "good life consists in the closest approximation to the state of nature . . . possible on the level of humanity" (1953, 282).[4] Alongside the hope that we can remake society to rid ourselves of evil is the hope that nature, in its goodness, will help us. Rousseau's epigraph to *Emile*, from Seneca's "On Anger," captures both of the high hopes inspired by Rousseau's theodicy: "We are sick with evils that can be cured; and nature, having brought us forth sound, itself helps us if we wish to be improved" (*E*, IV, 239; 31).

But nature's innocence may require its emptiness. Rousseau's physiodicy depends on the distinction between nature, on the one hand, and artifice and society on the other. Hobbes's error, Rousseau argues, was to read into human nature characteristics that human beings acquire only in society, including not only pride and love of power but also reason and language. But in the process of stripping human beings of the social acquisitions that make them inhumane, Rousseau cannot avoid also stripping away reason and language, which make them human. To teach that human beings naturally lack reason and language is, Strauss argues, to teach that nature provides no support for our humanity, or that "there is no natural constitution of man to speak of." The distinction between nature and society empties nature of substance, so that it becomes "absurd to go back to the state of nature in order to find the norm for man." Strauss suggests that Rousseau, who wishes to be a champion of nature, finally slays it for the sake of freedom:

Rousseau could not have maintained the notion of the state of nature if the depreciation or ex-inanition of the state of nature which he unintentionally effected had not been outweighed in his thought by a corresponding increase in the importance of independence or freedom.

If nature remains a standard at all in Rousseau, it is indistinguishable from a call for radical independence or a call to abandon all standards.

The very indefiniteness of the state of nature as a goal of human aspiration made that state the ideal vehicle of freedom. To have a reservation against society in the name of the state of nature means to have a reservation against society without being either compelled or able to indicate the way of life or the pursuit for the sake of which the reservation is made. The notion of a return to the state of nature on the level of humanity was the ideal basis for claiming a freedom from society which is not a freedom for something. (Strauss, 1953, 271, 274, 278, 294)[5]

Because, as we have seen, there is hope in supposing that our freedom to remake ourselves has no bounds, it is possible to greet the emptying out of nature with some cheer. Tracy Strong agrees with Strauss, Cassirer, and Melzer that Rousseau's understanding of nature depends on distinguishing it from society: "Nature is not even developmentally related to civil society." He agrees, too, that the stripping away of our acquired characteristics has the effect of emptying nature out. For Strong, the burden of the argument of the *Second Discourse* is that "in nature, humans are nothing"; "a human being has no natural qualities" (1994, 45, 140, 158). But far from being a cause for alarm, Rousseau's insight opens us to the experience of the "common" or "the human." The traditional pursuit of "a common core of human nature" is an obstacle to that experience. It is always, in effect, a means of making something out of others, instead of acknowledging them or "letting them be." Because "the world is always more than we can make of it," what purports to be a definition of nature is invariably "a form of domination." To empty out nature is not so much to leave us with nothing as to liberate us to pursue or at least to imagine multiple possibilities; it is to help us to accept "[our] own and others' multiplicity" and to "resist the temptation to define" (Ibid., 34, 28, 143).

To assume, on the other hand, that "our endowments have transcendental qualities" is both to fail to recognize ourselves and to impose our will on others. The "beginning of sin is the insistence that what one is, is privileged. What is unnatural is to claim that one is naturally any one thing" (Ibid., 140). The emptying out of nature, far from threatening to make us subhuman, is the very condition of our humanity.

Cassirer also welcomes nature's demise in Rousseau's thought. He admits that Rousseau's minimalist understanding of nature and his "thoroughly harsh and unsentimental" portrait of natural man lead him to "renounc[e] the guidance of nature." But the insight that "the specific gift that distinguishes man from all other natural beings is perfectibility" or that human nature is uniquely undetermined opens Rousseau to the radical possibility that man can "[devise] for himself a new form of existence that is his own" (Cassirer, 1989, 103, 105).[6] Cassirer, however, argues that Rousseau abandons nature in favor of not radical independence or multiplicity but moral freedom, the subjection of the will to ethical self-legislation. That is, Rousseau abandons nature for the sake of freedom understood as Kant would later understand it.

It is true that both Cassirer and Strong sometimes invoke nature. But Cassirer transforms nature's meaning so that it is no longer distinct from moral freedom and the capacity for man "to devise a new form of existence that is his own" (Cassirer, 1989, 105).[7] As for Strong, he uses nature to mean at least two things, both being not only consistent with but also dependent on the emptying out of nature I have described. Nature's first meaning is instantiated in the natural or original man of the *Second Discourse*, in which human nature is what remains when human beings are stripped of their historical acquisitions. On this understanding of nature, as we have already observed, "a human being has no natural qualities." Nature's second meaning is instantiated in the citizen of the *Social Contract*. This nature is something not given but achieved and emerges when "human beings find themselves in others and others in themselves." Human beings achieve their nature in this second sense when they "acknowledge that they are not anything" or that those substantive characteristics they may be tempted to call their essence are merely accidental. Only in this way can human beings acknowledge the "manner in which another is exactly the same as I am" and avoid making something of or dominating others (Strong, 1994, 122–23, 158, 141). Paradoxically,

if the human in nature is negativity, then the idea of human nature only makes positive sense in terms of the accomplishment of a complete denaturation and the translation of the negativities of the human into an actualized essence.... The problem for Rousseau, one might say, was to retain the original nothingness as an interior quality of the human itself. (Ibid., 47)

Though Cassirer and Strong both refer to the end of Rousseau's project as achieving nature, neither leaves any doubt that Rousseau's accomplishment was to understand more fully than Hobbes or Locke had that human nature is uniquely undetermined and that remedying human ills depends on our taking advantage of the capacity to remake ourselves. That remaking requires us to abandon the search for a natural "common core."

Rousseau justifies nature and God only by making them irrelevant to human beings. If we doubt the capacity of Strong's left-Nietzscheanism or Cassirer's neo-Kantianism to make freedom or perfectibility itself our guide, then despair must be regarded as one of Rousseau's legacies. Cassirer himself grants that if freedom itself did not provide a rule to human beings, their liberation would be cause for regret. When man renounces the guidance of nature, he "sees himself exiled to an unending road and abandoned to all perils" (Cassirer, 1989, 105). If Rousseau removes all content from nature, thereby making it incapable of guiding civilized human beings, then he opens us up not only to radical hope for what we can accomplish with our unique freedom but also to radical despair because we know neither how to use our freedom nor how to dissuade others from using theirs cruelly or destructively. We are left to mourn the loss of the consoling myth of nature and prevented from contemplating and acting on frightening extremes only by our arbitrary choice, our timidity, or the sense that extreme actions are no more meaningful or satisfying than inaction. Melzer, Strauss, and Strong all see in Rousseau Nietzsche's precursor (Melzer, 1990, 288; Strauss, 1953, 252–53; Strong, 1994, 92, 143, 149). If it is true that Rousseau returned to nature only to murder it, then he bears no small responsibility for ushering in the sense of liberation, danger, and hopelessness that Nietzsche's poetry captures and that our condition continues to inspire.

The Distinction Between Nature and History

Rousseau's physiodicy is not only worrisome because of its consequences but also strange because of its premise, which seems, at first, to be the distinction between nature and society but reveals itself as the distinction between nature and circumstances or history. It is strange and frustrating that Rousseau, of all thinkers, appears to exculpate nature for human ills by blaming society, for he is more attentive than any of his predecessors to "the fortuitous concatenation of several foreign causes" that brings human beings out of a primitive condition of goodness and into society. He emphasizes the "various chance occurrences that . . . from so remote a beginning finally bring man and the world to the point where we now find them" (*SD*, III, 162; I, 51) It is one of Rousseau's striking departures from Hobbes and Locke to put between man's natural state and society, both civil and precivil, a long series of accidents and multitudes of centuries – a history.[8] It is he, too, who strongly suggests that society could not have been wholly the product of human will by making natural man too stupid and brutish to engineer his own departure from the original state of nature. It is in his thought, above all, that blaming society begs the question of physiodicy by inviting the question of who or what is responsible for the long history that precedes society and renders it necessary. If nature is to be freed of responsibility for society, it must also be freed of responsibility for history.

Melzer, Cassirer, and Strong all acknowledge this aspect of Rousseau's thought. Strong observes that reading in nature, for Rousseau, means stripping "away from humans all that the passage of time has done to them so as to ask *what their being would be without time*" (1994, 40). As for Melzer and Cassirer, we should notice an ambiguity in their claim that Rousseau's great innovation was to blame human ills on society, not on nature or God. In a passage I have already quoted, Cassirer observes that in Rousseau's thought, "God is condoned and guilt for all evil is attributed to man" and goes on to argue that Rousseau blames evil on society. But in the same paragraph, almost immediately prior to the lines in question, Cassirer makes a slightly different argument:

Whereas Pascal had explained the insoluble contradictions of human nature by asserting that . . . man has a twofold nature, Rousseau . . . finds this conflict *in the midst of empirical existence and development*. This development has indeed *compelled* man to adopt a compulsory form of society, thus exposing him to moral evils. (1979, 156–57; emphasis added)

Between man's beginning and his entrance into society is a pre-social "empirical existence and development" that "compels" him to become social. If so, one must, in order to exonerate nature, distinguish not only between nature and society but also between nature and "empirical existence and development," or history. Similarly, Melzer, in a passage I have also already quoted, claims that Rousseau blames evil on "social *or* historical causes" (1990, 82; emphasis added). Elsewhere, he writes of "historical, social, or environmental causes" (Ibid., 17). He, too, implies that Rousseau's physiodicy must distinguish not only between nature and society but also between nature and history, and even "environment." Neither Cassirer nor Melzer considers the implications of this proposition. But the distinction between nature and history, or empirical existence and development, or man's environment, seems still more radical and debatable than the already radical and debatable distinction between nature and society. In order to decide whether Rousseau's thought implies the different but related consequences that Melzer, Strauss, Cassirer, and Strong think it does, one must decide whether Rousseau makes the distinction in question between nature and history.

NATURE AND HISTORY IN THE *SECOND DISCOURSE*

No one of Rousseau's works inclines us to think man's original state his natural state more than the *Second Discourse.* If the distinction between nature and history is a crucial premise of Rousseau's praise of nature, it is the crucial precondition of the very discovery of nature in the *Second Discourse.* The origin of inequality among men cannot be pinpointed without knowing natural man, and knowing natural man means knowing his beginnings. The study of human nature is the "study of original man" (*SD*, III, 126; Preface, 11):

How will man ever succeed in seeing himself *as Nature formed him,* through all the changes which the *succession of times and of things* must have wrought in his *original constitution,* and in disentangling *what he owes to his own stock* from what *circumstances and his progress* have added to or changed in his primitive state? (*SD*, III, 122; Preface, 1; emphasis added)[9]

Nature and circumstances, or nature and history, could not be much more sharply distinguished than this; man's career in history is different from, and even obscures and warps, his nature.

True, Rousseau emphasizes in the very next sentence changes that have occurred "in the lap of society" (Ibid.). Perhaps not all history but only social history degrades and conceals human nature. If so, we have misinterpreted Rousseau in suggesting that he means by original man more than the solitary primitive who is free of the passions, needs, and capacities that his miserable descendants will owe to society. First, however, Rousseau seems to include the "acquisition of a mass of knowledge and errors" and the "changes that have taken place in the Constitution of bodies" (Ibid.) among the alterations that have occurred in society, though significant developments in both areas occur prior to the advent of society (see, e.g., *SD*, III, 134, 165–66; I, 1, II, 5–8). Second, and more importantly, Rousseau reckons such physical, not social, circumstances as climate, air, and food among the causes of the variations within the human species that distinguish almost all existing human specimens from men in the "primitive state of Nature" (SD, III, 208; note x, 1). Physical and not social causes first alter human beings and draw them out of the original state. Accordingly, Rousseau opposes the builds and features worked into men by the "influence of the *Climate*" to the "*natural* constitution and complexion" (Ibid., emphasis added) of a population. Third and most important is what I am about to argue: According to Rousseau, man departs from the original state because he meets with and must overcome physical and animal rather than social obstacles to his survival and well-being in that state.

The division of the body of the *Second Discourse* into two parts reflects Rousseau's apparent distinction between nature and circumstances. Consider this statement near the beginning of the Second Part:

Such was the condition of nascent man ... but difficulties soon presented themselves ... the height of Trees which prevented him from reaching their fruits, competition from the animals. (*SD*, III, 165; II, 3)

The First Part, then, describes a natural man free not only of those characteristics that will much later be generated in him by society but also of those characteristics that will very soon be generated in him by his immediate surroundings. The Second Part narrates human history, the journey from the natural state to civilization, the first step of which coincides with the first impact of the environment on man's original constitution. Natural man is the man who has not yet taken that first step. The natural and the original, then, seem to be strictly equated, which is also to say that nature and history are strictly separated.

Objections to the Distinction Between Nature and History: First Indications[10]

The *Second Discourse* itself reveals that, whatever its role in Rousseau's physiodicy, the distinction between nature and circumstances or history has certain troubling consequences. One is already implicit in an assertion of the natural equality of men early in that work:

Men . . . , by common consent, are *naturally* as equal among themselves as were the animals of every species before various Physical causes introduced in some species the varieties which we observe among them. (*SD*, III, 123; Preface, 3; emphasis added)

Rousseau uses this observation to suggest that even the earliest noticeable differences among human beings are not natural but the result of external causes.[11] However, if we do not attribute to nature the differences among men produced by external causes acting on man's original constitution, we cannot attribute to it the differences among beasts produced by these same causes. Differentiation within a species, the formation of a variety, cannot be called natural, whether it is the separation of human beings into races or the separation of Galapagos turtles into the distinct varieties that inhabit different islands. Strictly physical differences, differences in size and coloration, which result from, among other things, the expansion of a species into new locales and environments, cannot be called natural. In short, what even Rousseau calls natural history (*SD*, III, 149, 214; I, 29, note x, 11) should not, strictly speaking, be called natural. While this conclusion does not simply reduce Rousseau's argument to absurdity, it is deeply counterintuitive and narrows nature's scope dramatically.

It is worth noting, too, that when Rousseau denies nature responsibility for variation within a species, he also denies it credit for certain advances. As physical causes altered different individuals in different ways and at different paces, "some were perfected or deteriorated and acquired various good or bad qualities *which were not inherent in their Nature*." The rest "remained in their *original state* for a longer time" (*SD*, III, 123; Preface, 3; emphasis added). Since it is a question of animals in this passage, "perfected" must mean something on the order of "best-suited to live and reproduce." Rousseau's apparent equation of the original and the natural implies that such perfection, when occasioned by physical causes, is not natural, that indeed a species is removed from its original state when it is so perfected. It does not take a full-blown evolutionist to balk at this conclusion. In fact, anyone should balk who thinks, as Rousseau himself does, that nature works like the law of Sparta by eliminating the less fit and, over time, rendering the species more fit (*SD*, III, 135; I, 4).

These doubts about variation among animals apply equally to human beings, for the distinction between nature and circumstances suggests that the natural man depicted in the First Part is not natural at all. This so-called original man is the product of the interaction between a being still more primitive than he and its environment. Rousseau grants that natural man may have developed from a more brutish animal predecessor, even as he rules such a creature out of his own study:

> However important it may be, in order to judge soundly regarding Man's natural state, to consider him from his origin . . . I shall not pause to search in the animal System what he may have been at the beginning if he was eventually to become what he now is. (*SD*, III, 134; I, 1)

Although he refutes, in note iii, certain arguments that man is naturally quadrupedal,[12] so denying, tentatively, one course of development for man, Rousseau writes of "the changes that *must* have occurred in man's . . . conformation . . . as he put his limbs to new uses and took up new foods" (Ibid.; emphasis added).[13] Even if one course of development did not occur, another surely did. Original man is not original; his body, at least, has already been altered by his encounter with the external world. If so, and if the natural and historical are strictly distinguished, the man with whom Rousseau begins cannot really be said to be natural man. And inasmuch as Rousseau acknowledges that variation can either perfect or corrupt, we cannot be sure that nature deserves credit or blame for any of the qualities Rousseau attributes to his "original" man.

One may think this objection easily dispatched. Rousseau puts aside the question of original man's predecessors because they differ from him only physically. That is, he puts them aside because knowing them is unimportant for human happiness. It suffices to say for now that such reasoning presupposes that the question of human happiness can be addressed without addressing the changes the human body has undergone and may yet undergo over time. That presupposition, whatever its basis may be, precedes and sets limits to the study of original man, which, rather than determining what human happiness is, is instead circumscribed and indeed distorted by some external standard of what does or does not count for human happiness. If so, however, the original, or the natural conceived as such, is not very, if at all, important. Either, then, nature is the original but its study has little or no bearing on human happiness, or it is not and must be reconceived, so that its study does bear on human happiness. However that may be, there is certainly a tension between Rousseau's distinction between nature and history and his depiction of a natural, "original" man who is a product of history.

The strangeness and implausibility of Rousseau's position can hardly be overstated. That position combines evolutionism[14] and primitivism. Evolutionism, by itself, does not necessarily force a rupture between nature and history. Buffon, for example, allows quite as much variation within species as Rousseau does without denying that nature causes it; "These changes are made slowly and imperceptibly. *Nature's great workman is Time*" (Buffon, *Histoire Naturelle*, Supplement, Vol. 5, 1778, 27. Quoted in Lovejoy, 1959, 104; emphasis added). But in Rousseau, evolutionism is added to primitivism, where primitivism is not a mere preference, on moral grounds, for what comes earlier, but the insistence that what comes earliest is the only thing natural. Rousseau treats primitivism not only as an ethical principle but almost as an ontology, and it is this odd understanding that leads him to deny natural status to all historical developments. Evolutionism, by implying that most biological phenomena are also historical phenomena, exacerbates but does not by itself create the difficulties brought on in the first instance by Rousseau's distinction between nature and history.

Objections to the Distinction Between Nature and History: Rousseau's Indications

Perhaps Rousseau was blinded to these difficulties by a desire to justify nature and God. We can forgo making much of the fact that Rousseau exposes them by making an unusual and apparently unnecessary analogy between human and animal variation. We would also have to set aside Rousseau's clear indication at the beginning of the First Part that original man emerges from the animal kingdom and is consequently himself a product of history. Even so, it hardly seems likely that Rousseau himself thought that nature and history could be strictly separated. For he posts clearer signs than those we have already seen that the man of the First Part, who is presented as natural man, has advanced a number of steps beyond man's original condition.

First, natural man's remarkable strength and agility issue from the impact of the environment on and over multiple generations of human beings:

Accustomed from childhood to the inclemencies of the weather and the rigor of the seasons, hardened to fatigue . . . men develop a robust and almost unalterable temperament; the Children, *since they come into the world with their Fathers' excellent constitution* and strengthen it by the same activities that produced it, acquire *all the vigor of which the human species is capable*. (*SD*, III, 135; I, 4; emphasis added)

The natural man Rousseau praises does not have man's original physical constitution. Physically, he has been not only developed but also perfected by external pressures. One of the characteristics Rousseau praises in natural man, then, is a product of history, rather than of nature.

Second, natural man survives not by means of his own instincts but by means of those he has acquired from other animals:

Men, dispersed among them, observe, imitate their industry, and so raise themselves to the level of the Beasts' instinct, with this advantage, that each species has but its own instinct, while man, perhaps having none that belongs to him, appropriates them all, [feeding] indifferently on most of the various foods. (*SD*, III, 135; I, 3)

Man appears to acquire his means of subsistence not from nature's beneficence but from contact with and adaptation to his surroundings. While Rousseau purports to be describing man's original state, he has incorporated into his description the first movements of human history.

We find a further indication that man's acquisition of instincts is bound up with history in Rousseau's description of natural man's "Metaphysical and Moral side" (*SD*, III, 141; I, 14) later in the First Part. There, Rousseau attributes man's capacity to feed on different foods, which he has already treated as part of man's physical nature, to freedom:

Thus a Pigeon would starve to death next to a Bowl filled with the choicest meats, and a Cat atop heaps of fruit or of grain, although each could very well have found nourishment in the food it disdains, if it had occurred to it to try some; thus dissolute men abandon themselves to excesses. (*SD*, III, 141; I, 15)

Shortly thereafter, however, freedom is set aside, and Rousseau attributes man's capacity to deviate from nature and make up for his want of instinct to perfectibility, that faculty which, "with the aid of circumstances, successively develops all the others" (*SD*, III, 142; I, 17). Perfectibility enables human beings, over time, to be altered or to alter themselves in response to circumstances; it is their ability to adapt or overcome their physical environment; it is the faculty that distinguishes an animal species, which is "after a thousand years what is was in the first year of those thousand" (Ibid.), from the human species, which has a history. As such, it may be that "which, by dint of time, draws him out of that original condition in which he would pass tranquil and innocent days" (Ibid.). Rousseau hesitates to admit perfectibility's guilt at this point, concluding only that it would be sad to be forced to admit it. But he indicates clearly enough that the same faculty that allows human beings to survive in the original state by acquiring instincts also makes them malleable in a way that animals are not and opens him to the possibility of error and excess. The same faculty that makes possible the praiseworthy characteristics of original man, such as his strength and acquired instincts, also makes man a historical being and all but guarantees his exit from the original state. Rousseau suggests not only that man's natural goodness is inextricably bound to his historicity but even that man's natural goodness is inseparable from his historical badness.[15]

Third, at the beginning of the Second Part, Rousseau treats man's need for exercise and his skill at comparing as results of a new development, of difficulties not present in man's original state: "but difficulties soon presented themselves" (*SD*, III, 165; II, 3). Yet the physical strength acquired through exercise and skill at comparing are attributes of the natural man described in the First Part (*SD*, III, 135, 136; I, 4, 6). We recall that the organization of the *Second Discourse* appears to mirror the distinction between nature and history. Original man is man unaltered by time or by things. Yet, in the Second Part, it transpires that a number of "original" man's advantages arise only when circumstances compel human beings to adapt.[16] They arise only when the equilibrium between man's requirements and nature's bounty that supposedly characterizes man's first condition (*SD*, III, 134–5, 143; I, 2, 19) is broken. We conclude that the dividing line between the two parts of the main body of the *Discourse*, and consequently that between nature and history, is not so sharp for Rousseau as it initially seemed.[17]

Doubting the Goodness of Nature

Up until now, I have tried to prove that Rousseau does not equate the original and the natural by showing that his description of natural man in the *Second Discourse* is shot through, in ways he could not have failed to notice, with historically acquired traits. Human beings develop out of and continue to develop because of their relation to a demanding natural environment. But this conclusion undermines Rousseau's case for the goodness of nature and the natural goodness of man.

In the *Second Discourse*, Rousseau's physiodicy seems to rest on his assertion that there is, in the beginning, an equilibrium between human nature and external nature. Recall John Scott's summary of Rousseau's argument for nature's providence: "The order of nature, including human nature, is found in our original or natural condition as physical beings embedded unproblematically in the physical whole of nature" (1992, 706). External nature, Rousseau claims, asks of human nature only what it can readily provide without altering itself or acquiring new, potentially corrupting, knowledge: "The Earth's products provided him with all the assistance he needed, instinct moved him to use them.... Such was the condition of nascent man" (*SD*, III, 164; II, 2–3). What is striking in Rousseau's account here, and in Scott's (Ibid., 702), is the banishment of perfectibility from the original state; absent is the admission that human beings had to *acquire* instincts to contend with a physical environment that did *not* provide for their needs. By leaving perfectibility out, Rousseau is able to portray a static natural condition in which an adequate and unchanging human nature exists within an external nature that provides for all its needs. But as my argument to this point has suggested, and as I will now show, Rousseau's considered view of nature depicts it as a dynamic condition, in which an originally inadequate human nature is repeatedly made to adapt to circumstances that are difficult from the outset. In that case, however, Rousseau's understanding of the goodness of both nature and man must be reconsidered.

The exigencies of nature propel human beings into history. Far from being the provider that gives human beings every reason to stay in place, external nature poses the obstacles that they cannot overcome without acquiring new knowledge and altering themselves in fundamental ways. In the Second Part of the *Second Discourse*, Rousseau writes as if a change had to take place in man's environment before the original equilibrium was broken and human beings were compelled to adapt in order to survive and prosper; but, again, "difficulties soon presented themselves" (*SD*, III, 165; II, 3). What kinds of difficulties, though? The "*height of Trees* which prevented him from reaching their fruits" (Ibid.; emphasis added). Were trees short in the original state? Or is it more sensible to conclude that a static equilibrium between human nature and external nature never existed?

Alternatively, one may conclude that at first enough fruits for everyone fell to the ground. When the population increased and the fruit that fell from the trees was no longer enough for everyone, human beings had to work for their meals by climbing the trees, whose height only then began to trouble them. This conclusion is supported by Rousseau's willing, even proud, admission that "an excessively large population ... results from the State of Nature" (*SD*, III, 222; note xvii). Population pressures introduced difficulties that did not exist in the original state; nature's providence is secure. But first, human beings also had to contend with "animals trying to eat these fruits" and the "ferociousness of the animals that threatened his very life" (*SD*, III, 165; II, 3). Are we to understand that the population of animals generally, and of frugivores especially, was small enough in the original state so that human beings did not need to defend themselves or climb trees, and that a general surge in population makes not only other human beings but also animals a problem for them for the first time? Second, and more obviously, if the ordinary and perfectly natural course of reproduction results in man's departure from the state of nature, then it is difficult to justify nature; setting man's corruption in motion is not much, if at all, more excusable than causing it to come about immediately.

Bear in mind that no change in the condition the First Part depicts need occur for history to get rolling. Though Rousseau credits migration into new climates for some early progress, human beings would have undergone considerable changes even if they had stayed in one place, for they are pressed by nature even in their first home. The natural men of the First Part wander "in the forests" (*SD*, III, 159; I, 46), and conditions in the forest call forth developments in man no less than in other habitats. In "forests they made bows and arrows and became Hunters and Warriors" (*SD*, III, 165; II, 4). The forest, with its tall trees and hungry inhabitants, man's original home, is no Eden.

Moreover, Rousseau sometimes admits the inhospitability of the original state, in spite of his usual insistence on the goodness of nature, and brings into the open nature's responsibility for driving human beings out of the original state. Nature itself presents the difficulties present at the dawn of history. Human beings "learned to overcome the *obstacles of Nature*" (*SD*, III, 165; II, 3; emphasis added). And Rousseau doesn't stop at blaming nature for the earliest human progress; he admits its part in progress at all stages of human development:

In all Nations of the world progress of the mind proportioned itself exactly to the Needs which Peoples received from *Nature* or to which circumstances subjected them. (*SD*, III, 143; I, 20; emphasis added)

What kinds of circumstances? The flooding of the Nile, Attica's infertile soil, the cold; differences in a people's physical circumstances, according to Rousseau, go some way toward explaining the differences between the civilized and uncivilized and among different varieties of civilization. Rousseau attributes these physical circumstances to a quasi-providential nature, except here, nature's providence does not retard but accelerates progress, where circumstances, *which it itself dictates*, demand it: "as if *Nature* wanted in this way to equalize things, by giving Minds the fertility *it* refuses the Soil" (Ibid.; emphasis added). This view is certainly a far cry from that of the polemical note ix, which condemns man for the civilization he has created against nature's will, the civilization that "beneficent Nature had taken care to keep away from him"; "it is not without difficulty that we have succeeded in making ourselves so unhappy" (*SD*, III, 202; note ix, 1). But in truth, nature can be separated neither from history, which it sets in motion, nor from our miseries, to which it gives rise. With these sorts of indications, Rousseau calls the goodness of nature into question.

Rousseau's usual approach is to hedge on the question of nature's responsibility for human development. Elsewhere, defending nature's innocence in man's ejection from the state of nature, Rousseau uses the word "little" (*peu*) three times in a single passage (*SD*, III, 151; I, 33) to describe nature's contribution to sociality and its part in the formation of language. As proof, he points out that primitive human beings have as little need for each other as monkeys and wolves (Ibid.). But in the Second Part, he reveals that monkeys, at least, "troop together" in almost the same way as human beings do in the course of the "initial progress" that "finally enabled man to make more rapid progress" (*SD*, III, 167; II, 10–11). The stage of more rapid progress is that of the "first revolution" that established families and a kind of property. The "little" need nature gave human beings for each other seems enough to set them on the road to society. In the same defense of nature's innocence, Rousseau describes nature's providence in relation to man: "The faculties he had in potentiality were to develop only with the opportunities to exercise them" (*SD*, III, 152; I, 33). But who provides the occasion? Is it human beings and "all [they] have done to establish the bonds" of sociability (*SD*, III, 151; I, 33)? They first had to be brought to the point of being able and willing to establish these ties, and for this development to come about, other occasions were needed. Man's first progress must be attributed to natural circumstances acting on naturally perfectible human beings. Here, a version of note ix's blame of human beings for their own corruption is accompanied by subtle indications of nature's own guilt.

Finally, nature, though only by example, shows human beings the way to metallurgy, a crucial element in man's move out of nascent society, which Rousseau praises, and into society proper, characterized by property, work, and misery. What is especially striking here is the way in which Rousseau couples his providential claim for nature with an admission, in the very same paragraph, of nature's share of the blame for human misery:

It might seem that *Nature* had taken precautions to withhold this fatal secret from us. The only remaining alternative, then, is that some extraordinary event, such as a Volcano throwing up molten metal, will have given its Witnesses the idea of imitating this *operation of Nature*. (*SD*, III, 172, II, 21; emphasis added)

Now it is true that Rousseau takes pains to indicate that human beings discover metallurgy only because of an "extraordinary event." Perhaps, he suggests, nature ought not to be blamed for so improbable an accident. Rousseau frequently emphasizes how unlikely the events that drive humanity toward society are, the chance meetings, the great floods, the lightning bolts, the volcanoes, in short that

fortuitous concatenation of several foreign causes which might never have arisen and without which he would eternally have remained in his primitive condition. (*SD*, III, 162; I, 51)

Yet Rousseau quietly warns readers to disregard this emphasis:

This will exempt me from expanding my reflections about how *the lapse of time makes up for the slight likelihood of events*: about the astonishing power of very slight causes when they act without cease. . . . It is enough for me to submit these issues for consideration to my Judges: it is enough for me to have seen to it that vulgar Readers need not consider them. (*SD*, III, 162–3; I, 53; emphasis added)

Rousseau suggests that it is the mark of a judicious reader of the *Second Discourse* to have these matters in mind, but such a reader will hardly be impressed by the unlikely or accidental character of events, since he has been warned that over vast periods of time, accidents will happen. Nature may make human progress or regression take a long time, but it also makes it inevitable. Consider the new concession Rousseau makes in the "Letter to Philopolis," in which Rousseau defends the argument of the *Second Discourse*:

Society follows from the nature of mankind not, as you maintain, immediately, but only, as I have proved, with the help of external circumstances which might have been or not been, *or at least might have occurred sooner or later*, and hence might have hastened or retarded the progress. ("Letter to Philopolis," III, 232; 9; emphasis added)[18]

Notably, this admission that man's departure from the original state may be inevitable is made nowhere explicitly in the *Second Discourse*. It is also noteworthy that the admission is drawn from Rousseau by his opponent's claim that nature, in the form of perfectibility, is the source of human sociality. In his response, Rousseau never denies this claim, which, from the perspective of the *Second Discourse*, should count against the goodness of nature. He goes so far, indeed, as to compare sociality to something of which nature is certainly the source, old age.

To be sure, old age "follows from the nature of man alone" whereas "society follows from the nature of mankind, not immediately...but only...with the aid of external circumstances" (Ibid.). This formulation leaves open the possibility that human nature is responsible for society and corruption in general in only a very limited way – that is, it is not incorruptible. All I would claim to have shown up until now is that external nature, contrary to Rousseau's argument for the goodness of nature to man, actually bears significant responsibility for human ills in the state of society and that Rousseau is well aware of it. It requires much more to show that Rousseau deliberately contradicts his assertion of the natural goodness of man. After all, the argument for that goodness hardly depends on human beings being good for themselves and others under every possible circumstance, however unlikely. If an asteroid were to strike the Earth, putting an end to human life, we might say that nature or God is indifferent or hostile to human beings but not that human nature is bad because it fails to protect us from asteroids. At the same time, Rousseau also leaves open a possibility that he had not allowed in the *Second Discourse*, namely, that circumstances are merely accomplices in a crime against human beings for which human nature bears primary responsibility. We would be especially tempted to draw that conclusion if it turned out that the situations human beings find themselves in ordinarily, not the situations human beings find themselves in rarely, push them toward society, or if human nature itself, not merely external circumstances, tended toward the changes that make the emergence of society all but inevitable.

Doubting the Natural Goodness of Man

It is tempting to argue that Rousseau's absolution of external nature is not nearly as important as his famous thesis of the natural goodness of man. Even if external nature, and not just society, made human beings bad, perhaps our internal nature, human nature, is still innocent. There are reasons for doubt, however. First among these reasons is the inadequacy of our original nature. We have already had occasion to notice that the advantages Rousseau assigns to original men – their strength, their acquired instincts, their mechanical prudence – are won in the course of this struggle to survive. Our internal nature, prior to the impact of circumstances, is wholly inadequate; human beings are weak and without prudence or instinct to guide them. The equilibrium between man's desires and his ability to provide for them is broken not only because nature makes demands on us but also because we are originally incapable of meeting almost any demand without being altered or altering ourselves. Nature is unkind to human beings not only when it comes to the environment in which it places us but also because it fails to endow us with the ability to get the goods we need without being drawn into misery. It is one thing to say that human nature is good, although human beings do not cope well with earthquakes, but it is quite another and far less convincing thing to say that human nature is good, except that it is not well suited to cope with the ordinary demands of its environment.

That said, Rousseau's argument for the natural goodness of man could perhaps be modified and rescued by pointing to the importance of metallurgy and agriculture in the story of human corruption. These inventions brought about the "great revolution" (*SD*, III, 171; II, 20) of the division of labor that pushes human beings out of still happy primitive societies into miserable civilized societies. While the inadequacies of human nature may have compelled human beings to develop certain faculties and skills, Rousseau asserts that the development of metallurgy requires a degree of imagination and foresight that even human beings who use tools, have leisure, and have acquired ideas of merit and beauty lack; only some extraordinary event could have made the use of iron ore known to human beings. In that case, while one might blame external nature for providing the volcano, whose operation human beings imitate when they develop metallurgy, one could hardly blame human nature, which is corrupted only because of an improbable accident.

Three initial responses can be made. First, the account of the development of metallurgy parallels Rousseau's account of the development of language. That is to say, Rousseau presents us with an almost impossible problem of how human beings make their way from one stage of development to a stage that is radically different without either the abilities or the incentive to get there. He then presents us with an inaequate and speculative solution to the problem.[19] Confronted with the near impossibility of accounting for the known facts on the basis of Rousseau's assumptions about human development, one defensible response is to suppose that Rousseau has exaggerated the extent to which nature has discouraged such development. Perhaps the obstacles nature and human nature present to the development of metallurgy are not as great as they seem. Second, at the stage of development that precedes metallurgy, human beings already have artificial needs and already practice, at the family level, a certain division of labor (*SD*, III, 168; II, 12–13). The new needs that human beings have may drive them actively to seek and be on the lookout for new tools; while the discovery of metallurgy remains improbable even under these circumstances, it is at least a little more probable. That human beings already know a kind of division of labor before metallurgy and agriculture are discovered similarly narrows the gap between the stage at which human beings find themselves before these discoveries and the stage they find themselves at afterwards. Third, the development of metallurgy is not the kind of accident described earlier, the equivalent of an asteroid striking the Earth. For one thing, it requires the active involvement of human nature, which, in discovering metallurgy and putting it to use, is an active participant in the chain of events that lead to the division of labor. For another, while the eruption of a volcano is a kind of accident, Rousseau does not insist that it is the only extraordinary event that could have led to the invention of metallurgy. The demands placed on human beings who find themselves in a position, at some point or another in their history, to observe some event or another that might suggest metallurgy to them seems closer to what I have called the ordinary demands of the environment than to the demands of a genuinely improbable event. The event itself is accidental, but that human nature is such that it responds disastrously to accidents that are not especially unlikely is an argument against the natural goodness of man.

However that may be, one can point to still clearer signs that Rousseau positively implicates human nature in history and human corruption and is not content to indicate its inadequacies in responding to the pressures of external nature. His account of the emergence of human beings from the state of nature casts doubt on not only the goodness of nature but also the natural goodness of man. Perfectibility, itself a part of human nature, makes human beings malleable. But in addition, it would be imprecise to describe human development as a series of alterations effected in human beings by their environment. At times, man's circumstances offer not pressure but only an opening into which he is coaxed by his own drives. Consider, for example, the development of new needs after men and women begin to live in fixed dwellings. "In this new state . . . men enjoyed a great deal of leisure which they used to acquire . . . conveniences unknown to their Fathers" (*SD*, III, 168; II, 13). Here, harsh circumstances push nothing on human beings. On the contrary, easy circumstances allow them to act not only on their interest in self-preservation but also on their interest in well-being. This latter interest, which is usually neglected by Rousseau's interpreters, is fundamental and is described in the same breath as the former. There are "two principles prior to reason, of which one interests us intensely in our *well-being and our self-preservation*" (*SD*, III, 125–26; Preface, 9; emphasis added). Indeed, interest in well-being may well be more fundamental than interest in self-preservation inasmuch as the latter may be regarded as a special, limited application of the former. Accordingly, primitive man, when he comes into contact with his fellows, will learn that not the interest in self-preservation but the "love of well-being is the *sole* spring of human actions" (*SD*, III, 166; II, 8; emphasis added). Yet it is the love of well-being that leads us into advantageous and not strictly necessary relations with others, which, in turn, lead to more dangerous and corrupting relations. And it is surely the love of well-being, too, that leads primitive human beings to take advantage of their leisure to acquire new things and, in short order, new needs, "the first source of evils they prepared for their Descendants" (*SD*, III, 168; II, 13). Of what consequence for the exculpation of nature is the argument that clothing or a dwelling is "not very necessary" (*SD*, III, 140; I, 12), a hedged claim even on its face, when human beings are not by nature driven by strict necessity? And the building of fixed dwellings is a crucial element in man's movement out of the natural state, part of the "first revolution" that brings about the establishment and differentiation of families.[20] Not only perfectibility but also the love of well-being is a force within our natures that drives us out of the state of nature.

Not only physical circumstances but also relations with other human beings trigger the appearance of previously unrealized aspects of human nature. These developments seem to emerge from within human nature at least as much as and probably more than they are injected from without. Circumstances help to bring human beings to the point of seeing each other regularly, but what circumstance induces them to sing and dance together and to wish to be looked at by others (*SD*, III, 169–70; II, 16)? *Amour-propre*, that great cause of misery (and some joy) for human beings, appears not so much as an alteration of man accomplished by foreign influences as a development that occurs as soon as the opportunity arises, an accident, to be sure, but one waiting to happen.[21] Of course, *amour-propre* needs more than the presence of other human beings to emerge; for example, one needs a certain ability to make comparisons in order to care about being better than others. But all such preliminary developments would not have the consequences Rousseau describes if a human being were not the sort of being to care what others think, if men and women were not disposed to form exclusive preferences, if they were insensitive to ideas of merit and beauty. No accidental circumstance compels or pressures human beings to develop these characteristics. Admittedly, the division of labor and increasing interdependence will ultimately press everyone to care what the others think. But Rousseau pointedly places all the developments in question prior to the revolution that introduces the division of labor (*SD*, III, 169–70; II, 15–17). In social relations, as in physical relations, human nature meets external nature at least halfway. Rousseau depicts the darkest side of this picture in connection with the love of dominance:

The rich, for their part, had scarcely become acquainted with the pleasure of dominating than they disdained all other pleasures . . . like those ravenous wolves which once they have tasted human flesh scorn all other food. (*SD*, III, 175–76; II, 28)[22]

We have come a long way from Rousseau's first sight of natural men in the First Part of the *Second Discourse*:

I see an animal . . . the most advantageously organized of all: I see him sating his hunger beneath an oak, slaking his thirst at the first Stream, finding his bed at the foot of the same tree that supplied his meal, and with that his needs are satisfied. (*SD*, III, 134–35; I, 2)

We have observed that the advantageous physical organization of human beings is a product of the same history that drives them out of the peaceful state here depicted, if such a state ever existed. We have observed that such a state probably never existed, since nature is harsh and does not leave human beings in peace. We have observed that Rousseau does not subscribe to a sharp distinction between nature and history, that he thinks nature not only harsh but also implicated in man's exit from the state of nature. With hindsight, we may observe, too, that this last conclusion is hardly surprising. How much sense did it make, after all, for Rousseau to argue that not nature but the physical environment (nature) acting on human faculties and desires (nature) is to blame for our ills?[23]

The great innovation of Rousseau's physiodicy as it has come to be understood is to make society the sole source of evil. Rousseau could not have intended this innovation or its consequences, since his considered thought does not allow a sharp distinction between nature and history, let alone society. Consequently, that thought supports neither the extravagant hopes nor the despair set in motion by the removal from nature of every trace of historical and social influence. But we are not out of luck or danger, since the collapse of the distinction between

nature and history may lead, as much as the distinction itself did, to
the depreciation of nature and to the conclusion that we must abandon it for the sake of freedom. For if nature is incapable of distinguishing among historical outcomes, or if all history is equally and indifferently natural, then nature is no guide for human beings. I now
turn to *Emile*, which rejects the distinction between nature and history
more clearly than the *Second Discourse*.[24] Through *Emile*, we will consider
whether rejecting the distinction between nature and history means for
Rousseau either that nature dissolves into history or that it should be
abandoned for the sake of freedom. Yet in *Emile*, Rousseau describes
a history according to nature, a history that, far from being indistinguishable from other historical outcomes, has so far taken place only in
Rousseau's imagination:

> It makes very little difference to me if I have written a romance. A fair romance
> it is indeed, *the romance of human nature*. If it is to be found only in this writing,
> is that my fault? *This ought to be the history of my species.* (*E*, IV, 777; 416; emphasis
> added)

NATURE AND DEVELOPMENT IN EMILE

In *Emile*, the method of the *Second Discourse* is abandoned. Whereas the
Second Discourse abstracts from progress and development in order to
know natural man, *Emile* assumes that natural man cannot be known
without knowing his progress and development:

> He would have to be seen wholly formed: his inclinations would have to have been
> observed, his progress seen, his development followed. In a word, the natural man
> would have to be known. (*E*, IV, 251; 41)

The natural man cannot be known before his education is complete. He
is not the original but the cultivated man. Moreover, the education of
nature is never or almost never successfully managed. That is why the
natural man is a "rare man" (Ibid.), so rare that perhaps he exists only in
Rousseau's fertile imagination.[25] That Emile is the man of nature and, at
the same time, unique in his development and accomplishments implies
that human nature consists in an end or perfection, or that Rousseau's
understanding of nature is teleological.

Roger Masters has another understanding of the difference between
the *Second Discourse* and *Emile*. Rousseau writes *Emile* in light of the irre-
trievable loss of the state of nature: "Evolution necessarily forces men to

live in society" (1968, 11, 26). Various accidents have made human beings social and developed in them faculties original man lacked. But:

It is perfectly comprehensible that, as a result of accidental causation, new forms or modes of being come into existence, which were not actually present at the outset and yet are natural. (Ibid., 426)

In *Emile*, Rousseau deems natural those characteristics that "do not distort man's basic nature." These characteristics, though new, are "based on the primitive dispositions of nature." "The same natural principles which governed the pure state of nature still operate in socialized human nature." Emile's conscience, for example, is a modification of pity, which is there from the beginning. The question *Emile* answers is, what is the natural unfolding of our primitive dispositions in our present stage of evolution? Obviously, we need not abstract from society to get our answer; rather, to describe the natural man living in society, one must abstract from "the artificial variations [in the development of our primitive dispositions] due solely to the peculiar human institutions found in various societies." More simply put, *Emile* describes our natural development in society, free from the distortion of particular social prejudices. The natural man will be the product of a certain development or progress – in this sense, he will be an end, not an origin. But this understanding of natural man "could be consistent with . . . non-teleological physics, since it does not prescribe an end" (Ibid., 9, 26, 27, 414). It merely describes the unimpeded development of our native endowment under hypothetical circumstances. Rousseau's understanding of nature is teleological only if it distinguishes between what I will call given and true nature, between, on the one hand, the undistorted development of the dispositions with which a human being comes into the world in whatever stage of evolution he happens to be and, on the other hand, the perfection of a certain set of dispositions with which a human being may or may not come into the world and by means of which he becomes a perfect being of his kind.

Emile certainly contains some evidence for Masters's interpretation. Nonetheless, I believe I can prove that Rousseau thinks there is a discrepancy between our given and true natures. That proof will consist in showing that Emile's governor selectively cultivates and perfects, and sometimes directly opposes, Emile's given nature with a view to his well-being, not only or even primarily as a human being made to live in society but also and above all as a human being simply. It will consist in showing that, for the true man of nature to emerge, aspects of Emile's native endowment must be overcome.[26] If so, the "nature" in "man of nature" refers to a teleological end, not, as Masters thinks, to the unimpeded development of our primitive dispositions in man's present stage of evolution.

Selecting a Pupil

Before moving on to the governor's selective cultivation and perfection of Emile's given nature, we should observe that Emile is selected from a pool of possible candidates for the natural education. First, one wants a student from the temperate zone because men "*are all that they can be only in temperate climates.*" Moreover, "the organization of the brain is less perfect in the two extremes. Neither the Negroes nor the Laplanders have the sense of the Europeans" (*E*, IV, 266–67; 52; emphasis added). This preference for the temperate zone reminds us, in its spirit if not in its details, of Aristotle, and here, as there, it implies that not all, or even most, natures are capable of realizing the true nature of a human being (Aristotle, 1958, 296 (1327b)). In any event, Rousseau is clearly concerned here not merely with the negative project of staving off the distorting influence of society but also with making men all they can be, a goal not easily met in the North or South and not met at all in man's original state. Second, one wants a healthy pupil instead of an unhealthy one "involved uniquely with preserving himself, [and] whose body does damage to the education of his soul" (*E*, IV, 268; 53). Nature produces natures that are unsuitable candidates for natural education. The governor accepts and rejects what nature gives according to a rule different from that by which empirical nature generally and our given natures specifically are governed when left to themselves.

It may be objected that the governor merely imitates the laws of empirical nature by weeding out the unhealthy. The *Second Discourse* indicates that nature, prior to the birth of societies, dealt with children as the law of Sparta did, favoring the stronger constitutions and leaving the weak to die (*SD*, III, 135; I, 4). However, Rousseau's approval of nature's harshness in this regard is merely another example of his judging empirical nature according to an external standard of goodness, perfection, or of true nature, since to approve of nature's extermination of weak natures is at least to call into question its production of them.[27]

Educating the Senses

The governor's education of Emile's senses perfects them in a way that their unimpeded development could not under any but the most contrived circumstances. For example, Emile learns to touch like a blind man:

The blind have a surer and keener touch than we do; because, not being guided by sight, they are forced to learn to draw solely from [touch] the judgements which [sight] furnishes us. Why, then, are we not given practice at walking as the blind do in darkness, to know the bodies we may happen to come upon ... in a word, to do at night without light all that they do by day without eyes? (*E*, IV, 381; 133)

To form natural man, the governor makes Emile into what his given nature fails to make him, a nocturnal and diurnal animal. Just as human beings in the *Second Discourse* are not limited to a particular diet as other animals are, Emile is now taught not to limit his actions to a particular time of day. No undirected combination of nature and experience could have produced or even tends to produce this result for Emile. Indeed, it is worth noting that the education of the senses begins where their unimpeded development leaves off. "The first faculties which are *formed and perfected* in us are the senses. They are, therefore, the first faculties that ought to be *cultivated*" (*E*, IV, 380; 132; emphasis added). The metaphor of cultivation that we encounter often in *Emile* is significant. A cultivator does not let a plant grow wild but assists, improves, refines, or directs growth with an end, an adult plant of a certain kind, always in view. However that may be, the education of nature, understood as a purely internal development, has already taken its course on Emile's senses by the time the governor begins his education of the senses in earnest. That education perfects the senses more than the education of nature alone, or even the education of nature and things alone, could.

Fear and Religion

In the midst of the education of his senses, Emile learns not to fear the dark. Before that, he learns not to fear what he does not know. Naturally, man "fears everything he does not know."[28] The governor conquers Emile's fear of the unknown by showing him a variety of unfamiliar things, "ugly, disgusting, peculiar animals" and masks ranging from the hideous to the pleasant. The education depends not only on showing a certain range of objects but also on showing them in a measured gradation. Emile sees new animals "little by little, from afar"; then, "by dint of seeing them handled by others, he finally handles them himself." The education of the masks succeeds if the governor has "arranged [his] gradation well" (*E*, IV, 283; 63).[29] Emile's given nature, of course, which tends toward fear of the unknown, cannot be made to produce the fearlessness characteristic of our man of nature without the aid of carefully contrived and controlled circumstances. Rousseau has not so much followed Emile's nature, if his nature consists in his primitive dispositions, as remedy its deficiencies.

The fear of darkness, like that of the unfamiliar, is natural. Night "naturally frightens men and sometimes animals as well." Further, Rousseau's description of the "natural cause" of this fear reveals a surprising understanding of what counts as natural:

What is this cause? The same one which makes deaf men distrustful *and the people superstitious*: ignorance . . . of what is going on about us. Accustomed to perceive objects from afar and to foresee their impressions . . . how – when I no longer see anything around me – would I not suppose there to be countless beings . . . in motion which can harm me?

The unimpeded development of our given nature brings the imagination into play along with our other faculties. This development is the source of our belief in phantoms. Rousseau leaves little doubt about the natural provenance of that belief when he explains that "instinct" sets the imagination in motion; our desire to preserve ourselves causes us to imagine unseen causes of danger, and our imagination, once it is activated, knows no boundaries. Thus, the unfolding of our given nature leaves the imagination dangerously unrestrained (*E*, IV, 382–84; 134–35; emphasis added).

Moreover, the imagination, when combined with ignorance or relative ignorance, causes not only the fear of darkness but also the religion of the first men:

The sentiment of our action on other bodies must at first have made us believe that when they acted on us they did so in a manner similar to the way we acted on them. Thus man began by animating all the beings whose actions he felt. Not only did he feel himself less strong than most of these beings, but, for want of knowing the limits of their power, he assumed it to be unlimited and he construed them to be gods. . . . During the first ages men were frightened of everything and saw nothing dead in nature. (*E*, IV, 552; 256)

The unimpeded development of human nature fails to protect human beings from superstition. The men of the first ages, who may be regarded as the products of such a development, have a natural tendency to judge what they don't know. Their given natures dispose them to prejudice and superstition. To be sure, certain circumstances set the imagination in motion. But darkness and danger are hardly the kinds of experiences we can call, in the language of the *Second Discourse*, accidental. That nature which ruins us when we are placed in unexceptional natural circumstances must be corrected; the product of that correction is Emile, the true man of nature.

For in contrast to primitives and, in fact, almost all human beings, Emile and the governor do not judge what they do not know:

A magician attracts a wax duck floating in a tub of water with a piece of bread. Although we are quite surprised, we ... do not say, "He is a sorcerer," for we do not know what a sorcerer is. Constantly struck by effects whose causes we do not know, we are in no hurry to make any judgments. (*E*, IV, 437; 173)

Emile's primary advantage over the savage is that, like Socrates, he does not think he knows what he does not know:

My pupil is that savage, with the difference that Emile, having reflected more, compared ideas more, seen our errors from closer up, is more on guard against himself and judges only what he knows. (*E*. IV, 535; 243–44)

This important difference between Emile and the savage has many implications. But, for our purposes, it suffices to note that Emile is protected by his education from a natural fear of great consequence and from the prejudices that result from it. Masters, we have observed, also thinks that Emile's education is directed against prejudice. But he does not attend to Rousseau's clear indications that our natural dispositions incline us toward prejudice. The inclination to judge what we do not know is one of the obstacles our given natures put in the way of the emergence of Emiles, true men of nature. Emile's restraint with respect to the truth and his ability to act in the dark without fear follow at least as much from the conquest of Emile's given nature as from removing impediments to the unfolding of that nature.

It is worth noting, however, that Emile, contrary to Rousseau's claims, is not free from prejudice. As a man, Emile will not fear the dark, in part because he associates it with pleasant images, with happy memories of the nocturnal games he played as a boy (*E*, IV, 387–88; 137). According to Rousseau, however, nothing "is so sad as darkness" (*E*, IV, 385; 135). The pleasant images Emile associates with darkness reflect the truth about it no better, if not worse, than the fearsome images others associate with it.

Emile's prejudice about darkness is one aspect of a prejudice about nature that his education instills. In the early stages of the education, the governor subjects Emile to the "heavy yoke of necessity." He commands

Emile so that the education and its restrictions seem to issue not from his own will, or from caprice, but from necessity. Yet the governor, unlike necessity, manifestly cares about Emile. Hence he is to grant "with pleasure; refuse only with repugnance," whereas natural necessity does not favor granting over refusing (*E*, IV, 320; 91). Further, the governor, when he is capable of protecting Emile from nature's harshness, subjects him to only those ills that will harden him against other ills (*E*, IV, 815; 443). The governor mimics nature and necessity imperfectly, in such a way that it may seem to Emile that nature cares about and favors human beings, or that nature is benevolent.

As in the case of the prejudice against darkness, the prejudice in favor of darkness, and more broadly in favor of nature, is connected to religion. Emile is inclined to love not only other human beings but also nature and nature's God "because he sees that everything approaching him is inclined to assist him (*E*, IV, 492; 213). Emile loves God not because he finds the world ordered (as he would even if necessity were harsh) but because he finds nature well disposed toward him. He is inclined to be virtuous

not only for the love of order, to which each of us always prefers love of self, but for the love of the Author of his being – *a love which is confounded with that same love of self.* (*E*, IV, 636; 314; emphasis added)[30]

Emile is inclined to obey God for the same reasons he is inclined to obey the governor, namely, gratitude and belief in the other's superiority and good intentions. Because Emile's beliefs rest on a distortion of necessity's appearance, we must regard them as prejudices.[31] Even the man of nature cannot do without prejudices, unless the fact that Emile's is a "common mind" (*E*, IV, 266; 52), coupled with the presence of a governor who is free even of Emile's prejudices, points to the possibility of a truer man of nature than the limited Emile.

It is worth noting that even Emile's disinclination to judge what he does not know may well depend on his prejudice in favor of nature. For savage religion and popular religion both appear, for Rousseau, to arise from fear and uncertainty above all. The imagination, as we have just observed, is set in motion when we feel threatened by the unknown. If Emile is anxious, then his imagination will be restless. But if he is persuaded that whatever the causes of things may be, their effects, on the whole, can be expected to favor him, then he will not be so desperate to know as to settle for fantasy.

Climate

Just as the governor makes Emile a nocturnal and diurnal animal, he trains him to live in a variety of climates and to withstand extremes of heat and cold. Emile should learn to live if he has to "in freezing Iceland or on Malta's burning rocks" (*E*, IV, 253; 42). His bathing regimen, in which the temperature of the water is gradually varied, is designed so that he is "able to adapt to various degrees of heat and cold without effort and without risk." He becomes "accustomed little by little to bathing sometimes in hot water at all bearable degrees and often in cold water at all possible degrees." Thanks to his training in water, Emile becomes "almost insensitive to the various temperatures of the air" (*E*, IV, 278; 60).

In what sense can this training be deemed natural? We may be inclined to call Emile's flexibility natural on the grounds that our given nature, before it comes into contact with external circumstances, is not yet Northern or Southern. As Rousseau explains in the *Second Discourse*, it is not nature that makes men in different locales so different from each other but rather the continuous action on successive generations of "Climates, air, foods, ways of life, habits in general" (*SD*, III, 208; note x, 1). Nonetheless, even if it is possible to abstract human nature from all these circumstances, the most we can say of it is that it is ready to live anywhere. We cannot say, as we can of Emile, that it is ready to live *everywhere*. Being fit for no particular human condition, as a nature untouched by circumstance would be, is something different from being "fit for all human conditions" (*E*, IV, 267; 52), as Emile will be. The latter fitness is arrived at not by leaving Emile's given nature alone but by pushing it beyond the limits it would exist within under all but the most improbable of circumstances. The governor's education does not so much follow Emile's given nature as prevent, as much as possible, that nature from limiting Emile's experience.[32] Indeed, Rousseau reveals a kind of frustration with nature's limits in his discussion of Emile's training in swimming, which comes as close as possible to turning Emile into an amphibian:

Emile will be in water as on land. Why should he not live in all the elements? If he could be taught to fly...I would make an eagle of him. I would make a salamander of him if a man could be hardened against fire. (*E*, IV, 379; 132)

Beyond the Necessities of the Age

One could argue that Emile must be able to live under a variety of circumstances because society, above all the society of his time, demands it. Rousseau suggests as much when he advances "the mobility of human things" and "the unsettled and restless spirit of this age" (*E*, IV, 252; 42) as reasons to prevent Emile from forming habits. Similarly, he explains that Emile must not be allowed to get in the habit of sleeping through the night, although that habit is "marked out by nature" because

civil life is not simple enough, natural enough, exempt enough from extreme changes and accidents for man properly to get accustomed to this uniformity to the point of making it necessary for him. (*E*, IV, 376; 129)

But natural circumstances do not allow human beings the luxury of sleeping through the night either. Rousseau reveals in the *Second Discourse* that "always near danger, Savage man must . . . be a light sleeper" (*SD*, III, 140; I, 13). Whatever its disadvantages, civil society is much more a friend to heavy sleepers than nature is. Far from undermining the habit of sleeping through the night, civil society makes possible a secure life in which that habit may be safely indulged. That society and progress make it possible for human beings *not* to be diurnal and nocturnal animals is also indicated in Rousseau's discussion of Emile's need to get his bearings in the dark. "We have lights, I will be told. What? Always machines? Who promises you that they will follow you everywhere in case of need?" (*E*, IV, 381; 133). It now appears that human beings ought to avoid habits not because of society's special demands but because society cannot be counted on always to save us from trying natural circumstances.

But, in fact, Rousseau admits elsewhere that the flexibility imparted to Emile is more than an adaptation to necessity, social or natural. Very soon after he blames the restless spirit of the age for the need to train Emile to live in a variety of circumstances, he suggests another, positive, advantage of such training:

To live is not to breathe; it is to act; it is to make use of our organs, our senses, our faculties, of all the parts of ourselves which give us the sentiment of our existence. (*E*, IV, 253; 42)

The governor's education makes possible a human flourishing that our given nature does not provide for and frequently obstructs. In this respect, the governor's education remedies not only the ills of society but also the deficiencies of Emile's given nature.

Timing

As we have already noticed, Rousseau concedes, in the "Letter to Philopolis," that human progress may be inevitable. He goes on to suggest that human beings have the power only to hasten or retard their progress as a species. Something similar may be said of the governor's power over Emile's faculties and desires. He cannot prevent them from emerging but is capable of influencing the timing of their emergence. This timing, however, turns out to be crucial. Our happiness depends upon a certain order, for which our given nature does not provide, in the emergence and development of our faculties and desires.

Consider, for example, the development of new needs. In the *Second Discourse*, as we have already noticed, these needs develop as soon as human beings acquire leisure, as soon as their strength exceeds their limited needs. The trouble is that, in the course of history, human beings develop strength and skills that their judgement and experience are not prepared to direct; that is how human beings can impose a "yoke" on themselves "without thinking of it" (*SD*, III, 168; II, 13). Emile's history is happier than the history of the species because as soon as he "has strength beyond what he needs," the governor takes pains to keep him out of trouble (*E*, IV, 426; 165). He limits Emile's curiosity and employment strictly to useful truths and objects, crushes the emergence of vanity, and teaches him to distinguish the arts that advance his security, preservation, and well-being from those whose value depends only on opinion. The history narrated in the *Second Discourse* shows that our given nature offers virtually no resistance to corruption once circumstances in which corruption is possible arise. As soon as we get leisure, we acquire new needs. As soon as we gather together with other human beings, we become vain. *Emile* is in part an inquiry into the possibility of correcting for or remedying the deficiencies of our original nature by making sure there is a certain order in our inevitable progress, that the development of our reason and judgment keep pace with our strength, sensuality, and needs. The natural education offered by the governor does not follow Emile's given nature but orders it with a view to his well-being.

Consider also the governor's attempt to delay Emile's puberty. Rousseau, in accordance with what most commentators have taken for his theodicy, first blames the need to delay puberty on society:

I gain time for him . . . by delaying the progress of nature to the advantage of reason. But have I actually delayed this progress? No, I have only prevented imagination from accelerating it.... While the torrent of our institutions carries him away, I attract him in the opposite direction by other institutions. (*E*, IV, 638–39; 316)

But does nature ensure that sexuality and the reason needed to check and guide it develop at the same pace? Rousseau points out that factors other than society can speed puberty's onset:

The transition... to puberty is not so determined by nature that it does not vary in individuals according to their temperaments and in peoples according to their climates. Everyone knows the distinction observable in this regard between hot and cold countries; and each of us sees that ardent temperaments are formed sooner than others. (*E*, IV, 495; 215)

In that case, reason can keep pace with sexual development only if it develops faster in Southerners and in ardent human beings. However, it hardly seems likely that reason develops more quickly in the mild climates of the South, in which, Rousseau asserts in the *Essay on the Origin of Languages*, men have little need for each other, arts, commerce, or laws (*Essay*, V, 400–401; 266–67).[33]

Moreover, Rousseau admits that nature, and not society alone, is responsible for making human beings sensitive before it makes them sensible. First, the project of the first part of Book IV is to counteract nature's tendency to do just that:

No matter what human art does, temperament always precedes reason. Up to now we have given all our care to restraining the former and arousing the latter, in order that man may as much as possible always be one. In developing his nature, we have sidetracked its nascent sensibility; we have regulated it by cultivating reason. (*E*, IV, 636; 314)

Delaying puberty is part of the governor's attempt to give reason a head start on sensitivity, even though our given nature proceeds in the opposite, dangerous, order. Second, Rousseau claims that "nature has no fixed point that can be moved ahead or back" when it comes to puberty; consequently, he argues, Emile's puberty can be delayed "without departing from nature's law" (*E*, IV, 640; 317). He implies that neither delaying nor accelerating puberty is a violation of nature's laws because nature has no law in this case; the timing most conducive to our happiness is therefore in no way guaranteed or even encouraged by our given nature. Third, the governor continues to sidetrack sensibility, even after puberty takes hold. He interests Emile in hunting because "violent exercise stifles the tender sentiments" (*E*, IV, 644; 320). That the effect of puberty must be combated even after nature's progress has been impeded as much as possible suggests that when nature is left to itself, puberty comes too soon. Insofar as nature does have a law regarding the timing of puberty, it impedes human happiness.

Consider, finally, the order of the development of the capacity for love and friendship. At first, Rousseau suggests that the latter develops out of the former. A "heart full of an overflowing sentiment likes to open itself. From the need for a mistress is soon born the need for a friend" (*E*, IV, 494; 214–15). But he also argues that this order is *reversed* in a good education: "the first sentiment of which *a carefully raised young man is capable is not love; it is friendship*" (*E*, IV, 502; 220; emphasis added). The *Second Discourse* reveals why this reversal may be important. In the history narrated in that work, the emergence of love is not prepared for, as it is in *Emile*, by the cultivation of the capacities for friendship and love of humanity.[34] When love stirs in human beings, hearts grows active, relations expand and bonds tighten; human relations are governed on the one hand by love and jealousy and, on the other, by vanity, for everyone "began to look at everyone else and to wish to be looked at himself, and public esteem acquired a value" (*SD*, III, 169; II, 16). Jealousy, envy, and resentment over slights stifle natural pity, which has already "undergone some modification," so that human beings become "bloodthirsty and cruel" (*SD*, III, 170–71; II, 17–18). While the state in which this cruelty exists remains, in Rousseau's estimation, best for man (much more on this in Chapter 2), there is no question that by cultivating friendship and humanity in Emile prior to love, the governor enables him to be a lover without becoming violent or cruel. The governor, in effect, corrects the deficient natural development of human faculties in order to prevent the emergence of the painful feelings that torment, on occasion, even the healthy savage. He seeks

to excite in [Emile] goodness, humanity, commiseration, beneficence, and all the attractive and sweet passions ... and to prevent the birth of envy, covetousness, hate, and all the repulsive and cruel passions which make sensibility, so to speak, not only nothing but negative and torment the man who experiences them. (*E*, IV, 506; 223)

The education in humanity and friendship, which takes place only when love is forestalled, is crucial to human happiness. But it is undermined by the order in which our given nature develops our capacities when it is left to itself.

The Limits of Nature

I think I have proved that Emile is the man of nature not because his primitive dispositions are allowed to unfold without social distortion but because, by means of the cultivation and perfection of some tendencies and the suppression or correction of others, he flourishes. His given nature allows but does not spontaneously tend toward or even always support his flourishing. There is a discrepancy between Emile's given nature and his true nature; we should understand the "nature" in "man of nature" teleologically to refer to an end or perfection. But I have not yet proved that the end in question is something other than freedom. Perhaps Rousseau uses "nature" as Cassirer and Strong do in different ways, so that it is indistinguishable from freedom. Emile's education removes limits, of climate, of time of day, of prejudices. Removing limits in this way makes possible either Strong's multiple self or Cassirer's autonomous self. Rousseau has emptied out nature after all.

But first, consider the importance Rousseau ascribes to natural "genius" or disposition. The governor must "spy out nature" (*E*, IV, 324; 94) to discover his pupil's particular tastes, talents, and penchants. In causing the child's genius to reveal itself, the governor prescribes to himself, in part, the direction and end of the education:

We put him in a position to develop his taste and his talent, to make the first steps toward the object to which his genius leads him, and to indicate to us the route which must be opened to him in order to assist nature. (*E*, IV, 465; 192)

The pupil's natural genius (as well as the character of his sex and of human beings in general) will determine the trade that suits him (*E*, IV, 474, 478; 198, 201). Plainly, natural genius is part of Emile's given nature but requires a favorable conjunction of circumstances to achieve a perfection toward which it points. In any event, natural genius imposes a limit on rather than removing an impediment to freedom. Thus, Rousseau tells of a lackey who is determined to become a painter. Though his zeal and perseverance take the place of talent up to a point, this painter will never be more than mediocre because he is naturally unfit for the work (*E*, IV, 474–75; 198–99; cf. *La Nouvelle Heloise, J*hereafter, II, 537; 440).[35] Rousseau's understanding of nature is not only teleological but also distinguishes nature from freedom.

Similarly, Rousseau's discussion of compatibility in love and marriage indicates that there are men and women who are simply not naturally fit for each other, whatever prejudices and social institutions may do to bring off a match. To predict whether a marriage will be happy, it is not enough to measure the strength of a couple's willful commitment. One must "consult nature" to discover whether the union is "in the order of nature." Each mind "has received its peculiar and determinate form . . . from the well-ordered or ill-ordered conjunction of nature and education." To arrange a good match, one must consider "natural compatibilities" and the "suitability of tastes, dispositions, sentiments, and characters" (*E*, IV, 764–65; 406–7). Like natural genius, character does not expand but limits our range of possible good choices.

CONCLUSION

If, as I think I have proved, Rousseau did not slay nature for the sake of freedom, then his legacy is, in many ways, founded on a misinterpretation of his thought. Commentators like Strauss, who raises grave doubts about the emptying out of nature, and like Strong and Cassirer, who raise great hopes about it, have mischaracterized Rousseau. Rousseau's thought, in fact, moderates the extravagant hopes for social reform that he is thought to have encouraged. First, Rousseau was a pessimist, not merely temperamentally but reflectively; he thought that, whatever our true nature, not just society but also our given natures pose tremendous obstacles to realizing it. Second, the idea of a true nature itself imposes limits on freedom; it rules out our suitability for certain ways of life. There is no question, however, that we need to know much more than I have said so far about what Rousseau thinks the contours of our true nature are and what way or ways of life are compatible with it. Only a careful study and description of Emile and his way of life, coupled with a similar study and description of extraordinary types and their way or ways of life (for which Rousseau's autobiographical works are an obvious source), can hope to meet this need. Let me try to say something very general, however, about Rousseau's vision of human nature and happiness.

Both Starobinski and Strong have drawn attention to Rousseau's early self-portrait in *Le Persifleur* (Starobinski, 1988, 53–54; Strong, 1994, 143–44). The theme of this portrait is Rousseau's variability. For example, "sometimes I am a harsh, fierce, misanthrope, while other times I wax ecstatic over the charms of society and the delights of love."[36] It is hard to know exactly what to make of so early and playful a comment, especially when the comment may be meant to describe not just Rousseau but the two writers, Rousseau and Diderot, writing under one pseudonym.[37]

However, this idea of Rousseau as an oscillating self reappears in the late autobiographical works, in which Jean-Jacques is said to swing frequently from one extreme to another, from solitude to sociality and from activity to passivity, among other opposites. Strong understands Rousseau to be lodging a protest against fixity, regularity, or definition (1994, 144). Starobinski, though he thinks Rousseau longs for a stable identity, agrees with Strong that he has failed to provide one for himself:

> The question then arises whether the notion of "nature" still makes sense. This oscillatory motion precludes the possibility that the soul will ever come to rest, that it will ever return to its natural state. Is there, then, such a thing as the natural state? At best it is an imaginary position, midway between two extremes.... Suppose we use the word *nature*... to refer to the very motion that makes stable identity impossible. (1988, 58)[38]

The middle point of the "true self" is abandoned in favor of the motion that better characterizes our existence.

My interpretation will emphasize this same variability of Rousseau's exemplary types, from the savage, who sings, dances, and competes for esteem with others while remaining capable of going off and living alone, to the rustic citizen, who serves the fatherland and then returns to the plow and almost to self-sufficiency. Unlike Starobinski and like Strong, I view Rousseau's oscillations as representing a considered view of what it is to be human, rather than a reflection of his troubled psyche. Consequently, my interpretation may seem to make Rousseau the first postmodern, in that it seems to reveal that Rousseau questions the stability of the self and finds multiplicity rather than unity at its core. I wish to dispel this impression from the outset.[39]

As my argument up until now has shown, Rousseau's nature is not another name for motion, or for man's lack of a nature. This entire chapter has shown that Rousseau did not intend, as postmoderns do, to deny that human nature has a common core. I propose the following thesis, which I will prove in the next chapter. Rousseau thinks oscillation desirable because human happiness is made up of certain disharmonious goods, solitary and social ones, for example.[40] His problem is to find a place in a life for those goods without setting himself in contradiction, like the bourgeois, who by seeking both sorts of goods attains neither. The incorporation of apparent contradictions into a single way of life is by no means limited to Rousseau's self-portrait. However dismissive Starobinski may be of the "imaginary position... between two extremes," Rousseau again and again seeks such a position. He thinks that the perfection of our nature demands the reconciliation of disharmonious goods; in this way, his teleological understanding of nature does not rule out the recognition of a plurality of human goods; that recognition is not, of course, necessarily postmodern. Rousseau's portrayals of the natural perfection of a naturally disharmonious being are the subject of the next chapter.

2

The Savage Pattern

In this chapter, I revisit the old controversy over individualism and collectivism in Rousseau's thought. Here is one way of describing that controversy. The *Second Discourse* is a hymn to nature and to a natural man more brutish, more solitary, and more limited in the scope of his passions than even the warlike natural man of Thomas Hobbes's state of nature. But the *Social Contract* is a hymn to the state and to a virtuous, dignified, and altogether socialized citizen. What support, if any, can be found in Rousseau's minimalist account of nature for his eloquent defense of the citizen? What support is there in indolent, isolated, natural man for virtuous members of a republican political community?

This formulation of the problem, however, assumes that Rousseau's account of nature is a "minimalist" one. My purpose in the last chapter was to prove that assumption incorrect. It is only on that assumption that a paean to nature and a paean to society must be an altogether baffling contradiction. Once it is abandoned, the tension in Rousseau's thought does not dissolve. But there is no question that the controversy over individualism and collectivism has been greatly exacerbated by the widely shared belief that when Rousseau praises nature, strictly speaking, he praises what must exclude society altogether.

My own interpretation of the unity of Rousseau's thought emphasizes not the extreme states Rousseau praises, such as the original man of the First Part of the *Second Discourse* and the citizen of the *Social Contract*, but above all the middling states, such as the savage of the Second Part of the *Second Discourse* and the "natural man living in the state of society" (*E*, IV, 483; 205) of *Emile*. If these middling states have been emphasized by few commentators, it is in large part because of the perceived radicalism of

Rousseau's understanding of nature. Where nature is perceived as a pure state of immediacy, solitude, and indolence that is fatally altered by the very first developments of history, let alone of civilization, there is little hope for compromise between natural and civil man. Indeed, it is hard, if one accepts the premise that Rousseau's praise of nature is the praise of a state hermetically sealed off from the impact of circumstances, not to think of him as engaged in a radical and dangerous quest. It is easy to think of him, as Jean Starobinki does, as a man who seeks to escape the ordinary "obligations of the human condition," who is unwilling to face the "uncertainty of life." It is easy to think of him, as Michael Sandel does, as a man "unwilling to abide disharmony," or as Irving Babbitt does, as a seeker of "dream unity" and an opponent of "sober discrimination."[1] It is nearly impossible to view him, as I do, as a thinker whose end is to accommodate the elements of a nature whose complexity and disharmony he understands well. Conversely, when one discards the false premise that Rousseau equated the original and the natural, one is better able to weigh the abundant evidence I will present in this chapter that the middling and not the extreme states Rousseau describes are the keys to understanding the unity of Rousseau's thought.

In his 1954 Introduction to Cassirer's *The Question of Jean-Jacques Rousseau*, Peter Gay described a problem that continues to dog Rousseau interpretation, though it was by then already fairly old: Is Rousseau a radical individualist whose model is the natural man of the *Second Discourse*, or is he a radical collectivist whose model is the citizen of the *Social Contract?* This problem and the opposing stands taken on it by Rousseau's interpreters raised another difficulty, which Gay also discussed: Is Rousseau's thought a unity, and if he is neither individualist nor collectivist, how can Rousseau's praise of natural man be reconciled with his praise of the citizen? In this chapter, I will show how two influential modes of interpreting Rousseau tend to magnify the incompatibility of man and citizen in his thought, even as they emphasize its unity. I will go on to argue that Rousseau regards the perfect individuality of original man and the perfect sociality of the denatured citizen as deficient remedies for the ills of divided civilized souls. I will make a case, primarily but not exclusively with respect to individuality and sociality, that the human good, in Rousseau's view, comprises disparate and disharmonious elements and that the coexistence of these elements, not the unity gained when one element or its apparent opposite is unreservedly embraced, is the end uniting Rousseau's various models of human happiness and projects of reform. If the argument of Chapter 1 is right, Rousseau seeks not some approximation of a natural beginning untouched by perfectibility, but a natural end or perfection for human beings. If the argument of this chapter is right, that end or perfection requires a difficult and delicate arrangement of conflicting goods. If both arguments are right, then the unity of Rousseau's thought consists in this: It is a reflection on the natural perfection of a naturally disharmonious being.

THE HOBBESIAN AND KANTIAN INTERPRETATIONS

I will call one mode of interpretation "Hobbesian" because it emphasizes Rousseau's debt to and radicalization of the thought of Thomas Hobbes (Melzer, 1990; Plattner, 1979; Scott, 1992; Strauss, 1953).[2] Hobbes "very clearly saw the defect of all modern definitions of Natural right." In particular, he understood the necessity of founding natural right on the strongest passions of human beings, rather than on reason, whose sway is very limited in the natural state and that is called into service by the passions. But, for Rousseau, Hobbes failed to see that "the same cause that prevents the Savages from using their reason, as our Jurists claim they do, at the same time prevents them from abusing their faculties" (*SD*, III, 153–54; I, 35). Hobbes exaggerated the scope of natural human passion and consequently gave human beings the knowledge (especially of death), social feelings (especially vainglory), and concerns (especially about providing for the future) that bring about the state of war. Had he thought through his insight into the interdependence of reason and the passions, Hobbes would have seen that the passions are calm and circumscribed and reason needless and virtually nonexistent in man's natural state. He could have buttressed this conclusion by conjoining his premise of natural human asociality with the observation that reason is coeval with language, which, in turn, appears to presuppose society. Hobbes would then have realized that the move from the natural state to the state of war requires an explanation, one that distinguishes not only between nature and civil society but also between original nature and the circumstances leading up to the state of war, or between nature and history.

He would have seen, moreover, that the original state is good, "the most conducive to Peace and the best suited to Mankind" (*SD*, III, 153; I, 35). For Hobbes, nature is a negative standard. His description of nature clarifies those problems to which civil society is the solution. When Rousseau radicalizes Hobbes's teaching, he finds nature good and worthy of use as a positive standard. Even though reflection on human history suggests that the original state is unrecoverable, it also reveals the extraordinary malleability of human beings and tells of the development of capacities, such as reason and foresight, that, though the cause of discontents so far, may, if properly employed, be our salvation. It may be that human art can bring about an approximation of the original condition for civil man. Guided by the model of natural man, man may re-create himself in his own, original image. Rousseau's so-called constructive projects and the advanced states he praises can be understood as attempts to recapture and perhaps augment the unity and freedom of humanity's first state.

The Hobbesian interpretation, then, unifies the individualist and collectivist sides of Rousseau in the following manner. Man was not in contradiction with himself in the state of nature, for he was naturally solitary and independent. His inclinations were not in conflict with his duties because he had no duties. Since he did not require the assistance of other men, his inclinations did not have to be suppressed or disguised for, and were only rarely frustrated by, other men. When, as the result of a series of accidents, man becomes social, when he comes to be interested in and even to need others, he is torn between his own inclinations and the demands placed on him by his fellows, on whom the satisfaction of his inclinations now depends. Fortunately, man's malleability, which is revealed in the story of the partial socialization of man, may provide the key to the restoration of his lost unity. The political art may be able to restore unity by further modifying man's inclinations in such a way that they are no longer at war with the common good, so that his desires are at odds with neither the just claims nor the whims of his fellows. If man can be fully socialized, then the unity of the most solitary condition of all may be recaptured in the least solitary condition of all, that of the citizen in the Rousseauian republic. Further, man was not subject to other men in the state of nature. The political art may restore freedom by substituting for dependence on men dependence on a polity constituted by self-made law. Subjection to self-made law does not violate and may even constitute human freedom. In this view, Rousseau reconciles individualism and collectivism by arguing that the particulars of original happiness described in the individualistic *Second Discourse* are irremediably lost to most civil men, but the core of original man's happiness is artificially reconstructed in the collectivistic *Social Contract*.[3]

The "Kantian" mode of interpretation emphasizes Rousseau's anticipation of Kant's thought (Cassirer, 1989).[4] In this view, Rousseau does not regard brutish, solitary, natural man as a model for the virtuous, social citizen. While the description of the original state demonstrates well how human beings have been led astray by history, return to original nature is neither possible nor desirable. Rather than retracing the path of nature, man must embark on the path of freedom; he must renounce the guidance of nature in favor of self-determination, which, unlike our physical natures, makes us truly human: "Rousseau did not hesitate in elevating this ethical conception of personality far above the mere state of nature" (Ibid., 25, 75, 56). Spiritual freedom, or the spontaneity of the will, which man gradually comes to know in the course of his history, is the thread and goal uniting Rousseau's constructive project, which consists in subjecting human beings to self-made, universally binding law.

The Kantian interpretation resolves the conflict between individualism and collectivism in Rousseau in the following manner. Nature made men independent of one another. By his own misguided efforts man emerges from the state of nature and becomes, on the one hand, partially cultivated but, on the other hand, subject to the ills described by Rousseau in the *First Discourse* and the *Second Discourse*. As Kant himself points out, Rousseau was not far off the mark in elevating the natural condition over this condition of merely partial cultivation: "Rousseau was not so mistaken in giving preference to the condition of the savage, if we omit the last step our species still has to mount."[5] But the history of our miseries reveals the reason and freedom that, while disastrous in their consequences so far, must be seized upon if we are to become truly and fully human:

With this they give up the independence of the state of nature, the *independence naturelle*, but they exchange it for real freedom, which consists in tying all men to the law. And only then will they have become individuals in the higher sense – autonomous personalities. (Cassirer, 1989, 56)

On the Kantian interpretation, then, the individuality of the *Second Discourse* is, indeed, abandoned, but only in favor of true individuality; the individualist and collectivist ideas are synthesized under the idea of law, through which, in Rousseau's words "'each one, uniting with all, nevertheless obeys only himself and remains as free as before" (*Social Contract, SC* hereafter, III, 360; 53).

The Hobbesian and Kantian interpretations share the following assessment of man's situation, which we find set down by Rousseau in a fragment:

What makes human misery is the contradiction one finds between our state and our desires, between our duties and our penchants, between nature and social institutions, between the man and the citizen; Make man one, and you make him as happy as he can be. Give him entirely to the state or leave him entirely to himself; but if you divide his heart, you tear it. ("Of Public Happiness," *Oeuvres Completes*, III, 510)[6]

They further agree that a kind of unity on the individual level exists by nature, that a harmful disunity of duties and inclinations, of social and selfish demands, arises in history, and that salvation lies in the restoration of unity on the social level,[7] whether this restoration is an artificial imitation of nature or the complete emergence of a new, "intelligible" nature. While both groups of interpreters offer a resolution of the tension between individualism and collectivism in Rousseau, they agree that man and citizen are polar opposites and that, for the sake of human happiness, one or the other must be embraced.[8] The attempt to embrace both types results at best in "less perfect"[9] solutions and at worst in the bourgeois, a man who, according to Rousseau, is "always in contradiction with himself . . . good neither for himself nor for others" (*E*, IV, 249–50; 40).

For the Kantian interpreter, who sees the departure from the original state as essentially connected to the fulfillment of human destiny, the solitary unity of natural man is precisely what must be rejected. Whatever the necessity or goodness of certain elements of our physical natures, any conception of man's estate that embraces our beginnings as on a par with the attainments of civilization compromises our very humanity. Certainly, any halt on the way to the realization of our intellectual selves out of love for our asocial origins is unthinkable. The Hobbesian interpreter arrives at a similar conclusion by a different route. Original man remains a standard for him. But because original man's happiness is dependent on characteristics like stupidity, asociality, and immersion in the present that are negated by the most minimal attainments of civilization, there is little hope for compromise between natural man and civil man;[10] the formal unity of original man may be recaptured but only by abandoning his substantive characteristics in favor of their opposites.

It is worth reminding ourselves that the minimal and negative character of natural man's happiness is necessitated only by the equation of the original and the natural. That equation renders natural happiness not only bestial but also very fragile and little capable of adjustment to new circumstances, with the surprising result that only the most extreme artifice, the completion of civilization in the form of an absolute state, is the perfect solution to man's historical misery. It is in this way that when we suppose that Rousseau's thought turns fundamentally on a radical bifurcation of nature and history, we are bound to think him as an extremist whose uncompromising and radical understanding of nature commits him to an equally uncompromising and radical understanding of society. Yet in Rousseau's thought, the praise of "middling states," from what I will call the "savage nation" to the small society at Clarens in *Julie*, to the man of nature in society in *Emile,* is the rule rather than the exception. When we discard the equation of the original and the natural, we are free at least to entertain this thesis: Rousseau prefers such middling states to the extremes, which he describes, in fact, less frequently. In what follows, I offer what I take to be compelling evidence for that thesis.

THE SUPERIORITY OF THE SAVAGE STATE

To understand how Rousseau pursues what his interpreters and he, himself, sometimes seem to discourage, namely combining the individualistic and collectivist elements in his thought, we should begin by considering his praise of the savage nation in the *Second Discourse.* This praise implies not only that collective existence is compatible with a high degree of independence of individuals but also that this compatibility makes possible the best state for man.

One of Rousseau's criticisms of his early modern predecessors, especially of Hobbes, follows from the individualistic perspective opened up by Rousseau's description of solitary natural man. These predecessors mistook historical accretions for parts of the essential core of man. Even when they claimed that society is the product of a contract, of an act of human will, rather than of human nature, they ascribed to the contracting parties characteristics that could have been acquired only in societies:

All of them, continually speaking of need, greed, oppression, desires, and pride transferred to the state of Nature ideas they had taken from society; they spoke of Savage Man and depicted Civil man. (*SD*, III, 132; Exordium, 5)

Rousseau's predecessors took human beings to be more social, and therefore much worse, than they are.

But Rousseau has another disagreement with his predecessors, too. Consider the following criticism of Hobbes, which, in agreement with the first criticism, seems to take its bearings from an individualism more radical than Hobbes's:

By reasoning on the basis of the principles he established, this Author should have said that, since the state of Nature is the state in which the care for our own preservation is least prejudicial to the self-preservation of others, it follows that this state was the most conducive to Peace and the best suited to Mankind. He says precisely the contrary because he improperly included in Savage man's care for his preservation the need to satisfy a multitude of passions that are the product of Society. (*SD*, III, 153; I, 35).

Had Hobbes followed through his individualistic, minimalistic principles to the end, Rousseau claims, he would have realized that the natural state is more conducive to peace than is society, that this state is, indeed, the best for man.

But Rousseau himself denies that the natural state is the best for man, thus breaking with what he regards as Hobbes's position rightly understood. For Rousseau, the state "reached by most of the Savage Peoples known to us" (*SD*, III, 170; II, 17) is "the happiest and the longest-lasting epoch . . . the least subject to revolutions, the best for man" (*SD*, III, 171; II, 18). The savage state is characterized by the coexistence of independence and social relations. Savage men and women "enjoy the sweetness of independent commerce with one another" (*SD*, III, 171; II, 19).[11] Men and women gather, sing, dance, and contest for public approbation (*SD*, III, 169–70; II, 16) without becoming utterly reliant on the others and without losing a taste for the pleasures associated with "spending [one's] life alone in the depths of the forests, or fishing, or blowing into a poor flute without ever managing to draw a single note" (*SD*, III, 220; note xvi, 1). That the social aspect of the savage state is an important part of its charm is indicated by the story behind the frontispiece of the *Second Discourse*, an illustration of a young man who returns not to the natural state, at least if the natural is the original, but to the savage state. The young man resolves "'to live and die in the Religion, the ways, and the customs of [his] Ancestors'" (*SD*, III, 221; note xvi, 4).[12] The return to the savage state, then, is a return not only to independence but also to community and rootedness. Each savage nation is "united in manners and morals, and character, not by Rules or Laws, but by the same kind of life and of foods, and the influence of a shared Climate" (*SD*, III, 169; II, 15).[13]

The savage state, then, shows up the deficiencies not only of civil society but also of the original state, for the latter is wholly lacking in community. Rousseau regards this advantage so highly that he is willing to prefer to the original state one in which "vengeance became terrible, and men bloodthirsty and cruel" (*SD*, III, 170; II, 17), "everyone was sole judge and avenger of the offenses he had received" and "the terror of vengeance had to take the place of the Law's restraint" (*SD*, III, 170–71; II, 18). Rousseau's disagreement with Hobbes could hardly be more marked; the original state is clearly superior to the savage state from the standpoint of peace yet Rousseau praises the latter more highly. His criticism of Hobbes, then, is twofold. On the one hand, he thinks that Hobbes has failed to recognize the outcome of his own principles, namely that lone, completely uncivilized natural men are better off than their more advanced and communal counterparts. On the other hand, he thinks that Hobbes's principles exaggerate human asociality, thereby mistakenly narrowing the scope of man's ends and the requirements of his happiness.

I have suggested that Rousseau's description of brutish original man could, from a certain angle, appear to be a caricature of radical individualism. And indeed, the description of the savage state and Rousseau's higher praise of it do point up the deficiencies of the original state and of the individualism on which the account of it is based. At least two objections may follow. First, the savage state is no mean between individualism and collectivism. Rather, it represents Rousseau's abandonment of individualism, which leaves us subhuman, in favor of community, which makes us human. As we have seen, savages are united in a nation. The morals and character of a particular savage nation appear to be a spontaneous outgrowth of a shared way of life fitted to the requirements of shared circumstances. This organic community, in which morality first appears on the scene (*SD*, III, 170; II, 18), is a precursor of the contrived community of the *Social Contract*, whose citizen virtue is an incalculable advance over rudimentary savage morality. The rootedness of savages in ancestral religions, ways, and customs, far from representing individualism, is a collectivism that is destined, under the guidance of a manipulative Legislator, to be overcome by the more perfect, and arguably more sinister, collectivism of the *Social Contract*. Alternatively, following the Kantian reading, the savage state is a first stage in the abandonment of an individualism of instinct and appetite in favor of a truly human individualism. The beginning of morality in the savage nation is an initial but far from complete subordination of instinct to duty, of natural freedom to moral freedom, and of the individualism of appetite to the individualism of ethical personality. What begins in the savage nation ends in the polity of the *Social Contract* with the fusion of individualism and collectivism made possible by law.

We can begin to address both objections by reminding ourselves of the language Rousseau uses to praise savage society. Savages enjoy "the sweetness of independent commerce." Independence and community are given equal weight. This independence, moreover, exists not because of communal life but despite it. Savages, though they undertake certain tasks in common, perform the most needful ones without assistance. They "applied themselves only to tasks a single individual could perform." Their happiness is in jeopardy "the moment one man [needs] the help of another" (*SD*, III, 171; II, 19). Savage independence is, in addition, not the capacity to conquer one's appetites, but rather the capacity to satisfy one's needs without assistance.

On at least one occasion, Rousseau gives independence more weight than community in his depiction and praise of savage nations. It is above all the pleasure of being alone that the savage knows and the civilized man simply cannot imagine:

After a few observations they can readily see that all our labors are directed at only two objects: namely, the comforts of life for oneself, and consideration from others. But how are we to imagine the sort of pleasure a Savage takes in spending [his] life alone in the depths of the forests, or fishing or blowing into a poor flute. (*SD*, III, 220; note xvi, 1)

Thus, this variety of independence, the capacity to live and take pleasure in solitude, is not the precursor of a new and self-conquering kind of individualism; if anything, it hearkens back to original man.

In at least one respect, however, independence is different for the member of the savage nation than it is for original man. Savage man is conscious of the goodness of his independence. Rousseau argues that savages are not attached to their way of life by mere habit (*SD*, III, 221; xvi, 3). They adamantly resist being civilized. "They consistently refuse either to adopt political society in imitation of us, or to learn to live happy among us" (*SD*, III, 220; note xvi, 1). They refuse not because they are prisoners of tradition but because they reason that civilized life is directed toward comforts and consideration and judge that these goods are inferior to the pleasures they derive from material and psychological self-sufficiency. While Rousseau's original man may be regarded as individualistic only in the sense that his description seems to be grounded on a radically individualistic understanding of human nature, the savage is individualistic in reflectively and fervently desiring his independence. It is true that savages risk their material self-sufficiency by acquiring new needs "without thinking of it" (*SD*, III, 168; II, 13) and that they, equally without forethought, risk their psychological self-sufficiency by allowing public esteem to acquire a value (*SD*, III, 169–70; II, 16). One therefore has reason to doubt that the savage in the savage nation fully understands the goodness or the conditions of his own way of life. It may be that the man of the frontispiece, who returns to savage life after experiencing civilized life, is in a better position to understand how a mean between individualism and collectivism can be preserved in the face of the inevitable and not in itself undesirable cultivation of the human faculties and arts that cannot fail to alter the character of communal life. However that may be, the imperfections of savage life point not toward a transformation in the direction of perfect collectivism or "true" individualism but rather toward the self-conscious preservation of a middle way for which the spontaneously arising savage nation is a model.

Rousseau says that the savage state is best for man, an assertion that contradicts those who argue that Rousseau's end is either an individual or a collective unity. The savage is a human being who knows and tastes the pleasure of being alone while also enjoying those social pleasures that cause him, even if they do not obligate him, to consider the desires of his fellows. That Rousseau draws to our attention not only the bourgeois but also the savage implies that communal and purely individual goods may lure men in different, seemingly opposite, directions without tearing them apart.[14]

At this point, another objection may be raised. Even if the savage takes others into consideration in his thoughts and deeds, it is surely significant that he is not obligated or compelled to do so. There is an important distinction between savages and citizens, and one must acknowledge a wide gap between an endorsement of sociality and an endorsement of collectivism. That said, the sociality of the savage nation does point in the direction of collectivism. First, the savage may be obligated in some sense, even if there is only the terror of vengeance to compel obedience; there are already the "first duties of civility" (*SD*, III, 170; II, 17) among savages, though the character of these duties is not much elaborated. Second, Rousseau couches the distinction between man and citizen in such a way that community of any kind is a departure from individualism in the direction of collectivism. If natural or original man is an "absolute whole" and the citizen is "a fractional unity dependent on the denominator" (*E*, IV, 249; 39), the savage is on the road to citizenship and is in some ways already like the citizen. Since he already values "public esteem" and wishes to be looked at by others (*SD*, III, 169; II, 16), his happiness is already partially dependent on "the denominator." Insofar, then, as Rousseau offers as the best, if not most practicable, solution to the division of bourgeois man something other than a stark choice between the individual and the community, he may also be said to offer a middle way between individualism and collectivism.

But is Rousseau's praise of the savage condition representative of Rousseau's considered thought? Heinrich Meier makes this praise a case study in the danger of "capitulating to Rousseau's rhetoric" (1988–89, 214). He argues that when Rousseau describes tribal savages as "bloodthirsty and cruel," he deliberately leaves the discerning reader a clue that he should reject them after all. But it hardly seems obvious that "the more philosophical readers" (Ibid.) to whom, on Meier's account, the *Discourse* reveals itself would regard the violence of savage society as decisive grounds for rejecting it (Ibid.). Meier also argues that the three uses of the term "sociable," all negative, in the *Discourse* are damning for sociability. This is a very striking and correct observation, but it does not explain or do away with Rousseau's sometimes benign use of related terms like "society."[15] Finally, Meier's explanations of Rousseau's rhetorical intention in praising the tribal savage are not very convincing. He suggests that Rousseau, in praising heathens, rejects Christianity and, in praising a state in which our faculties are not fully developed, underscores the anti-teleological character of his history (Ibid.). It is hard to understand why Rousseau's praise of the original man would not serve both purposes well enough. Besides, even if praising the tribal savage serves both of the rhetorical purposes Meier discusses, there is no reason to suppose that there is nothing genuine in it. I have already stated my reasons for thinking that Rousseau's homage to the tribal savage and his preference for that savage over original man are genuine in at least one respect. Rousseau congratulates him on maintaining his independence amidst the pleasures and dangers of sociality, an accomplishment on which neither original nor civilized man may be congratulated. In the next several sections of this chapter, I will show that this feature of savage life can be discerned, to various degrees, in Rousseau's other exemplary figures.

THE SAVAGE PATTERN IN EMILE

In *Emile*, Rousseau seems to offer precisely the stark choice between individualism and collectivism that I deny he offers. Natural man is "entirely for himself," a "unity," an "absolute whole," while civil man is a "fractional unity"; his "value is determined by his relation to the . . . social body" (*E*, IV, 249; 39–40). The task of social institutions is to transform isolated natural individuals into social men, and this involves nothing less than a "denaturing":

Good social institutions are those that best know how to denature man, to take his absolute existence from him . . . ; with the result that each individual believes himself no longer one but a part of the unity. (*E*, IV, 249; 40)

Man and citizen are "necessarily opposed objects" (*E*, IV, 250; 40) requiring different educations. Attempts to combine the two educations produce divided men:

> He who in the civil order wants to preserve the primacy of the sentiments of
> nature does not know what he wants. Always in contradiction with himself, always
> floating between his inclinations and his duties, he will never be either man
> or citizen.... He will be one of these men of our days...a bourgeois. (*E*, IV,
> 249–50; 40)

The end of public education is the Spartan or Roman, a man raised for
others who loves "the country exclusive of himself" (*E*, IV, 249; 40). Domestic education, on the other hand, raises a man "uniquely for himself"
(*E*, IV, 251; 41). The education that attempts to raise a man for himself
and for others is the "education of society," which, by "tending to two
contrary ends, fails to attain either" (*E*, IV, 250; 41). Rousseau seems to
insist on a choice between an individualist and a collectivist education,
implying a similarly exclusive choice between individualist and collectivist
solutions to the problem of the bourgeois. But he quickly suggests that a
third alternative is possible and that, perhaps, Emile's education will be
guided by it.

> What will a man raised uniquely for himself become for others? If perchance the
> double object we set for ourselves could be joined in a single one by removing
> the contradictions of man, a great obstacle to his happiness would be removed.
> (*E*, IV, 251; 41)[16]

On the other hand, Rousseau warns that one cannot judge the success
of this enterprise until one has read *Emile* and seen the student of the
domestic education, or of the education of nature, fully formed (Ibid.).
With this in mind, let us examine the adult Emile to see whether he, like
the savage, is both social and independent.

   At the end of Book III, Emile remains nearly asocial and a good model
for the individualistic side of Rousseau's thought:

> He considers himself without regard to others and finds it good that others do
> not think of him.... He is alone in human society; he counts on himself alone.
> (*E*, IV, 488; 208)

But a difficulty, or an opportunity, presents itself in the form of Emile's
need for a companion:

> The blood ferments and is agitated; a superabundance of life seeks to extend itself
> outward.... One begins to feel that one is not made to live alone. It is thus that
> the heart is opened to the human affections and becomes capable of attachment.
> (*E*, IV, 502; 220)

The governor uses Emile's "second birth" (*E*, IV, 490; 212) to make a second, social man of his pupil. By turns, Emile is led to experience humanity,

romantic love, and attachment to his country and countrymen. He acquires not only inclinations but duties, and if the first birth produced a happy man, the second produces a virtuous one. The question arises: Does the second, social Emile efface, or at least greatly outstrip in importance, the first, solitary Emile – as Cassirer suggests when he makes duty and citizenship the ultimate end of the education (1989, 121–27), or do the two Emiles coexist on something close to an equal footing – as Allan Bloom suggests when he argues that "Emile stands somewhere between the citizen of the *Social Contract* and the solitary of the *Reveries*" (1979, 28)?

Certainly, the Emile of the first three books does not disappear in society. Indeed, Rousseau emphasizes the way in which Emile is "in the midst of a group the same as he is when alone." Emile presents himself in a "natural and true" way, and his manners are frank because "he loves freedom above everything" (*E*, IV, 665, 666; 335, 336). All this is not the result of a newly acquired ethical character but rather an "effect of his first education." This first education is the source, especially, of Emile's disdain for display: "He will not resort to the gilded frame" (*E*, IV, 669; 338), the kind of frame rejected more literally in Book II (*E*, IV, 399; 145); he does not babble because he "knows enough about things to assign them all their true value." Here, true value is not judged with reference to a transcendent ethical standard but rather by utility, a criterion Emile learned to respect before his second birth: "He says only *useful* things" (*E*, IV, 666; 336; emphasis added); the "sphere of his knowledge does not extend farther than what is *profitable*"; "Emile is a man of good sense" (*E*, IV, 670; 339; emphasis added).

It is true that Emile now has pride and is not indifferent to the opinions of others (*E*, IV, 670; 339), but pride is the particular form of *amour-propre* characteristic of great souls (*E*, IV, 494; 215). It is an early goal of Emile's second education to direct Emile's concern for his position with respect to others in such a way that he believes himself to be in the first rank:

> As soon as *amour-propre* has developed . . . the young man never observes others without returning to himself and comparing himself with them. . . . I see from the way young people are made to read history that they are transformed, so to speak, into all the persons they see. . . . If in these parallels [Emile] just once prefers to be someone other than himself . . . everything has failed. (*E*, IV, 534–5; 243)

Moreover, although Emile already feels compassion for others, it is not the characteristics of the new, social Emile that place him in the first rank.

The characteristics Emile prides himself on and which will be preserved, in part, by Emile's pride are recognizable as the virtues of the solitary learned in the first three books:

If he judges them well, he will not want to be in the place of any of them.... The goal of all the torments they give themselves is founded on prejudices he does not have.... For him, all that he desires is within his reach. [He is] sufficient unto himself and free of prejudices.... He has arms, health, moderation, few needs, and the means of satisfying them. Nurtured in the most absolute liberty, he conceives of no ill greater than servitude. (*E*, IV, 536; 244)

At least one aspect of Emile's second education, then, is designed to preserve the benefits of the first. Emile will have the tastes and merits of a solitary even after he develops a taste for and competence in society.

Even love does not do away with the Emile of the first three books, for Sophie "wants to reign over a man whom she has not disfigured" (*E*, IV, 810; 439). To be sure, she is attracted to Emile's virtue and his attachment to duty, but she is also attracted to the good sense Emile acquired before he was a lover. She despises the "petty jargon of gallantry" (*E*, IV, 754; 399) and wants young men "to be *useful*" (*E*, IV, 753; 399; emphasis added) when they speak seriously, as does Emile, who is guided in his speech by the criterion of utility. Sophie loves Emile for characteristics that include both social virtues and the virtues he practiced in his imagination on Crusoe's island, namely,

esteem of true goods, frugality, simplicity, generous disinterestedness, contempt for show and riches. Emile had these virtues before love imposed them on him. How, then, has Emile truly changed? He has new reasons to be himself. This is the single point where he differs from what he was. (*E*, IV, 801; 433)

Moreover, Emile continues to pursue and enjoy solitary pleasures both when he is looking for Sophie and after he finds her. When he looks for Sophie, he travels on foot with his tutor and becomes so interested in pursuing his natural science, the study, pursued especially in Book III, of man's relation with physical objects, that "if Sophie is not forgotten before we have gone fifty leagues," the governor's skill or the pupil's curiosity must be deficient (*E*, IV, 773; 412). When he is in love with Sophie and courting her,

the days when he does not see her ... he is Emile again. *He has not been transformed at all.* Most often he roams through the surrounding countryside. He pursues his natural history. (*E*, IV, 804; 435; emphasis added).

Rousseau explicitly warns the tutor not to lose sight, in making the man, of the ends achieved in educating the child:

Prolong the good habits of childhood during youth; and when your pupil is what he ought to be, fix it so that he will be the same at all times.... What misleads teachers ... is their belief that one way of life excludes another and that, as soon as someone is grown up, he ought to renounce everything he did when he was young. (*E*, IV, 799–800; 431–32)

Thus Emile does not trade in his solitary independence, even when he acquires virtue, or moral freedom. Writing of the habits that must be maintained, Rousseau describes a kind of freedom and activity that has nothing to do with citizenship or even with sociality:

Emile ... in his childhood did everything voluntarily and with pleasure. In continuing to act the same way ... he therefore only adds the empire of habit to the sweetness of freedom. The active life, work with his hands, exercise, and movement have become so necessary to him that he could not give them up without suffering.... He needs fresh air, movement, toil. (*E*, IV, 801; 432)

None of this is to deny that Emile learns virtue, that he even becomes in some measure a citizen, or that these changes are significant. These concessions undoubtedly bolster the position of the Kantian interpreter. But, even here, Rousseau does not suggest a thoroughgoing abandonment of individual independence in favor of social virtue. Indeed, the most striking and perhaps the first display of genuine virtue on Emile's part is connected with his agreement to leave Sophie for two years. This exercise in virtue is meant not only or even primarily to force Emile to learn about citizenship or to prevent him from wanting to have Sophie, even at the price of his morality. The governor advises Emile not to extend his attachments through virtue but to "restrain [his] heart within the limits of [his] condition" (*E*, IV, 819; 445). Virtue will enable Emile to conquer those passions that make him dependent on goods and human beings that can be lost, without making it impossible for him to enjoy them. "You will possess them without their possessing you" (*E*, IV, 820; 446). In my view, Rousseau's emphasis on virtue is neutral with respect to the argument between individualist and collectivist interpretations of Rousseau; virtue can serve to draw man into or out of himself. As for citizenship, Emile will rarely, if ever, be called to serve; but if he is summoned, he will serve like the Romans, who "went from the plow to the consulate" (*E*, IV, 860; 474), with the implication that he will return to private life when his task is done. Emile's citizenship has room for Emile's individual, even solitary, pleasures.

By showing that Emile, like the savage, maintains independence and certain solitary tastes within society, or that the individual Emile of the early books continues to exist alongside and on a level with the social Emile of the later books, I have gone some way toward showing that the praise of the tribal savage in the *Second Discourse* is not an anomaly in Rousseau's thought. But unlike the savage, whose way of life is clearly described as best for man, Emile, who is an ordinary child living in conditions under which true public education is not to be had, is not obviously the best man. The possibility that more radical alternatives, both social and individual, exist for certain men or societies of Rousseau's time must not be discounted. Let us consider, then, what look to be such alternatives in Rousseau's thought, to see whether they indicate that Rousseau prescribes unity on either the individual or the social level for the best men or for men in the best of circumstances.

THE SAVAGE PATTERN IN ROUSSEAU'S SOLITARIES

Rousseau tells us that Emile has a "common mind" and that his education is meant to serve as an example only for common minds. At the same time, he mentions another type, who needs no education; some men "raise themselves in spite of what one does" (*E*, IV, 266; 52). Allan Bloom suggests that Rousseau himself is such an exceptional type (*E*, 482, note 21), and Rousseau's personal embrace of solitude might suggest that the solution to the discontents of bourgeois life presented in *Emile* is meant for ordinary people who cannot attain to the superior solution for exceptional men of breaking with society altogether. Is Rousseau's vision of the best life, after all, radically individualistic?

At one point in the fourth book of *Emile*, Rousseau describes the life he would lead if he were a rich man. This life is undoubtedly more solitary than Emile's. Rousseau would have no wife or child, and most of the pleasures he plans to enjoy would have nothing to do with others. However, he will gather in his country house "a society." This society, more than Emile's, is reminiscent of the savage nation. It displays a commerce that, while still more independent than savage commerce, is a kind of commerce nonetheless:

Each of us, openly preferring himself to everyone else, would find it good that all the others similarly preferred themselves to him. From this cordial and moderate familiarity there would arise . . . a playful conflict a hundred times more charming than politeness and more likely to bind together our hearts. (*E*, IV, 687–88; 351–52; emphasis added)

Even the most independent alternative in *Emile* seeks to combine solitary and social pleasures. Sociality is much less prominent here than in
Emile's life, but even the solitary Rousseau is exposed to the full, effusive
pastoral treatment – complete with peasants, country celebrations, and
rustic songs – a treatment that suggests not only radical individualism but
also a sentimental attachment to a certain kind of community.

But one has reason to suspect Rousseau's self-presentation in *Emile* because he introduces it as "an example that is more evident and closer to
the morals of the reader" than Emile is (*E*, IV, 678; 344). Arthur Melzer
has argued that Rousseau promoted a popularized version of his individualistic teaching that he meant to attract readers for whom citizenship,
for various reasons, was no longer an option (1990, 279). A life of retreat
among family and friends, for such readers, is the best possible alternative
to civilized corruption. Perhaps Emile, who is virtuous, if not fully a citizen, is also too lofty a model for such readers. Rousseau is a better model
for the corrupted reader in that he is selfish and seeks happiness instead
of virtue. For all the unnaturalness of civilized life and the artificiality of
civilized pleasure, civilized Frenchmen remain pleasure-seekers and are
consequently closer to nature than to Sparta. Rousseau can expect to have
some effect by offering himself as a model for the intelligent hedonist.
But Rousseau can serve as a such a model only by concealing the depth
of his asociality, which is as much out of the reach of the corrupt reader
as Emile's virtue is. Rousseau's self-portrait in *Emile*, then, as much as or
more than his portrait of Emile, is a compromise with the weakness of
his readers and the sad conditions of his time. But if neither the *Second
Discourse* nor *Emile*, both of which have been regarded as examples of
the individualistic side of Rousseau's teaching, contains the individualistic teaching in full measure, what work does? There remain Rousseau's
autobiographical works, in which Rousseau's laziness, solitude, and immersion in the moment bring to mind the original man of the First Part
of the *Second Discourse*.[17]

Rousseau's self-portrayal in the autobiographical works undeniably
constitutes a great praise of the solitary life. Yet Rousseau consistently
denies that his love of solitude precludes a powerful longing for attachments. He repeatedly affirms that his heart was made for intimate attachments, especially in small groups:

I knew he had always fled high society and loved solitude. But I also knew that in
small social groups he had formerly enjoyed the sweetness of intimacy as a man
whose heart is made for it. (*D*, I, 786–7; 98)[18]

He fled society not because he disliked men or company but in order to combine solitary pleasures and independence with social charms. "He liked seclusion not in order to live alone, but to *bring together the sweetness of study and the charms of intimacy*" (*D*, I, 676; 14; emphasis added);[19] "the indomitable spirit of liberty . . . is why, although the ordinary commerce of men is odious to me, intimate friendship is so dear to me, because there are no longer duties for it" (*Letters to Malesherbes, M* hereafter, I, 1132). The desire for friendship without loss of independence; the desire for respite, even from one's friends, in solitude; the insistence that the love of solitude is not misanthropy – all these are prominent themes in Rousseau's autobiographical works.[20]

It is telling that when Rousseau's ways lead to a bitter estrangement from his friends, his solitary pursuits continue to have a social component. When he walks alone, he imagines himself among friends, "creatures after his very heart" (*D*, I, 816; 121):

My imagination did not leave the earth . . . deserted for long. I peopled it soon with beings after my own heart . . . I formed myself a charming society. . . . I made a golden century with my fancy. (*M*, I, 1140)[21]

This golden century Rousseau makes for himself must be set alongside the golden age he imagines for Emile (*E*, IV, 859; 474) and "the genuine youth of the World" (*SD*, III, 171; II, 18), in which savage nations flourish. When alone, Rousseau longs for intimate society; hence the *Dialogues*, which are a praise of solitude, end with the promise to form a small society:

Add to that the sweetness of seeing two decent and true hearts once again open themselves to his own. Let's temper in this way the horror of that solitude in which he is forced to live in the midst of the human race. . . . Let's arrange for him the consolation for his final hour that his eyes will be closed by the hands of friends. (*D*, I, 976; 245)[22]

In the *Reveries*, however, Rousseau seems finally to have outgrown his longing for society. He characterizes his expulsion from society as an unintentional favor granted by his enemies, a stroke of luck:

When men later reduced me to a life of solitude, I found that in isolating me to make me miserable, they had done more for my happiness than I had been able to do myself. (*Reveries of the Solitary Walker, R* hereafter, I, 1015; 52)

Such are his disdain for his fellows and his joy in solitude that he has ceased to long for reconciliation with his fellows, however favorable the terms (*R*, I, 998; 30). At this stage, Rousseau asserts, his imagination has dimmed[23] and no longer fills his solitude with companions (*R*, I, 1004; 37). But the end of hope and the weakening of imagination have forced Rousseau to withdraw into himself, and there he finds happiness (*R*, I, 1002–1003; 35–36).[24] Arguably, the last of Rousseau's autobiographical works reveals the desire for society to be a delusion and the imagination to be simply a villain; once these are finally cast off, Rousseau enjoys, like natural man, freedom from hope and fear and the sweet sentiment of present existence.

Even in this most radically individualistic of works, however, Rousseau opens by describing himself as the "most sociable and loving of men" (*R*, I, 995; 27). Even in the greatest celebration of solitude in the book, the description of life on the island of St. Peter, Rousseau has company, "Thérèse, . . . the Steward, his wife and his household" (*R*, I, 1041; 83). On the island, Rousseau, in pastoral mode, lends a hand to laborers at the harvest (*R*, I, 1043; 85) and ends his day laughing, talking, and singing some old song with his small island circle (*R*, I, 1045; 87). In the Eighth Walk, which begins with one of the strongest statements in favor of withdrawing into oneself (*R*, I, 1074; 123), Rousseau, in spite of an imagination that is "dried up" (*R*, I, 1075; 124), still dallies with "the children of my imagination, the creatures of my heart's desire, whose presence[25] satisfies its yearnings" (*R*, I, 1081; 131). Further, the Ninth Walk dwells on a kind of sociality. It contrasts the amusements of rich men and men of letters with the innocent pleasures to be had among children, pensioners, and the Swiss – human beings who, because of their innocence, isolation, or citizenship elsewhere, are free from Parisian corruption. Finally, the Tenth Walk, which describes Rousseau's life with Mme. Warens, emphasizes the coexistence and even the interdependence of solitude and independence, on the one hand, and sociality on the other:

> *The taste for solitude and contemplation grew up in my heart along with the expansive and tender feelings which are best able to nourish it.* Noise and turmoil constrain and quench them, peace and quiet revive and intensify them. I need tranquillity if I am to love. . . . I needed a female friend after my own heart, and I had one. . . . I could not bear subjection, and I was perfectly free, or better than free because I was subject only to my own affections and did only what I wanted to do. (*R*, I, 1099; 154; emphasis added)[26]

It must be admitted that sociality has a relatively small and qualified place in the *Reveries*. Rousseau's companions on St. Peter's Island cannot be called friends; they are simple and good people but not Rousseau's peers. As for the sociality of the Ninth Walk, much of it is arranged and observed but not fully participated in by Rousseau.[27] However that may be, Rousseau's autobiographical writings, while they offer a model of a still more solitary and independent life than either the savage or Emile leads, cannot be said to deny that sociality, especially the kind that exists in small, intimate societies, is part of the economy of human nature and happiness. In its alternation between solitude and society, the way of life Rousseau claims to prefer is closer to the savage state than it is to the original one.

THE SAVAGE PATTERN IN ROUSSEAU'S CITIZENS

Emile is addressed to men for whom citizenship is not a viable alternative. For moderns, the dedication to the fatherland characteristic of Sparta or Rome has been supplanted by devotion to a Father tied to no particular land and to His otherworldly kingdom. Consequently, "public instruction no longer exists and can no longer exist, because where there is no longer a fatherland, there can no longer be citizens (*E*, IV, 250; 40). We cannot conclude from the fact that Emile is not a citizen in the full sense, or that his individuality is not completely absorbed in a whole, that citizenship is not the best way of life. Arthur Melzer has argued that Rousseau wished to rescue republicanism for the few states that were still capable of it but worked toward a limited moral reform for the states, the majority, that could not escape despotism (1990, 253–82). Perhaps, after all, Emile is not a citizen merely because he cannot be; perhaps Emile is second best.

Yet the goodness of Emile's life on the fringes of society undermines the argument for collectivist politics. That argument is predicated on the claim that the alternative to collectivism is brutishness:

Although in this state he deprives himself of several advantages given him by nature, he gains such great ones, his faculties are exercised and developed . . . to such a point that if the abuses of this new condition did not often degrade him . . . he ought ceaselessly to bless the happy moment that . . . *from a stupid, limited animal* [*made him*] into *an intelligent being and a man. (SC*, III, 364; 56; emphasis added)

Here, as we will see in more detail later, Rousseau argues as if there is a direct transition from original man to civil society. Yet we cannot think this is the case if we attend to Rousseau's writings as a whole. They present not only brutish original man but also savage man, Emile, or even Rousseau, the solitary walker as alternatives to the citizen.[28] Since a considerable measure of intellectual and moral development is to be had without recourse to full citizenship, it is hard to understand why the best life is that of the citizen. Even if not everyone can be an Emile because existence on the fringes of society depends on those who are more closely attached to society, then citizenship is only necessary, not best. A closer examination of his political writings shows that even where Rousseau seems most collectivistic, some measure of individualism remains and is, moreover, useful for politics.[29]

Those who argue that politics is the antithesis of nature, or that the *Social Contract* argues for complete artificial social unity where the *Second Discourse* argues for complete natural, solitary unity, regard Rousseau's description of the legislator in the former work as telling:[30]

> One who dares to undertake the founding of a people should feel that he is capable of changing human nature, so to speak; of transforming each individual, who by himself is a perfect and solitary whole, into a part of a larger whole from which this individual receives, in a sense, his life and his being. . . . So that . . . each citizen is nothing, and can do nothing, except with all the others. (*SC*, III, 381–82; 68)

However, the argument of the *Second Discourse*, that a considerable change in man had to happen before there could be any need or desire for society, suggests that the legislator does not deal with perfect and solitary wholes. Historically, Rousseau claims, civil society begins at a time when men can no longer do without each other, when men are already social in the worst possible way:

> Much less than the equivalent of this Discourse was needed to sway crude, easily seduced men who . . . had too much business to sort out among themselves to be able to do without arbiters, and too much greed and ambition to be able to do for long without Masters. (*SD*, III, 177; II, 32)

Why, then, does Rousseau exaggerate the independence of the men who are to enter society? One reason is suggested by the context of the passage just quoted. The proposal that seduces men – that all men's forces should be gathered into a supreme power and that institutions of justice and peace to which all are obliged to conform should be enacted by the whole – is similar to Rousseau's formula for legitimate power in the *Social Contract*. But, as the subsequent history described in the *Second Discourse* attests, even legitimate power is bound to be abused when citizens prefer tranquility to freedom. Consider Rousseau's argument against the notion that "Peoples initially threw themselves unconditionally and irrevocably into the arms of an absolute Master" (*SD*, III, 180; II, 37).

This argument proceeds from the premise that men remain "proud and untamed" (Ibid.), that they continue to appreciate a freedom so primal as to be compared to that of "Animals born free and abhorring captivity" (*SD*, III, 182; II, 39). But we have already learned that, in fact, men, far from being jealous of their freedom, "ran toward their chains" (*SD*, III, 177; II, 32). Rousseau appears guilty of disregarding the facts until we learn that he examines "the facts in terms of Right" (*SD*, III, 182; II, 41) in his argument against tyranny, contrary to his earlier procedure in which "moral proofs [were] without great force in matters of Physics" (*SD*, III, 215; note xii, 4). Rousseau argues not that tyranny was impossible because men were proud and untamed but rather that the maintenance of legitimate politics, the success of the "principles of political right," requires that men be proud and untamed, that they be jealous of their freedom. The success of the social contract demands that the objects of legislation be independent, in some sense, like original man is independent.

Nonetheless, Rousseau is mindful that original men and animals have no reason to join societies. The most fitting people for legislation is one that "though already bound by some union of origin, interest, or convention, has not yet borne the true yoke of laws" (*SC*, III, 390; 74), one in which the legislator finds "the simplicity of nature together with the needs of society" (*SC*, III, 391; 74–75). From this observation, we may conclude that the ideal object of legislation is not an original man but rather a savage or an Emile, for these latter types are between solitude and citizenship, independence and sociality in such a way as to meet the legislator's needs. But that is not to say yet that the citizen, the product of legislation, maintains an attachment to natural freedom and his own good. Perhaps he abandons it in favor of a freedom that is indistinguishable from subjection to law and a good that is indistinguishable from the common good. What is suitable for the object of legislation is not necessarily suitable for the product of legislation. However, in the *Second Discourse*, when Rousseau argues in favor of man's natural love of freedom and against the inclination to servitude, he writes of "all free Peoples" (namely citizens), "naked savages," and "Animals" as if their attachments to freedom are in some sense attachments to the same "one good" (*SD*, III, 181–82; II, 39). Citizenship does not preclude – and may even require – an attachment to a kind of primal freedom. We are reminded of Emile's continued attachment to the sweet freedom and independence of the early stages of his education, even after he becomes acquainted with the hard freedom of self-conquest.

The *Constitutional Project for Corsica* contains further and more striking proof that Rousseau's political thought has room for individualism. In the *Social Contract*, Rousseau names Corsica the only country in Europe still fit for legislation (*SC*, III, 391; 75). Consequently, the *Constitutional Project*, though unfinished, may be expected to reflect a kind of high point of politics, for Rousseau does not think himself compelled to compromise with a deeply rooted, corrupt political tradition, as, for example, in *Considerations on the Government of Poland*.[31] Yet in the *Constitutional Project*, more than in any other political work of Rousseau's, the coexistence and mutually reinforcing character of independence and sociality in the polity is a theme. The Swiss, Rousseau's models for the Corsicans, spend half the year separated from one another by snow; each is compelled to be "sufficient unto himself and his family" and to practice "all the necessary arts." In addition to practicing the useful arts, which free him from the dependence entailed by the division of labor, each Swiss is also a farmer, and this, too, fosters self-sufficiency: "Each, living on his own land, succeeded in making it satisfy all his needs." Far from making men completely asocial, however, independence makes for sweet, if limited, social ties. "Since needs and interests did not conflict, and no one depended on anyone else, their only relations with one another were those of benevolence and friendship" (*Constitutional Project for Corsica, C* hereafter, III, 914; 295). What is more, the Swiss not only associate with each other but also are capable of uniting effectively for the common defense. This ability is related directly to their purely private enjoyments and independence:

This hard-working and *independent* life attached the Swiss to their fatherland.... When you consider the constant unity that prevailed among men who had no masters and practically no laws ... it is no longer difficult to understand the prodigies they performed in defence of their country and independence. (*C*, III, 915; 296; emphasis added)

Unlike the savages of the savage nation, the rustic Swiss have farmers, masons, carpenters, and even rulers. But the gap between the Swiss and the savages with respect to the arts should not disguise an essential similarity in their ways of life. Like savages, the Swiss combine independence,[32] even self-sufficiency, with a communal existence founded on a shared way of life:

Their isolated and simple life made them independent as well as robust; each recognised no other master than himself; but all, having the same tastes and interests, found it easy to unite in pursuit of the same objects. (*C*, III, 916; 297)

Notably, and in accordance with the previous analysis, the independence of Swiss individuals preserves the Swiss people from corrupt rulers:

The ambition of their leading men made them change their principles; they felt that, the better to rule the people, they would have to give them less independent tastes (Ibid).

Moreover, the importance of independence does not cease with the acquisition of more laws. Rousseau could not be more concerned about restoring an agricultural way of life to the Corsicans: "The whole basic tendency of our new constitution is to make this calling happy in its mediocrity, and respectable in its simplicity" (*C*, III, 925; 310). While Rousseau has more than one reason for fostering agriculture, he makes its connection with independence clear, for shortly after the sentence just quoted Rousseau reveals that the plans he has in mind aim at the fostering of independence at every level:

What local magistrates and heads of families should do in each region, parish and household to make themselves independent of the rest, the central government of the island should do to make itself independent of neighbouring peoples. (*C*, III, 926; 310)

But Rousseau highlights the connection between farming and independence most strikingly in a discussion of the importance of watching closely the proportion between taxes paid in kind, which indicate the predominance of agriculture in a society, and taxes paid in money, which indicate the predominance of industry. Though agriculture is to be encouraged, a great disproportion of taxes in kind to taxes in money is a danger sign:

It will be a sign that agriculture and population are doing well, but that useful industries are being neglected; it will be proper to re-animate them somewhat, lest the private citizens,[33] by becoming too *isolated, savage*[34] *and independent* no longer place sufficient value on the government. (*C*, III, 935; 323; emphasis added)

Notably, Rousseau is only somewhat concerned with the excessive independence of citizens. "This defect . . . will always be little to be feared and easily remedied" (Ibid.). The argument for farming, which fosters self-sufficiency at the same time that it attaches men to the land or fatherland, is an argument for a way of life that combines independence, even relative isolation, and sociality.

Rousseau also regards the rustic Swiss as a suitable model for urbane Geneva. In the *Letter to D'Alembert*, Rousseau lauds the mountaineers of Neufchatel, who represent to him not only themselves but also a way of life that should be preserved and of which a remnant seems to exist in Geneva.

Thus Rousseau defends the relevance of the mountaineers to the debate over the establishment of theater in Geneva: "My supposition ought not to be objected to as chimerical. . . . Take away some circumstances and you will find other Mountaineers elsewhere; and *mutatis mutandis*, the example has its application" (*Letter to D'Alembert* [*LA* hereafter], V, 59; 64). As in the *Constitutional Project for Corsica*, the rustic Swiss are very independent and materially self-sufficient: "Each is everything for himself, no one is anything for another" (*LA*, V, 56; 61). Yet the numerous inhabitants enjoy "both the tranquility of a retreat and the sweetness of society" (*LA*, V, 55; 60), a formulation that calls to mind the independent commerce enjoyed in the savage nation.

The need to preserve rustic life runs through Rousseau's political works,[35] finding a place in the *Political Economy* ([*PE* hereafter], III, 259; 222), *Considerations on the Government of Poland* (III, 1003–1004, 1008–1009; 224–25, 230–31), and the *Social Contract*. In that latter work, rusticity is embodied in Swiss peasants, whom others would do well to emulate: "Among the happiest people in the world, groups of peasants are seen deciding the affairs of State under an oak tree" (*SC*, III, 437; 108). In Rome, too, that "model of all free Peoples" (*SD*, III, 113; Dedicatory, 5),[36] the harsh image of citizen is softened by the more pastoral image of the rustic peasant or villager. To Rome's preference for "rustic tribes" is attributed "the preservation of its mores and the growth of its empire"; "all who were most illustrious in Rome lived in the country and tilled the soil." The Romans had a "taste for country life" and honored "the simple and hardworking life of village people" (*SC*, III, 445, 4 46; 114). We have already noted the connection between the agricultural life and both independence and love of country. This impression in the Roman case is reinforced by the status of the Roman citizen as a model for both Emile and the Corsican; in both cases, Rousseau uses the Roman example to suggest that independent, nearly self-sufficient, private men will serve the fatherland and return to the plow after they have served (*E*, IV, 860; 474; *C*, III, 925; 310).

In light of Rousseau's evident concern for the independence of individuals, one should not be surprised to encounter certain liberal elements in Rousseau's thought.[37] He takes care to show that the sovereign's power leaves the individual free in a sphere that cannot be claimed for the community:

In addition to the public person, we have to consider the private persons who compose it and whose life and freedom are naturally independent of it. . . . It is agreed that each person alienates through the social compact only that part of his power, goods, and freedom whose use matters to the community. (*SC*, III, 373; 62)

He does lead us to doubt the importance of this qualification when he adds: "But it must also be agreed that the sovereign alone is the judge of what matters." Even if the sovereign, by definition, acts only for the common good, the very need of the polity, suggested by the importance of the legislator, for citizens who are nothing without the others indicates that the common good encompasses a great many things. Indeed, the extent to which the people must be manipulated and transformed has led some to accuse Rousseau of fostering totalitarianism.[38] Had Rousseau specified no limit to the demands of the common good, such a charge would probably be justified. In the chapter on civil religion, however, Rousseau applies his theory of the limits of sovereign power to advocate religious toleration:

The right that the social compact gives the sovereign . . . does not exceed, as I have said, the limits of public utility. . . . Now it matters greatly to the State that each citizen have a religion that causes him to love his duties; but the dogmas of that religion are of no interest either to the State or to its members; except insofar as these dogmas relate to morality. . . . Everyone can have whatever opinions he pleases beyond that, without the sovereign having to know what they are. (*SC*, III, 467–68; 130)

While this limitation of the power of the whole hardly meets contemporary standards of liberalism, it lends substance to Rousseau's claim that a distinctly private, untransformed liberty is both compatible with the good of the republic and demanded by the principles of political right. Not all citizens have to think alike and not all the inner thoughts of the citizens must be transparent to the community.

That the citizen is nothing without the others, moreover, does not have to mean that the private ceases to exist. Consider how Rousseau presents the advantages and disadvantages of political society. Though Rousseau speaks of a transformation in man – the acquisition of morality and moral freedom – he also justifies political society in terms of the very goods man enjoyed in the state of nature, which he will enjoy more securely, if more narrowly, in civil society:

What man loses by the social contract is his natural freedom and an unlimited right to everything that tempts him and that he can get; what he gains is civil freedom and the proprietorship of everything he possesses. . . . One must distinguish carefully between natural freedom, which is limited only by the force of the individual, and civil freedom, which is limited by the general will; and between possession, which is only the effect of force or the right of the first occupant, and property, which can only be based on a positive title. (*SC*, III, 364–65; 56)

In the last stage of the state of nature – the state of war – the life, freedom, and goods of men are at risk. Although these essential elements of a human life are not created by society, they are protected by the state, and, in this sense, it may be said that without the state's protection a citizen is nothing. Rousseau puts it in these terms in the *Second Discourse*:

[W]hy did they give themselves superiors if not to defend them against oppression, and to protect their goods, their freedoms and their lives, which are, so to speak, *the constituent elements of their being.* (*SD*, III, 180–81; II, 37; emphasis added)

Whatever distinctly public or collective goods civil society may provide, whatever the importance of morality and virtue, there can be no question that the freedom and the goods of the state of nature, goods that are distinctly private and as recognizable to savages as to citizens, must be defended by civil society. In this respect, then, the private individual does not dissolve in the whole. Thus an individualistic component remains even where Rousseau's collectivistic tendency peaks.

Similarly, in the very section of the *Political Economy* in which the importance of public-spiritedness is emphasized, Rousseau argues that love of country is instilled when the state protects the property, lives, and freedoms of its citizens:

Do we want peoples to be virtuous? Let us then start by making them love their homeland. But how are they to love it . . . . if they did not even enjoy civil safety there, and if their goods, life, or freedom were at the discretion of powerful men? (*PE*, III, 255–56; 219)

Further, though the citizen is subject to the law, the definition of law implies that each private individual is protected; no individual may be sacrificed, even on the altar of the whole:

Rather than that one ought to perish for all, all have engaged their goods and their lives for the defence of each one among them, in order that private weakness always be protected by public force, and each member by the whole state. (*PE*, III, 256–57; 220)

Rousseau is certainly no liberal. He emphasizes the need for virtue and a genuine social bond and is willing to meet that need with sumptuary laws and other limits on freedom. Nonetheless, it is a considerable exaggeration to assert that perfect citizenship is, for Rousseau, that which best does away with our solitary and individualistic natures. As Emile is transformed into a moral being without losing the taste for and enjoyment of the sweet freedom and private pleasures he knew as a child, so man is transformed into a citizen without losing the taste for or enjoyment of the pleasures and freedoms he knew in the childhood of the species, as original man and as savage. Undoubtedly, the citizen is much more social than either Emile or the savage, and, moreover, his distinctly private freedoms, if not his pleasures, are more narrowly circumscribed than Emile's or the savage's. However, those who claim that Rousseau offers as his best alternatives a choice between artificial social unity and natural individual unity will have to explain the abiding presence of individualism in Rousseau's most collectivistic works. Any attempt to explain that presence in terms of the impracticability of eliminating original nature altogether must come to terms with the evidence that suggests that untransformed individual freedom is both a good intrinsically because it is sweet and a good instrumentally because only independent citizens are vigilant defenders of freedom.

In the best case, republican life is sweetened not only by community but also by relief and protection from community, by the citizen's provision for his own needs and his own pleasures with his own resources in his own home. Rousseau's portrait of that life cannot fail to remind us of the savage in the savage nation. The man of nature is preserved, modified, but hardly beyond recognition, in Rousseau's politics.

UNITY AND EXTENT

In this chapter, I have argued against the view that unity is the goal of Rousseau's constructive projects. But Arthur Melzer has proposed that not only unity, which characterizes the original state, but also extent of existence, which is added to unity in the state of the social contract, guides Rousseau's praises and blames of the different men Rousseau describes: "[L]ives are to be evaluated by their degree of existence, by their measure or 'extent' and especially of unity of soul" (1990, 90). On Melzer's argument, Rousseau can laud the savage state and other middling states, in which men have "slightly compromised their perfect, animal-like unity of inclination" because the loss of unity is

more than compensated for by the greater development of their faculties, the elevation of their sentiments, and their rudimentary social contacts based on pure affection or identification. . . . These changes clearly increased their capacity to "feel life." (Ibid., 70)

Melzer's proposed criterion of unity and extent is a powerful tool for explaining the wide range of states Rousseau praises. I offer three objections.

First, Rousseau does not regard all kinds of extent as equal. In *Emile*, Rousseau describes an expansive active principle that seems every bit as formal as Melzer's idea of extent. The child

senses within himself, so to speak, enough life to animate everything surrounding him. That he do or undo is a matter of no importance; it suffices that he change the condition of things. (*E*, IV, 289; 67)

Yet Rousseau clearly prefers certain playings out of the active principle to others. If the rejection of tyranny can be readily explained in terms of the need to preserve psychic unity, what of other projects, like building things or destroying them, that do not necessarily involve us in dependence on others but do not produce, as, for example, family life does, "the sweetest sentiments known to man" (*SD*, III, 168; II, 12)? Rousseau seems to elevate one kind of extent, the kind that involves other people, above other kinds of extents. This elevation of sociality cannot be explained satisfactorily in terms of Rousseau's interest in solving the problems of those men, the vast majority of his readers, who cannot be expected to abandon society. As we have already seen, Rousseau does not spend his own solitude solely in communion with nature, one plausible means of extending existence, or in communion with imaginary abstractions, another such means. His reveries often take the form of imagining beings and small societies after his own heart. Rousseau could have used his powerful imagination to pursue art for art's sake, seemingly a pursuit offering infinite possibilities of expansion. That he instead pursues art for the sake of approximating or perfecting the kind of happiness to be found in societies is a powerful statement that a merely formal extension of being is not Rousseau's object.

To be sure, Melzer describes the mechanism of extent as a "capacity for 'identification.'" Insofar as human beings identify especially strongly with other people, it is perhaps not surprising that Rousseau would favor the social version of extent. But Melzer also insists on the purely formal character of the standard of extent: "Any way of life of reasonable extent is good, regardless of content, provided only that it is internally consistent." "Any content will do as long as it is self-consistent." Our impulse for self-extension is "a pure goalless expansiveness" that can be directed into "any number of forms," not all of them social. Melzer also argues, as we saw in Chapter 1, that once man leaves the state of nature he "is now on his own, homeless and free, without nature or instinct to guide him, an accidental being who must try to invent an altogether new life and happiness for himself" (1990, 44–45, 89–90). I think that the standard of extent is not formal but substantive and that human beings are therefore much more restricted and guided by their natures in pursuing happiness than Melzer implies. Sociality, not extent alone, is a component of human happiness.

Second, Rousseau does not regard all kinds of unity as equal. I have discussed the sweetness of the independence of original man, savage man, or Emile in the first stage of his education. This sweetness is something substantively and altogether different from the harsh, self-conquering, sometimes almost ascetic virtue exemplified by the Spartan or by Emile in the second stage of the education. I do not deny that this virtue confers a kind of unity and that it is an aspect of the human good, but I do deny that the latter kind of unity can substitute for the former. Rousseau seeks to preserve elements of what are regarded as his individualistic prescriptions, even in his collectivist works, precisely because he thinks that the presence of one kind of unity does not make up for the absence of another. Like the standard of extent, the standard of unity is not purely formal.

Third, and in a related vein, Rousseau avoids going to either the individualistic or the collectivistic extreme, not only tolerating but actually preferring states in which the goods associated with solitude and independence are available along with the goods of society. The criteria of unity and extent allow for the existence of such states along the continuum of states praised by Rousseau. Logically, these states could be an incidental result of Rousseau's attempt to attain the maximum degree or extent of existence compatible with a high degree of unity. They do not explain Rousseau's *preference* for middling states, the pervasiveness of what I have called the savage pattern in his work.

CONCLUSION

In my treatment of the *Second Discourse*, I made much of Rousseau's praise of the savage in the savage nation, which is higher than that given to original man. That independent commerce is superior to independence alone suggests one way of looking at the relation between Rousseau's praise of the bestial, solitary original state and his praises of more advanced, distinctly human states. First, these latter states are praised for having something the original state does not have; the original state is deficient because it lacks a component of human happiness. The advanced states redress a deficiency in our original condition. Additionally, the advanced states are praised for retaining an element of the happiness of original man, which does not cease to be a part of the human good merely because it is not the whole human good. That solitary and social pleasures cannot be enjoyed at the same time does not deter Rousseau from preferring the savage state, a state of disunity, if not, on the individual level, destructive disunity, to a unified state in which one or the other type of pleasure is lost. That Rousseau calls the savage state best implies such a conclusion. The pattern of the savage state, in which goods that cannot be enjoyed together or synthesized are enjoyed, nonetheless, separately, is repeated throughout Rousseau's works, including the most individualistic and collectivistic of them. The pattern laid out in *Emile*, in which bourgeois disunity can be addressed only by a wholehearted embrace of natural individuals or artificial societies, is the problem Rousseau sets out to resolve, not Rousseau's own solution to it. Recall his observation that "if perchance the double object we set for ourselves could be joined in a single one by removing the contradictions of man, a great obstacle to his happiness would be removed" (*E*, IV, 251; 41). The savage, the rustic democrat in his pastoral Swiss or more hardened Roman manifestation, Emile, and even Rousseau himself are different examples of men who avoid the destructive disunity of the bourgeois, not by uniting the disparate goods each pursues into a harmony but by finding a place for each. The model for human happiness is an arrangement of disharmonious tastes, goods, and aims in such a way that the individual is not torn apart, not the natural grant or artificial imposition of unity.

The problem of balancing or arranging conflicting but good tendencies in human nature is not limited to the area of individualism and collectivism. For example, the savage state not only balances the demands of independence and sociality but also occupies "a just mean between the indolence of the primitive state and the petulant activity of our vanity" (*SD*, III, 171; II, 18).[39] The "primitive state," which is not as far from the "first state of Nature" as the savage state, occupies more than one middle, "placed by Nature at equal distance from the stupidity of the brutes and the fatal enlightenment of civil man, and restricted by instinct and by reason alike" (*SD*, III, 170; II, 17). *Emile*, too, suggests a coexistence of apparently contradictory human goods. Emile's "active principle" (*E*, IV, 289; 67), which inclines him to make and unmake, has a tendency to draw him out of himself, endangering his sense of his own existence. For that reason, there is the stoic injunction in *Emile* to "restrain your heart within the limits of your condition" (*E*, IV, 819; 445) and an embrace of the negative happiness characteristic of original man, freedom from hope, fear, and, except for necessity, the outside world. But there is another strain of *Emile* that counsels against passivity because our very sentiment of existence is dependent on acting:

> To live is not to breathe; it is to act; it is to make use of our organs, our senses, our faculties, of all the parts of ourselves which *give us the sentiment of our existence*. (*E*, IV, 253; 42; emphasis added)

Indeed, we are born without the sentiment of existence (*E*, IV, 279–80; 61) and do not experience it until that period in which the "first developments of childhood" (*E*, IV, 298; 74), learning to walk, talk, and feed oneself, occur. Activity and passivity each are conditions of the sentiment of existence, and Emile therefore must negotiate a middle position between acting in the world and restraining himself or staying in place.

Consider, also, another reason that we are born without the sentiment of existence, or are at least incapable of enjoying it. We lack self-consciousness, which, in turn, depends on memory. Here is how Rousseau describes the end of "infancy, strictly speaking":

> It is at this second stage that, strictly speaking, the life of the individual begins. It is then that he gains consciousness of himself. Memory extends the sentiment of identity to all the moments of his existence; he becomes truly one, the same, and consequently already capable of happiness or unhappiness. (*E*, IV, 301; 78)

Self-consciousness and extension over time, though necessary for our happiness, are in tension with its other preconditions. The happy savage, Rousseau argues in the *Second Discourse*, "lives in himself," whereas the unhappy "sociable man [is] always outside himself" (*SD*, III, 193; II, 57). But to be self-conscious is to be detached from oneself, to be on the outside looking in. In order to enjoy the unity of their existence, human beings must first become divided. Similarly, original man's happiness is bound up with its immediacy, its immersion in the present. Like Rousseau's soul, whose happiness emerges only when "time is nothing to it," when there is "no need to remember the past or reach into the future" (*R*, I, 1046; 88), so original man's happiness depends on the concentration of his entire being in the immediate. "His soul, which nothing stirs, yields itself solely to the sentiment of its present existence, with no idea of the future, however near it may be" (*SD*, III, 144; I, 21). Yet in order to enjoy existence one's memory must extend to all the moments of one's existence, and perfect, effortless, and timeless unity must give way to a problematic and ultimately artful fusion of our past, present, and future selves.[40]

While I have tried in this chapter to offer new insight into the old problem of individualism and collectivism in Rousseau's thought, I think that I have also made a strong case for this general proposition: Rousseau views the human good not as a unity but as a set of disharmonious attributes or tendencies that must somehow be arranged in a life so as not to tear the human being apart.

Let me return to the old, familiar, and still very common charge that Rousseau was the founder of modern democratic totalitarianism. I believe that I have proved, by insisting on the strains of rustic and liberal individualism that persist even in Rousseau's most collectivist works, that Rousseau was not a totalitarian. To be sure, he is also no liberal, and one can point to his elaborate schemes for extensive civic education to suggest that a totalitarian element exists in his thought alongside the rustic and liberal individualism to which I have drawn attention. However, much of the rhetorical weight of the charge against Rousseau is that it connects him to the worst crimes of the twentieth century. That "Hitler is an outcome of Rousseau,"[41] as Bertrand Russell claimed, is what we mean when we say that Rousseau is a totalitarian. In this sense, to call someone who favored civic education and civil religion[42] a totalitarian is to empty that term of its moral seriousness and to stretch it to capture the whole of the republican tradition, from Aristotle to Jefferson.

Rousseau's insistence on rustic and liberal individual freedom is perhaps the most powerful defense he has against the charge of totalitarianism. But I want to focus, to end this chapter, on another argument for the defense. Implicit and sometimes quite explicit in many of the assaults on Rousseau's thought is an assault on his character. J. L. Talmon's influential work is representative. Rousseau is a totalitarian, in large part, because he "was one of the most ill-adjusted and egocentric natures who have left a record of their predicament." The "secret aspect of [his] dual personality was that the disciplinarian was the envious dream of the tormented paranoiac." Both the state of nature of the *Second Discourse* and the denatured state of the *Social Contract* are responses to the "agony" Rousseau attributes to man living in modern society, though it is, in truth, the agony of a "motherless vagabond starved of warmth and affection, having his dream of intimacy constantly frustrated by human callousness, real or imaginary" (Talmon, 1952, 38–39). Rousseau emerges from Talmon's analysis as a neurotic who just can't take the vicissitudes and complexities of society, as a child driven by a child's urge for simplicity or unity, or as an ineffectual madman who prepared the way for the more dangerous madmen of the twentieth century.[43]

I certainly do not mean to deny that Rousseau was paranoid or even, sometimes, quite mad. Nonetheless, it is at least a secondary purpose of this book to show that when we examine what we know more or less for sure, what Rousseau wrote down, and decline to deduce his thought from our speculations about his mental health, a more balanced picture of Rousseau emerges. Far from being unable to confront complexity or disunity, Rousseau kept the disharmoniousness of the elements of human happiness constantly before his eyes. Far from impatiently seeking unity at the cost of human freedom, Rousseau was willing to preserve tension in order to give the plurality of human goods their due. Far from being "unable to abide disharmony," as Michael Sandel has argued, Rousseau made the savage nation, a nation characterized by struggle, a pattern for his visions of the good life. Rousseau is not a moderate, to be sure, but his critics have been too ready to dismiss him for an immoderation of which he is not guilty. Indeed, Rousseau, in spite of his radicalism, may be more sober than contemporary thinkers who dismiss him, but I will save that argument for Chapter 4. In the next chapter, I come to a problem that has been, in a way, hanging over the argument of the past couple of chapters, that of Rousseau's rhetoric.

3

Rousseau's Rhetorical Strategy

Up until now, we have set aside the question of Rousseau's rhetorical strategy. We have not yet asked why Rousseau sometimes quite boldly equates the original and the natural, even though he does not think they are equivalent. It seemed enough to show that he ultimately rejects the proposition that nature is that which exists at the beginning and accepts instead the proposition that nature is an end or perfection. Whatever reasons Rousseau may have had for advancing the equation of the original and natural in the Preface to the *Second Discourse*, I believe I have demonstrated, in light of subsequent developments in the *Second Discourse*, and in light of *Emile*, that he does not, finally, endorse it. Similarly, it did not seem necessary to ask why Rousseau sometimes makes it appear that unity is both what human beings need above all for happiness and the objective of his political, social, and moral prescriptions. It seemed enough to show that the objective of those prescriptions is instead the "savage pattern," in which opposing elements of the human good, which cannot be unified or synthesized, are able at least to coexist. While my arguments have taken Rousseau to be a careful writer, they do not rest on any particular conception of Rousseau's rhetorical strategy. Up until now, I have done my best to base my reading on the preponderance of textual evidence, without recourse to controversial theories about how to interpret a text. While I attack one mode of interpreting Rousseau at the end of Chapter 2, that attack is a conclusion from rather than the basis of the long argument that precedes it.

To be sure, taking Rousseau to be a careful writer at all may be thought to be controversial. My argument could not avoid, for example, the claim that Rousseau's most striking statements are sometimes undermined by less striking, if more abundant, evidence. Nor could it avoid the claim that Rousseau constructed his works artfully, intending to achieve certain objectives. Such claims, however, are implicit to a greater or lesser degree in every interpretation of Rousseau with which I am familiar, not excepting Jean Starobinski's psychoanalytic interpretation[1] or even Jacques Derridas' deconstructionist one.

The study of Rousseau's rhetoric is an enterprise that should require little justification. Rousseau, after all, wrote in, among other contexts, the context of the French Enlightenment. Reasonable people disagree about the extent to which Plato or Aristotle may have seen the need not merely to state the truth to all who would listen but to propagandize. However, there is no disagreement, as far as I know, regarding the eighteenth-century philosophes and their conscious understanding of themselves as constituting a party among many parties with differing interests and objectives, and as requiring a mastery not only of the science of nature but also the science of tactics to succeed. The philosophes were mindful of the the need to sway different audiences, aristocratic and popular, for example, and of the difficulties this situation posed for them as rhetoricians.[2] Taking the historical context into account, then, the thesis that Rousseau, unlike his contemporaries, was unmindful of such considerations is more shocking and requires more justification than the opposite thesis. Yet explicit accounts of Rousseau's rhetorical strategy are rare, confined mainly to Straussian interpretations of his thought.

Perhaps it is out of reluctance to be associated with Leo Strauss and his students that some recent interpreters have avoided a thematic discussion of Rousseau's rhetoric. Even Asher Horowitz, who concedes that Rousseau's writings have some of the characteristics of a "dramatic production" in which "there are a number of voices and characters present, suggesting ... the author's less than full identification with any one of them,"[3] criticizes "Strauss and his followers" for suggesting "a conscious intention on Rousseau's part to convey two different meanings to two different audiences, a vulgar and a philosophical audience" (Horowitz, 1987, 11 n.30). To impute such an intention to Rousseau is to risk being associated with the elitism it assumes and with the naivete of supposing it possible to discern an author's intent. Horowitz dissociates himself with the "historical effort to elicit a thinker's conscious intentions" and leagues himself mainly, though not exclusively, with a second methodological approach that attempts the "educated but imaginative reconstruction of the significance of Rousseau's thought" (Ibid., 9). Yet Horowitz's own interpretation cannot help but distinguish between Rousseau's real position and the "rhetorical garb" with which it is covered, between the "rhetorical theme" of the *Second Discourse* and the "much more subversive theory" that is at least "partially obscured by it," or between the "polemical purposes" of the *Second Discourse* and Rousseau's real analysis of history, which discloses itself to careful readers; Horowitz cannot help writing about how Rousseau "hints at but leaves out" certain implications of his argument and suggesting that Rousseau does so in part to distinguish himself from opponents whom he resembles more than it is useful for him openly to admit (Ibid., 46, 51, 87, 142). Regardless of whether such a reading points to a difference between the philosophic few and the vulgar many, it certainly points to the necessity of taking Rousseau to be a careful writer who deploys rhetorical strategies.[4]

If we believe that Rousseau is a careful writer, we cannot in good conscience state that Rousseau sometimes says what he does not mean and leave it at that. In the course of our argument, we have noticed instances in which Rousseau cannot fail to understand that he is contradicting himself. As Arthur Melzer has pointed out in a somewhat different context: "[I]t strains credulity to think that [Rousseau] could have been simply unaware of the obvious contradictions that every college freshman sees in his works" (1990, 6). Our argument will therefore be more plausible if we can provide satisfactory answers to the following questions that it raises. First, why does Rousseau claim that the original is the natural when he does not think so? Second, if Rousseau thinks that nature cannot be fully understood without reference to ends or perfections, why does he not state this view more directly and often than he does? Third, why does *Emile* reveal more clearly than the *Second Discourse* does both the untruth of the equation of the natural and the original and the importance of the study of ends or perfections in the investigation of nature?

There is another important reason for investigating Rousseau's rhetorical strategy. It is possible that our arguments up until now, however much textual evidence may be cited in their favor, have concentrated on superficial elements of Rousseau's presentation rather than on the core of his argument. Rousseau himself warns readers of the difficulty of his writings and of the care he took to present them so that they would be useful to the public:

I unfolded my ideas only successively and always to only a small number of Readers. I spared not myself but the truth, in order to have it pass more readily and make it more useful. Often I went through great trouble to try to condense into a single Sentence, a single line, a single word tossed off as if by chance, the result of a long chain of reflections. The majority of my Readers must often have found my writings poorly structured and almost entirely disjointed for want of perceiving the trunk of which I showed them only the branches. But that was enough for those capable of understanding, and I never wanted to speak to the others. ("Preface of a Second Letter to Bordes," III, 106; 115)

Of course, Rousseau, who includes among his works a didactic and very popular novel, and who more than any other modern writer insists on the tension between philosophy and art, on the one hand, and the health of society on the other, considered the impact of his writings on those who did not read him carefully. Attending to Rousseau's rhetoric therefore means attending not only to the effect he hoped to have on careful readers but also to the effect he hoped to have on the majority of his readers. In any case, no reading of Rousseau can afford to ignore altogether the possibility of mistaking the branches for the trunk, or of being duped by Rousseau's rhetoric. While this chapter cannot hope to foreclose that possibility entirely, we are much less likely to fall victim to rhetoric when we are on the lookout for it.

A full account of Rousseau's rhetoric would require a full account of the characteristics of Rousseau's audiences as Rousseau understood them. One would need to distinguish between, among many others, urbanites and provincials, skeptics and believers, subjects and citizens, and academicians and the broader public. One would also need to bear in mind the features Rousseau thought all audiences have in common and the problems that political thinkers and writers are likely to face in all societies. In this chapter, I will sometimes distinguish between Rousseau's different audiences. The difference between citizens and subjects will play a role in the argument, and the idea that Rousseau's rhetoric could be effective assumes a distinction between those who read carefully and well and those who do not. In addition, I will, especially in the part of the argument that concerns ends and perfections, appeal to political considerations I think Rousseau understood to be permanent. But most of this chapter concerns different implications of a single feature that characterizes most of Rousseau's audiences – that they are either modern sophisticates or tempted by modern sophistication. I choose the term "sophistication" because it captures a range of characteristics from urbanity to being under the influence of philosophers and the doctrines they willingly teach and even advertise. I qualify the term with "modern" because the love of progress and the idea that applied knowledge is the key to the solution of human problems, which Rousseau observed and sought to combat, characterize the modern much more than thay characterize the ancient or medieval worlds.

That Rousseau was concerned about sophistication and its consequences is uncontroversial. It is also uncontroversial that Rousseau's attack on sophistication and its consequences is, at least at times, more
extreme than Rousseau's considered view of the costs and benefits of civilization warrants. Even that most indignant critic of Rousseau's romantic
tendencies, Irving Babbitt, concedes that Rousseau has a moderate
and conciliatory side and that his apparent intemperance is balanced
by "shrewdness and at times something even better than shrewdness"
(Babbitt, 1968, 11). But although critics have frequently recognized
the polemical character of Rousseau's attack on the arts and sciences,
they have not usually been inclined to see the same intention at work
in Rousseau's more radical attack on perfectibility, history, and society
altogether; his embrace of original man as the only natural man; and
of the original condition as the only natural condition. But, in my view,
the latter attack, which is much more implausible and extreme than
the former, invites the suggestion that it is part of an exaggerated assault on the prevailing doctrines and prejudices of Rousseau's time and
place.

THE NATURAL AND THE ORIGINAL

Satire

According to A. O. Lovejoy, Rousseau's praise of man's original[5] or
primeval state is nothing new. What is remarkable about Rousseau's
description of this state, Lovejoy observes, is how unappealing it is.
Rousseau's state of nature and his brutish natural man are even less attractive than their counterparts in Voltaire and Pufendorf, yet Voltaire and
Pufendorf intended to *disparage* them (Lovejoy, 1948, 18–19).[6] Lovejoy
thinks that Rousseau, on the whole, means to disparage them, too. If
Rousseau sometimes slips, and praises nature ardently and sincerely, that
is only because he is not yet altogether free of the hold of traditional
primitivism. One may take issue with Lovejoy's assumption that ardent
and apparently sincere praise cannot be one aspect of a satire. One may
suspect, too, that Lovejoy is too quick to assume that Rousseau cannot possibly mean to praise a state that civilized beings find repulsive. However
those things may be, we are more concerned for now with Lovejoy's central claim, namely, that Rousseau could have introduced the primitivistic
sense of nature, that sense in which the natural is equated with the original, for the purpose of disparaging the primitive. Another way of putting

the claim is this: When Rousseau equates the original and the natural, he is engaging in satire.

Lovejoy may be right to identify primitivism as one target of Rousseau's satire. However, as we observed in Chapter 2, Rousseau says explicitly that his description of the state of nature and an assessment of that state as "best suited to Mankind" can be arrived at by "reasoning on the basis of the principles [Hobbes] established" (*SD*, III, 153; I, 35). Rousseau's later assertion that the violent, lawless, yet more advanced state of the savage nation is "best for man" (*SD*, III, 171; II, 18) appears to underscore his disagreement with Hobbes and his rejection of that understanding of human nature which follows from the consistent application of Hobbes's principles. Insofar as Rousseau's description and praise of the original state of nature may be regarded as a satire, then Hobbes is at least as likely a target as the primitivists to whom Rousseau, after all, does not choose to draw our attention. Hobbism, while not obviously a feature of modern sophistication, does seem to be one for Rousseau, who includes a seemingly Hobbesian doctrine among those that philosophers hawk in the public square (*First Discourse* [*FD* hereafter], III, 27; 24).

In what sense should we regard Rousseau's original state of nature as the necessary consequence of Hobbes's principles? Hobbes failed to draw the necessary consequences of his principles because "he improperly included in Savage man's care for his preservation the need to satisfy a multitude of passions that are the product of Society" (*SD*, III, 153; I, 35). The Hobbesian principle of which Rousseau's original state of nature is the consequence is that of the natural asociality of man. As I argued in Chapter 2, that Rousseau ultimately prefers the social savage nation to the asocial original state reflects his disagreement with Hobbes's radical individualism.

One may object that Rousseau misreads Hobbes, who does not explicitly state that human beings are naturally asocial. While Hobbes does seem to think that we are concerned above all with ourselves and our own, this natural selfishness can take on distinctly social forms, like vanity and the love of dominion over other human beings. Therefore, Hobbes concedes that however individualistic human beings may be, social life appeals even to the people least fit to live in it, namely the prideful: "It is one thing to desire, another to be in capacity fit for what we desire; for even they who, through their pride, will not stoop to equal conditions, without which there can be no society, yet desire it" (Hobbes, 1993, 110).

However, Hobbes advances the thesis of natural human asociality in a very radical form when he claims that speech and reason, which make society possible, are not natural but artificial, or invented by human beings:

> But the most noble and profitable *invention* of all others, was that of SPEECH, consisting of *names* or *appellations*, and their connexion . . . without which there had been amongst men neither commonwealth, nor society, nor contract, nor peace, no more than among lions, bears, or wolves. (1985, note 16; emphasis added)

Hobbes claims that these invented faculties enable human beings to raise themselves above beasts, not only with respect to their capacity to form societies but also with respect to their intellectual capacities more generally:

> Besides sense, and thoughts, and the train of thoughts, the mind of man has no other motion, though *by the help of speech and method* the same faculties may be improved to such height as to distinguish men from all living creatures. (Ibid., 14; emphasis added)

Human sociality, even humanity itself, are products not of nature but of artifice. Although Hobbes does not draw the necessary consequence of his principles, Rousseau has a plausible argument to back his claim that his description of original man as an asocial brute is the product of Hobbesian premises. Rousseau equates the original with the natural in the First Part of the *Second Discourse* in order to criticize those premises.

To be sure, one should not be too quick to accept at face value Hobbes's most radical claims about the natural asociality of human beings, any more than one should accept at face value the less radical claims. The liberal tradition is too often dismissed by communitarians as beholden to an indefensibly "atomistic" theory of the self. This criticism neglects the possibility that a thinker might have offered a description of the self in order to make his prescriptions more likely to succeed. Although Machiavelli, for example, often seems to advance the theory that human beings are bad, the *Prince* teaches that human beings are almost never bad enough. It is very difficult to learn to be bad. Machiavelli describes human beings as bad at least in part in the hopes of making them bad, that is, in the hopes of weaning them from the irrational attachments and beliefs that stand in the way of rational politics. By the same token, Hobbesian "atomism" certainly could be understood as an exaggeration designed to serve Hobbes's practical end, to dampen the social passions, like vainglory, that threaten peace. However, it is beyond the scope of this chapter to determine what the right reading of Hobbes is. Therefore we cannot pursue the question of whether Rousseau read Hobbes correctly or the related question of whether the disagreement between Hobbes and Rousseau is primarily theoretical or practical, even though we need to answer both questions in order fully to understand and assess Rousseau's rhetorical strategy. Nonetheless, I think I have said enough to make this argument plausible: Rousseau equates the original and the natural, even though he does not believe the equation is true, in order to attack Hobbes.

The Innocence and Benevolence of Nature

Arthur Melzer has argued that Rousseau's writings "offer essentially *no* political hope and *no* political advice to decadent Europe" (1990, 278). Rousseau's political teaching is addressed primarily to "the tiny, threatened world of actual or potential republics" (Ibid., 271). For the monarchies of Europe, civilized corruption is advanced and irreversible. Rousseau therefore offers the individual subjects of such monarchies not a political teaching but an apolitical teaching, even a teaching against politics. He offers what Melzer calls a popular "individualistic solution." While Rousseau's own extraordinary and radically individualistic way of life does not serve as a model for ordinary human beings, Rousseau's audience in monarchical Europe may benefit from a "modified ethic of withdrawal and inwardness" (Ibid., 29). What interests us especially in this solution is Rousseau's attempt to persuade his audience to pursue nature as an alternative to politics and to modern sophistication more broadly speaking:

The lyrical praise of wilderness and isolation in the *Reveries* and other works, and in a different way Rousseau's botanical writings, helped to foster the new romantic cult of rustic retreat, of solitude and reverie, of communing with "nature" defined as the nonhuman world. (Ibid., 280)

One might add, as Melzer also notes, that the individualistic solution pits natural spontaneity against social constraint and appeals not only to wild nature but also, as in the *Profession of Faith*, to an ordered, providential nature. In this section, I will argue that Rousseau equates the original and the natural, even though he does not believe they are equivalent, in order to make nature appear kinder than it is, so that his audience will love it more. But before I make that argument, I will elaborate on and diverge somewhat from Melzer's claims about Rousseau's strategy.

Melzer distinguishes fairly sharply between Rousseau's individualistic and republican solutions. They are "two opposite solutions to the human problem" (Ibid., 282). But if the argument of Chapter 2 is correct, then these solutions are not simply opposites, and one can expect more overlap than Melzer expects between Rousseau's intentions for republican Geneva and his intentions for monarchical Europe. That overlap makes it easier than it would otherwise be to explain how Rousseau could address a book like the *Second Discourse* to both Geneva, to whose people he dedicates the work, and France, where he enters it into a contest sponsored by the Academy of Dijon. Melzer's explanation is elegant. The *Second Discourse* teaches the natural goodness of man. That doctrine benefits citizens of republics because it criticizes modern sophistication so powerfully and makes the case for a simplicity and austerity that republicans need, even if it overshoots the mark. An urgent part of Rousseau's mission for republican Europe is to "combat the fateful allure of everything that was Paris" (Ibid., 276). The doctrine is more obviously good for the subjects of monarchies because it detaches them from societies that are hopelessly corrupt and encourages them, for the sake of their happiness, to withdraw into the family, or the wilderness, or natural religion, or all three (Ibid., 280). By teaching the natural goodness of man, Rousseau addresses himself simultaneously to two different audiences in two different ways. The difficulty with Melzer's explanation is that it is very hard to see how modern republicans, who are in Rousseau's estimation far from impervious to corruption, can be made to get the message that is appropriate for them, without being corrupted by the ethic of withdrawal and inwardness that, in Melzer's account, Rousseau thinks is sharply opposed to the republican solution. But if we take the argument of Chapter 2 seriously, that Rousseau wishes and thinks it possible to find a place for individualism and retreat even in his otherwise republican politics, then the messages Rousseau expects different readers of the *Second Discourse* to extract are not as radically opposed as Melzer suggests they are. Rousseau's rhetorical task is thereby rendered somewhat easier and the suggestion that he is engaged in such a task is rendered more plausible.

In addition, there is a practical reason that Rousseau could not pursue a republican solution that was radically opposed to his individualistic solution. We have already observed that Rousseau pursues the individualistic solution in monarchical Europe because civilized corruption is advanced and irreversible. But there is at least one sense in which there is no going back for republican Europe either. Christianity has meant, for good or for ill, that "there is no longer and can never again be an exclusive national religion" (*SC*, III, 469; 131). The civic profession of faith Rousseau proposes in the *Social Contract*, while it is certainly different from the more individualistic profession of faith proposed by the Savoyard priest in *Emile*, does not cause citizens to love their native cities more than their souls.[7] After Christianity, the kind of devotion to politics that characterized the ancient republic is impossible to sustain, at least absent a revolution for which Rousseau does not hope or pray. Moreover, the extent to which politicians can use Christian virtue to sustain civic virtue is limited, at best, both because the spirit of Christianity is antithetical to the spirit of good citizenship and because the attempt to use a robust Christianity for political purposes typically ends in the overpowering of the interest of the state by the interest of the priest (*SC*, III, 469; 131). For these reasons, one cannot expect republican virtue to carry the day by itself, even in Geneva. Just as most Parisians will have to look to a less demanding and more individualistic model for personal virtue than Emile, like Rousseau's rich man, so also will most Genevans have to look to a less demanding and more individualistic model for political virtue than the Roman. For the same reason that Rousseau must pursue an individualistic solution for monarchical Europe he must also pursue an at least somewhat individualistic solution for republican Europe. And for that reason, at least some of the elements of what Melzer calls Rousseau's individualistic solution to the human problem may also occur in – I have shown that they in fact do occur in – Rousseau's republican writings, including the appeal to a rustic or pastoral nature.

But the strategy of retreat into nature is complicated because nature is not obviously good. As I argued in the Chapter 1, nature cannot be regarded as good if it is responsible for "the fortuitous concatenation of several foreign causes" (*SD*, III, 162; I, 51) that lures us into society and brings about our deplorable present state. If human development is driven by demanding, even harsh, external circumstances, if these circumstances trigger internal tendencies, toward pride, for example, that are not purely artificial but latent, then nature is not obviously a worthy object of longing. It may even be an object of resentment. If nature is to be a refuge for and not an enemy to man, as Rousseau's strategy would seem to require, then nature must be made innocent of history. The equation of the original and the natural radically separates nature from history. It is a physiodicy, a claim that nature is not responsible for the terrible human misfortunes chronicled in the *Second Discourse*.

That Rousseau is prepared to use rhetoric to defend nature's innocence should be obvious to any careful reader of note ix of the *Second Discourse*, in which Rousseau declares nature not only innocent but also providential. Here, Rousseau answers a "famous Author" who concluded that the evils of human life greatly exceeded the good and takes up directly the question of physiodicy:

If [that author] had gone back to Natural man, it is likely that he would have reached very different results, that he would have noticed that man suffers almost no evils but those he has given himself, and that Nature would have been justified. It is not without difficulty that we have succeeded in making ourselves so unhappy. (*SD*, III, 202; note ix, 1)

Nature is not only freed from blame for human ills, as it is when Rousseau equates the original and the natural, but also praised for attempting to stave off those ills. Rousseau urges us to

deplore man's blindness which, in order to feed his insane pride and I know not what vain self-admiration, causes him eagerly to run after all the miseries of which he is susceptible, and which beneficent Nature had taken care to keep from him. (Ibid.)

This justification of nature, as we noticed in passing in Chapter 1, is uncharacteristic of the *Second Discourse*. It is uncharacteristic both in clearly attributing an intention to nature and in placing responsibility for human ills squarely on human shoulders. As we have seen, the more characteristic argument of the *Second Discourse* is that human nature, though originally good, is disfigured by history, by circumstances "which might never have arisen and without which he would eternally have remained in his primitive condition" (*SD*, III, 162; I, 51). The latter argument prevails for a good reason. The road back to nature appears to terminate in a human beast who is incapable of exercising freedom or, in any case, of having responsibility for his actions in any meaningful sense. Bestial human nature cannot be to blame for the events or actions that disturb the supposed equilibrium of the original state and draw human beings out of "that original condition in which [they] would [have spent] calm and innocent days" (*SD*, III, 142; I, 17). Rousseau draws our attention to this problem in a remarkable way. He appends note ix to his description of perfectibility, that faculty which distinguishes human beings from animals. Perfectibility stands in the place of human freedom, about which Rousseau admits there can be some disagreement. Perfectibility, which develops our faculties with the aid of circumstances, introduces ambiguity into the question of human responsibility for human progress or corruption. Unlike freedom and its consequences, perfectibility and its consequences are not obviously to be blamed on human beings who, as Rousseau's account allows one to conclude, may be more playthings than makers of history. The most emphatic argument to be found in the

Second Discourse for natural providence, then, is appended to a passage in which blaming human beings rather than nature for human ills is shown to be most dubious.

The equation of the original and the natural is a justification of nature that is needed once Rousseau substitutes perfectibility for freedom. If human progress is driven not by willfulness but by the impact of a multitude of external circumstances, then nature can be justified only if it is distinguished from those circumstances. While the move from freedom to perfectibility tends at least partially to exculpate human nature by rendering it an essentially passive victim of history, the equation of the original and the natural tends to exculpate external nature by insisting, albeit unconvincingly, that only the original state, that original set of circumstances which supposedly does not force human beings into history, is natural. As I argued in Chapter 1, Rousseau understands that his physiodicy is open to a number of objections, objections he understands to be decisive. Even if the distinction between nature and history were entirely successful in maintaining the innocence of external nature, it would leave human nature wanting and consequently open to blame. When one peels away man's historical acquisitions, one is left either with no nature or with a nature that is inadequate with respect to its own needs. Such natural needs, along with the love of well-being and with the aid of perfectibility, cast human beings out of the original state and therefore must bear some of the responsibility for human ills. Rousseau nonetheless means to persuade his readers of the goodness of nature, so that they will love it; he signals this intention when he appends a powerful defense of natural providence to a passage that undermines the theory of freedom that is the basis of that defense. He indicates that intention, too, by trying to have it both ways rhetorically. Although there is obviously a contradiction between defending nature by blaming freedom and defending nature by blaming circumstances, Rousseau employs both defenses in support of his cause. We are compelled to assume either that Rousseau has missed the "obvious contradictions that every college freshman sees in his works" and that his placement of note ix is a matter of chance, or that Rousseau thinks that rhetoric must be brought to bear to defend the goodness of nature.

It is worth noting that Rousseau does not limit his argument for nature's providence to the claim that nature resists progress. As we observed in Chapter 1, Rousseau does not hesitate to incorporate the results of man's first progress, such as physical strength and mechanical prudence, into his description of natural or original man. Rousseau, indeed, sometimes both affirms and denies the presence of a human trait in man's original condition, in order to give nature credit for the good consequences of that trait and free it from blame for the bad consequences. Consider Rousseau's treatment of foresight. On the one hand, foresight may distract us from the sole sentiment of our present existence, cause us to worry about our deaths, and enable us to conceive projects to escape our original condition. Nature's goodness is assured only if original man has "no idea of the future" (*SD*, III, 144; I, 21). The Carib, who is already at some remove from the original state, still has so little foresight that he sells his bed in the morning, not foreseeing that he will need it in the evening (Ibid.). On the other hand, foresight appears to be a necessary condition of pity's effect in the state of nature. Pity "will keep any sturdy Savage from robbing a weak child or an infirm old man of his hard-won subsistence if he hopes he can find his own elsewhere" (*SD*, III, 156; I, 38). Yet one needs foresight to know whether it will be possible to find food elsewhere. Rousseau grants original man foresight when that foresight tends to enhance the standing of nature and denies him foresight when it tends to diminish the standing of nature. The same can be said of imagination, which is said to depict nothing to human beings (*SD*, III, 144; I, 21) when Rousseau wishes to underplay the tendencies that propel human beings out of the natural state but is allowed to put us in the place of others when Rousseau wishes to exaggerate the impact of pity on brutes. Rousseau advances two different arguments, neither of which he thinks entirely true, in order to enhance nature's reputation.

Moreover, Rousseau argues both that nature means to keep us in the original state, demonstrating "how little care Nature has taken to bring Men together" (*SD*, III, 151; I, 33), and that nature means to keep us in the more advanced and social state of the savage nation by withholding the discovery of metallurgy from us (*SD*, III, 172; II, 21). In this way, Rousseau lets nature have it both ways. He suggests both that nature is free of responsibility for the ills that are already present in the savage nation, such as artificial needs, and that it is responsible for what is good in the savage nation, which is, after all, "best for man." One may be inclined to reflect that if nature really meant to keep us in the original state, then it would be guilty of trying to deprive us of a better state, the savage nation. But Rousseau, far from helping us to this reflection, clouds the issue by using the term "savage" to apply indifferently to original man, the men of the savage nation, and all men between those two states. The effect of this otherwise puzzling straddle is to enable nature to get credit for everything good and evade responsibility for almost everything bad.

erhaps Rousseau could have avoided the tension between his praise kind of progress and his praise of origins by crediting nature with bringing about a measured progress in which an equilibrium between the development of human faculties and needs is always maintained. He makes such a claim for nature once in the *Second Discourse*:

> It was by a very wise Providence that the faculties he had in potentiality were to develop only with the opportunities to exercise them, so that they might not be superfluous and a burden to him before their time, nor belated and useless in time of need. In bare instinct he had all he needed to live in the state of Nature, in cultivated reason he has only what he needs to live in society. (*SD*, III, 152; I, 33)

As I suggested in Chapter 1, the history recounted in the *Second Discourse* is, in many ways, an extended proof that this characterization of nature is overly generous, that when human nature is left to itself in perfectly ordinary circumstances, new developments occur before we are in a position to profit from them. Nonetheless, we have already seen that the falsity of an argument is, for Rousseau, no obstacle to its use for winning over readers to nature's side. Why, then, does Rousseau so rarely characterize nature as the guardian of cautious progress? I will argue later in this chapter that Rousseau thought a prejudice against progress salutary. For that reason, Rousseau is rarely forthright when he praises the good things that arise only in and through history. To praise nature too often and openly as progressive would have cut against the important anti-progressive rhetoric of the *Second Discourse*.

Individualism

Original man as Rousseau depicts him is entirely solitary. The equation of the original and the natural tends to exaggerate human independence to the point of making human beings completely asocial. Rousseau claims in the *Second Discourse* that his predecessors who sought the state of nature did not go back far enough and consequently "transferred to the State of Nature ideas they had taken from society" (*SD*, III, 132; Exordium, 5). By equating the original and the natural, Rousseau exhibits his determination to go all the way back and thereby eliminate every last vestige and spring of sociality from human nature. Original man is man at his most individualistic, lacking not only social virtues but also those needs, desires, and faculties that give him the motive and the means to enter into society. But as I argued in Chapter 2, Rousseau is not a radical individualist.

Indeed, he thinks that modern societies, or theorists of modern societies like Hobbes, have exaggerated human asociality and suppressed the social sentiments that human happiness requires. Why, then, does Rousseau, by advancing the equation of the original and the natural, insist upon human asociality?

First, the well-being of the small republic, for which Rousseau admittedly does not hold out much hope, demands that human beings be made independent before they can be made good citizens. As I argued in Chapter 2, Rousseau thinks that human beings, by the time civil society is necessary, are all too ready to welcome their chains. Because of their "greed and ambition" and all the business they have with each other that needs to be sorted out by arbiters, the denizens of the last stage of the state of nature cannot and do not wish to live without masters. If Rousseau insists, nonetheless, that men remain so "proud and untamed" as to be compared with "Animals born free and abhorring captivity," he does so in the context of examining "the facts in terms of right," that is, of setting down the conditions that must be met for the principles of political right to succeed (*SD*, III, 177, 180, 182; II, 32, 37, 39, 41). The success of these principles requires that human beings be jealous of and vigilant about protecting their freedom. Where individuals, because of their business with and dependence on others, prefer tranquility to freedom, they allow the ambitious to rule over them and to render them politically powerless:

The People, already accustomed to dependence, repose, and the comforts of life, and already past the state where they could break their chains, consented to let their servitude increase in order to secure their tranquility. (*SD*, III, 187; II, 48).

It is such individuals, too, who are willing to pay representatives to rule them and mercenaries to defend them. Even perfectly good laws cannot keep such citizens free. Even before good citizens can be made, independent individuals must be made. While the task of the legislator, as the *Social Contract* says, must be one of transforming independent and solitary wholes into corporate beings, his prior task must be one of transforming dependent, comfort-loving beings into independent and solitary wholes. Yet Rousseau finds the small republics besieged by the tempting and triumphant ways of modern sophistication. While social man is always dependent on others, modern philosophers encourage mutual dependence and the concentration of men in cities (*Preface to Narcisse* [*PN* hereafter], II, 967–68; 104–105; *J*, II, 19–20; 13–14). It is, therefore, hardly surprising that Rousseau exaggerates in favor of independence, even to the point of asserting falsely that human beings are asocial, independent, and solitary wholes before the legislator molds them into citizens.[8] Just as Melzer suggests, then, though in a rather different way than the one he proposes, the *Second Discourse* can serve a purpose for republican Europe by fostering the love of sweet freedom that republicans require. The equation of the original and the natural, though it exaggerates human asociality, is useful in that it offers natural man as a model of independent and solitary wholeness.

It is worth noting just how pervasive Rousseau thinks dependence is and how little Rousseau thinks his contemporaries value independence. After all, it is not only tranquility that is preferred to independence. Even prior to the establishment of civil society, when human beings are a good deal less dependent on each other than they will be later on, they prefer to live in the most horrible state of war, rather than to flee one another:

> They would have dispersed if the evil had been swift . . . but they were born under the yoke; by the time they felt its weight, they were in the habit of bearing it, and were content to wait for the opportunity to shake it. Finally, as they were already accustomed to a thousand comforts that forced them to stay together, dispersion was no longer as easy as in the first times. (*SD*, III, 222; n. xvii)

It is not only that human beings for a long time have tended to prefer tranquility to independence; they also on the whole prefer war to independence. Long before the advanced corruption characteristic of eighteenth-century European monarchy set in, human beings not only failed to value their independence very much but also valued the fruits of their dependence so much that independence and solitude became evils more terrible to contemplate than the state of war. How much different these men, who prefer war and dependence to peaceful independence, are from the savage of the savage nation, who prefers a bloody independence to servitude and who, far from fearing solitude, knows the pleasures of being alone. Civilized human beings are so far from this pleasure that they cannot even imagine it (*SD*, III, 220; note xvi, 1). If Rousseau exaggerates the asociality of human beings so much, it is not only because the task of making independent human beings comes first but also because that task is so daunting as to require powerful and misleading rhetoric.

Second, Rousseau's individualistic solution for monarchical Europe also demands that human beings be made independent before they can be made fit for healthy social relations of any kind. An Emile is expected to be attached to his own family, to neighboring families, and even, in a very limited way, to foreigners (*E*, IV, 854–55; 471). But such ties are destructive for a human being only so long as he remains in a state of civilized dependence. Material dependence makes him want to exploit his "fellows" through force or fraud. He becomes "knavish and artful with some, imperious and harsh with the rest." The need human beings have for each other turns them into secret enemies. They were not secret enemies when they were "free and independent." Similarly, psychological dependence, or *amour-propre*, "instills in all men a black inclination to harm each other" (*SD*, III, 174–75; II, 27). As the character "Rousseau," who I think in this particular case speaks for the real Rousseau, puts it in the *Dialogues*:

[A]s soon as . . . absolute love degenerates into amour-propre and comparative love, it produces negative sensitivity, because as soon as one adopts the habit of measuring oneself against others and moving outside of oneself in order to assign oneself the first and best place, it is impossible not to develop an aversion for everything that surpasses us, everything that lowers our standing, everything that diminishes us, everything that by being something prevents us from being everything. Amour-propre is always irritated and discontent, because its wish is that each person should prefer us to all else and to himself, which is impossible. (*D*, I, 806; 112–13)

Negative sensitivity is contrasted with positive sensitivity, which is "directly derived from love of oneself" (*D*, I, 805–6; 112) without reference to comparison with or the opinions of others and which attaches us to other human beings. Like material dependence, psychological dependence poisons our relations with others; no reform of those relations can succeed unless it begins by helping us to overcome our deep-seated dependence on others. In my view, Rousseau exaggerates human independence into human asociality for that reason, among others. Both the *Second Discourse* and *Emile* advance early on powerful and, I have argued, exaggerated claims for human asociality. In the second part of the *Discourse* and in Books IV and V of *Emile*, in the account of the savage nation, on the one hand, and of compassion, love, family, and politics on the other, sociality is given its due and place in human life. The design of these two works very roughly follows the necessary design of the individualist solution, which must establish human independence before seeking to make, or in order to make, men fit for healthy social relations.

Of course, the *Second Discourse* begins not with the individualistic First Part but with the republican dedicatory letter. And Rousseau's *First Discourse* places much more emphasis on the Spartan and Roman models than it does on primitive ones. It would be foolish to insist that independence, or detachment from unhealthy social relations, must come before dependence, or the establishment of healthy social relations in a more than formal way. Among other things, such a rigid formula would obscure the extent to which Rousseau seeks independence even after healthy social relations are established, and the extent to which whatever independence most human beings are capable of depends on healthy social relations, as Emile depends on the governor and on Sophie. Accordingly, Rousseau pursues simultaneously the strategies of stirring longing in his readers for a certain kind of society and disgust at the vast majority of existing societies. Indeed, even when he counsels people for which there may be great political hope, like the Corsicans, he oscillates between individualist and collectivist rhetoric. This is no surprise, since Rousseau thinks that the best citizens must have both individualist and collectivist beliefs. Even American citizens are or at least once were encouraged to entertain the logically contradictory but politically salutary ideas that Americans, disdaining assistance, pull themselves up by their bootstraps, and that they owe it all to their country – that they would be nothing without it. How much more so Rousseau's citizens, who in the best case are both more independent and more socialized than Americans.

The Question of Progress

By equating the original and the natural, Rousseau moves as far as one can from the view that nature's instrument is progress. We have seen, however, that Rousseau praises and gives nature credit for some instances of progress, the development of the foresight and imagination that set pity in motion, for example. It would seem, as I suggested earlier, that Rousseau's own project of exculpating and almost deifying nature would be advanced by the depiction of nature as the instigator and guardian of measured progress. Instead, Rousseau gives the equation of the original and the natural much greater prominence than his rare open admission that nature sanctions certain kinds of progress. He depicts an original man who, in his fortunate independence from and disastrous vulnerability to history, inclines us to regret progress. Why, then, does Rousseau think a prejudice against progress desirable?

The *First Discourse* is the first of Rousseau's writings in which he argues in favor of this prejudice.[9] In it, Rousseau denies that the restoration of the sciences and the arts has contributed to the purification of morals and thereby seems to deny that progress in and consequent to the sciences and the arts has so contributed. He admits, to be sure, that men like Bacon, Descartes, and Newton are "Preceptors of Mankind" who can, especially when kings spur them on, "contribute to the happiness of the

Peoples to whom they have taught wisdom" (*FD*, III, 29–30; 59). But this admission is one of the few retreats in the *Discourse* from an otherwise relentless attack on the arts and sciences. In fact, Rousseau seems to take it back almost immediately when he declares virtue "a science of simple souls" (*FD*, III, 29–30; 60) and thereby implies that human beings have no need for preceptors in the most important matters. What is essential in such matters has long been known and is potentially undermined by novel teachings. Progress and corruption are in that case synonymous. It is not without reason, his protests notwithstanding, that some of Rousseau's critics took him to be attacking the pursuit of the arts and sciences altogether.[10]

In his replies to critics of the *First Discourse*, Rousseau does not abandon by any means his polemic against the arts and sciences. But he is more explicit both in admitting that it is good for some to pursue them and in specifying the true object of his assault:

Greece owed its morals and its laws to Philosophers and to Legislators. I quite agree. I have said a hundred times over that it is good that there be Philosophers, provided the People do not pretend to be Philosophers. (*Last Reply*, III, 78; 30)

The true villains of the *First Discourse* are not the arts, the sciences, or philosophy, nor do advances in or consequent to them have to harm societies. Rather, it is the widespread taste for and pursuit of such learning and brilliance that must be vigorously attacked. In the *Preface to Narcisses*, Rousseau recapitulates the argument of the *First Discourse*, holding "a taste for study and letters" responsible, in part, for the deterioration of morals in modern societies (*PN*, II, 965; 78).[11] This sophisticated taste, born of and tending to nourish luxury, idleness, and vanity, softens and corrupts human beings; it undermines, for the sake of novel theories, the law, tradition, and virtue that hold societies together while, at the same time, it makes human beings all the more dependent on each other. The prejudice in favor of progress, then, which so dominates modern life and characterizes modern sophisticates, is disastrous for societies. The contrary prejudice is, to be sure, hardly free of difficulties. Rousseau is compelled to defend himself against the charge that he prescribes burning down libraries (*PN*, II, 963–64; 12). And even if it is true that those suited to philosophy need no teachers and little encouragement (*FD*, III, 29; 59), they surely need not to be executed, as Socrates was, by suspicious citizens. Nonetheless, it is not difficult to see why, especially when a "crowd of Popularizers" and "Anthologizers of works" have helped to make science and philosophy far more fashionable in Rousseau's Europe than they were in Socrates' Athens, Rousseau thinks a prejudice against progress needful (*FD*, III, 28–29; 59).

One may object that Rousseau's acknowledgement that Greece owed its morals and laws to philosophers and legislators does not prove that his argument against progress is meant to instill a prejudice rather than a truth. After all, Rousseau claims that the duties of a citizen are discovered early. Once they have been discovered, progress in philosophy or in legislation really is synonymous with corruption:

The first Philosophers earned great renown by teaching men to perform their duties and the principles of virtue. But before long these precepts had become commonplaces, and in order to achieve distinction men had to strike out in opposite directions [;] one is horrified to see how far the maxims of our ratiocinating century have carried the contempt for the duties of man and citizen. (*PN*, II, 965–66; 20)

Similarly, Emile learns from his tutor that

[A]ll the ideas which are salutary and truly useful to men were the first to be known; that in all times they constitute the only true bonds of society; and that the only way transcendent minds can now distinguish themselves is by means of ideas that are pernicious and destructive for mankind. (*E*, IV, 670; 339)

While progress may have been salutary once, long ago, Rousseau really thinks, and does not merely profess to think, that it is pernicious in his time.

Set aside the obvious answer that Rousseau's prejudice against progress, as the *Second Discourse* reveals, covers not only recent progress but all progress since the very beginning of the human story. However that may be, there are other reasons to think that when the governor teaches Emile that only the first truths were salutary and useful, he teaches him a prejudice, just as Rousseau, according to my argument, teaches his readers a prejudice in the two *Discourses*. For he reveals in his discussion of the political teaching Emile receives that the science of "political right has yet to be born, and it is to be presumed that it never will be born. Grotius, the master of all our learned men in this matter, is only a child" (*E*, IV, 386; 458). The science of political right is furthered by Rousseau and remains in a state of infancy even after Rousseau's innovations. Inasmuch as this science clarifies the character of social ties and sets forth the conditions of the social pact that in turn defines the duties of citizens, it cannot be true that all the ideas that are useful for human beings were the first to be known. One might add that, since Rousseau claims to advance the study of natural law, which has been left in a state of confusion by ancients and moderns alike, there may be progress not only in our knowledge of the duties of citizens but also in our knowledge of the duties of men (*SD*, III, 124–25; Preface, 6).

Rousseau connects Emile's prejudice against new ideas to the young man's "good sense." One part of Emile's good sense is that "the sphere of his knowledge does not extend beyond what is profitable" (*E*, IV, 670; 339). Because most new ideas, at least in the civilized society into which Emile is to be introduced, are clever rather than useful and offered to the public only to elicit its admiration, a prejudice against new ideas can be expected generally to draw sensible conclusions. Emile's good sense may require the support of such a prejudice against the onslaught of civilization. It is Emile's good sense, his attachment to the useful and profitable, that leads him to ask always "What is that good for?" when he is confronted with new learning (*E*, IV, 446; 179). That skeptical question itself may be thought to reflect Emile's arguably unnatural and prejudiced refusal to indulge himself in wonder.

It should be noted that Rousseau gives Emile's curiosity considerable latitude within the confines of prejudice and good sense. When it is directed toward the thought experiment of living on Robinson Crusoe's island, for example, Emile's pursuit of knowledge is praiseworthy: "He will want to know everything; he will want to learn the reason for everything. From instrument to instrument he will want always to go back to the first; he will accept no assumption" (*E*, IV, 460, 188). And when it comes to certain questions, which at least point in the direction of "the great relations he will have to know one day in order to judge well of the good and bad order of civil society," Emile's curiosity yields nothing to the philosopher's: "He is all alone philosophizing for himself in his corner. He questions me; I refuse to answer; I put him off to another time. He gets impatient; he forgets to eat and drink; he burns to get away from the table" (*E*, IV, 462–63, 190).[12] Soon enough, Emile's compassion and love will be used to turn his curiosity more directly to the great relations he begins to glimpse in the course of this exercise, in which he reflects on the labor and materials required to produce an opulent meal. What this story suggests is that the pursuit of learning and of progress in the arts and sciences by ordinary human beings is safe and good for societies when it is restrained by the criterion of utility and, as Rousseau argues in many other places, when it does not lead to an undue dependence on tools or on others.[13] While Emile resists dependence and disdains the useless as a result of his careful education, it may well be that other human beings can be led to ask "What is that good for?" only by a prejudice that is still stronger than the one Emile is taught, the kind of prejudice that the equation of the original and the natural will tend to instill.

A Useful Abstraction

I began this section by building on A. O. Lovejoy's claim that Rousseau's original man is, at bottom, a satire against primitivism. I went on to argue that the equation of the original and the natural and Rousseau's praise of original man are part of a rhetorical strategy directed against sophisticated modern society and the errors of its great theorists. But it is important to note that Rousseau's description of the original state is not merely an elaborate deception, meant only to discredit what it appears to stand for. By equating the natural and the original, or by separating nature from history, Rousseau isolates what he regards as a genuine and permanent aspect of human happiness. As I argued in Chapter 2, original man embodies the immediacy, inactivity, independence, and solitude that are irreplaceable components of that happiness. Though original man is an abstraction, inasmuch as human beings have never been altogether free of the impact of history, he is an abstraction that serves both to show forth clearly an aspect of human nature and to indicate the peculiar combination of fragility and permanence that characterizes it. Rousseau's recounting of the corruption by history of a nature that is not itself historical implies both that nature is easily corrupted and that it is never eradicated. "It is, so to speak, the life of your species that I will describe to you in terms of the qualities you received, which your education and your habits could deprave, but which they could not destroy" (*SD*, III, 133; Exordium, 7).

ENDS AND PERFECTIONS

If the argument of Chapter 1 is right, Rousseau understands human nature to consist not in a beginning untouched by perfectibility, which original man represents, but a natural end or perfection for human beings, which the cultivated Emile represents. If so, however, why must one expend so much effort to uncover this conception of nature, which hardly seems so politically or otherwise charged that it ought to be hidden? At first glance, at least, this question may seem reason enough to dismiss the argument which, however much it relies on evidence that Rousseau leaves more or less out in the open, nonetheless requires us to extract with no small trouble an argument that Rousseau nowhere makes straightforwardly, in spite of the obvious and great importance of nature in his thought. Surely Rousseau would not have been so coy about a matter of such great importance were he not somehow compelled to be.

It is easy enough to excuse the interpretation I have offered by casting stones at the others. After all, as much as a more straightforward interpretation of Rousseau's conception of nature seems a reasonable demand, there exists no such interpretation. Indeed, no thoughtful interpretation of Rousseau's thought could have the audacity to claim that Rousseau's interpretation of nature is easy to get at. To mention just one reason, the reader of Rousseau's work is confronted by the apparent contradiction that we noticed in Chapter 2 between the procedure of the *Second Discourse*, which strips away progress and development to get at the natural man, and *Emile*, which insists that natural man cannot be known until the results of a certain progress and development have been observed. While Rousseau is notorious for the difficulties unifying his thought presents, the difficulty of finding a univocal conception of nature in his thought may be suspected of being more challenging than most such difficulties, at least if the paucity of treatments of this undeniably important problem in the vast literature on Rousseau is any indication of how challenging it is.

In any case, it would be wrong to assume that Rousseau has no good reason for discussing the idea of nature as an end or perfection cautiously. We have already given one reason in this chapter. If it is part of Rousseau's rhetorical strategy to equate nature with humans beginnings, that same strategy can be expected to lead Rousseau to dissociate nature from ends. In that case, it is necessary for Rousseau to conceal or at least downplay his view that the question of human nature is inseparable from the question of what a perfected human being is.

Arthur Melzer suggests another reason Rousseau may have for keeping his considered view of nature in the background of his works. He argues that Rousseau follows Hobbes in "being obsessed with closing off every possible challenge to the law." Both Hobbes and Rousseau think that the foremost threat to political stability comes from "ambitious ideologues who escape and subvert the law through the appeal to some higher law." Rousseau does not "deny altogether the existence of an objective standard of justice" grounded in the nature of things and "discoverable by the wise" (Melzer, 1990, 125, 133, 135). He also acknowledges, more openly than Hobbes chooses to,[14] vast inequalities among human beings, some of which imply that a few are more fit to rule than the many. There is, in Rousseau's thought, a "pervasive Platonic strain, recognizing the need for an absolute rule of wisdom" (Melzer, 1990, 232). However, Rousseau rejects both natural law and natural rule in favor of consent and natural equality. He does so, according to Melzer, for a variety of reasons. One reason, and the one that concerns us most here, is that human beings are typically both unwise and unreasonable. They are incapable of discerning an objective standard of justice in nature. "Rousseau... denies that the mass of men have become so rational as to have access to a true understanding of justice." Moreover, they cannot solicit nature's guidance through wise intermediaries, for "being unwise, they cannot see the value of the wise man's commands or tell him apart from all the false claimants to wisdom" (Ibid., 136, 240). Under these circumstances, the assertion that nature offers political guidance and establishes inequalities aids those "sophists and counterfeit philosophers" who, by claiming to know and draw on a transcendent or natural standard, establish their own authority and advance their own interests at the expense of the state and of civil peace (Ibid., 137). Insofar as Rousseau remains concerned with the future of republican Europe, the suppression or downplaying of that assertion must be part of his rhetorical strategy.

Yet Rousseau's own idea that nature consists, at least in part, in an end or perfection suggests that nature offers political guidance, in that there may be a naturally best way of life toward which politics ought to be directed. It also suggests that nature establishes inequality, in that some may be more or less capable of understanding and of pursuing natural human perfection. Rousseau's own understanding of nature tends not to be straightforwardly asserted in his work because it would be of no use to most human beings and, if promulgated and vulgarized, of use to those pretenders to philosophy who would like to be kings or, at least, advisors to kings. While Rousseau does suggest, to be sure, in the *First Discourse* that philosophers could be advisors to kings, that suggestion is based on the dubious assumption that the conclusions of the philosophers will be in perfect accordance with virtue, that sublime science of simple souls that is identical to citizen morality. That is, the philosophers must not reveal the tension between nature and even the best politics that Rousseau, himself, points to in other places and that a straightforward account of his conception of nature would bring to the surface.

Of course, as Melzer points out, Rousseau does appeal to nature when it is a question of his individualistic solution for monarchical Europe. Rousseau's doctrine of conscience asserts that nature provides moral guidance. This doctrine, however, is both individualistic and egalitarian, attributing to each an infallible guide within. It does not incline us to listen to outsiders who claim to be wise (1990, 148).[15] Rousseau evidently does not expect his individualistic solution to promote widespread dissatisfaction with legitimate, or at least relatively good, republican politics. Similarly, though Rousseau appeals to nature in the *Second Discourse* and even suggests that the study of original man will resolve a host of political questions (*SD*, III, 125, 126; Preface, 8, 11), his argument tends to draw nature still further from politics, and even from recognizable human life, than had his predecessors and, indeed, to raise serious questions about the very existence of natural law. This appeal is not of the sort to provide comfort or cover to ambitious pretenders to wisdom, and bestial original man is still less likely than the individualistic man of conscience to lure citizens away from decent regimes.

THE "CLARITY" OF *EMILE*

We can extract from the *Second Discourse* the conclusion that Rousseau does not subscribe to or think tenable his provisional equation of the original and the natural. Our "given" nature can never be separated from circumstances or our history. But it is only in *Emile* that the whole mode of describing and investigating nature takes on a historical or developmental character and in which the inadequacy of our origins comes to the surface. Similarly, though there are certain indications in the *Second Discourse*, it is only in *Emile* that nature comes to light as not merely that which emerges in and through history but as an end or perfection. Why, then, does *Emile* admit more plainly than the *Second Discourse* does the falsity of the equation of the original and the natural and the importance of ends or perfections in the study of human nature?

We can begin to answer this question by falling back on the imperfect but useful distinction often made between Rousseau's critical and constructive works. Readers as diverse as Immanuel Kant and Allan Bloom have observed that the two *Discourses* are especially concerned with criticizing and exposing the ills of sophisticated modern societies. Other works, like *Emile, Julie,* and the *Social Contract,* propose and work through possible or experimental remedies for those ills (Bloom, 1979, 29; Ferrara, 1993, 25–26; Kant, 1963, 61; Todorov, 2001, 11; Wokler, 1995, 31–32). As I have argued in this chapter, the equation of the original and the natural, which is most prominent in the *Second Discourse,* supports a radical and hyperbolic attack on civilized progress and sociality. It belongs especially, though not exclusively, to the critical side of Rousseau's project.

The independence, inactivity, and immediacy of original man are, to be sure, components of a positive vision of human happiness. Nonetheless, we can agree in part with Kant that original man is meant not so much to illustrate Rousseau's vision as to expose the manifold corruptions of civilized man. As Cassirer puts it:

Kant judges that Rousseau's purpose did not involve inviting man to go back to the state of nature but rather to look back to it in order to become aware of the errors and weaknesses of conventional society.

Natural man is "a contribution to ethical and social criticism" (1963, 25, 20). As Kant himself argues:

Rousseau did not really want to go back to the state of nature but rather to *look* back on it from where he now stands. He assumed that man is good *by nature* (as it is bequeathed to him), but good in a negative way, that is he is not evil of his own accord and on purpose but in danger of being . . . corrupted by evil or inept guides and examples. (Kant, 1963, 168)

Cassirer goes on to argue that Rousseau's constructive works, especially the *Social Contract* but including *Emile*, substitute for the "negative" natural man a positive and complete idea of natural human goodness as consisting in man's capacity for freedom:

For him, the goodness of man, which he affirmed and championed now as before,[16] was not an original quality or feeling but a fundamental orientation and fundamental destiny of man's will. . . . Man is "by nature good" – to the degree to which his nature is not absorbed by sensual instincts but lifts itself spontaneously and without outside help to the idea of freedom. (1989, 104–105)

On this understanding, the critical works compel us to imagine a human being untouched by progress so that we will see the extent to which history as it has actually unfolded has corrupted us. We will then be prepared to consider history as it should have been or ought to be, as leading up to and culminating in freedom. The negative understanding of nature, to which the equation of the original and the natural gives rise, is provisional and prepares us to grasp our true, ethical nature. It is not surprising, then, that the falsity of that equation is revealed most clearly in a constructive work like *Emile*, nor is it surprising that the constructive works manifest more clearly than the critical ones Rousseau's view that the question of man's nature is inseparable from the question of his end or perfection. Though Cassirer gives Rousseau only partial credit for deliberately de-vising a rhetorical strategy, he indicates clearly enough the difference in emphasis between the critical and constructive works:

> Throughout, Rousseau's interest and passion were given to the doctrine of man. But he had come to understand [in his later works] that the question, What is man? cannot be separated from the question, What ought he to be? (Cassirer, 1989, 65)

As I have indicated, especially in Chapter 2, I do not agree on the whole with Rousseau's Kantian interpreters, who think that Rousseauian morality requires the conquest of Rousseauian nature. To doubt that view, it suffices to recall that history as it ought to be, as narrated in *Emile*, culminates in a man of nature who, though he is capable of self-conquest and morality, derives much of his happiness from the sweet freedom and simplicity we encounter in the *Second Discourse*. The portrait of original man is not merely negative or critical but embodies an aspect of the human condition and of human happiness that remain an object of Rousseau's constructive works. However that may be, we can agree in part with Kant and Cassirer. Rousseau was, indeed, willing, more deliberately than they thought, to advance a misleading conception of nature that was very effective in discrediting civilized sociality and progress. But while the equation of the natural and the original was instrumental in understanding the consequences of history as it actually unfolded, that equation had ultimately to be abandoned in *Emile* when Rousseau set out to tell what "ought to be the history of [his] species" (*E*, IV, 777; 416). A proper account of that history, as I argued in Chapter 2, requires us not to abandon nature for a rational telos, as the Kantian interpretation proposes, but to consider nature as an end or perfection. One might add that the reader of the *Second Discourse*, which exaggerates in favor of individualism and inculcates a prejudice against progress, will be inclined to take *Emile*'s qualified endorsement of sociality and progress with due caution. Like Emile himself, such a reader will be shielded by his or her previous education from the dangers that even measured progress and a limited social life entail.

To be sure, the view that nature must be considered as an end or perfection is not advanced in all of Rousseau's constructive works, nor is it advanced simply or straightforwardly in *Emile*. That is not surprising. We have already seen how downplaying or concealing this view is part of Rousseau's rhetorical strategy, especially as it regards republican Europe and its future. The *Social Contract*, whose implications for republican Europe are obvious, occasions a stricter application of this strategy than

Emile, or *On Education,* whose announced subject matter, domestic rather than public education, appears inapplicable to republics.

We should observe, however, that *Emile* may be misleading where it seems to be clearest about natural ends. In his discussion of love, sex, and marriage, Rousseau has recourse to nature's intention in support of his claim that men and women are naturally directed toward each other and that their relations are meant to culminate in monogamous marriage. Each sex is said to fulfill "nature's ends according to its own particular purpose." Man and woman have not only different bodies but also different characters, tastes, skills, and duties, so that "each contributes equally to the common aim, but not in the same way" (*E,* IV, 693; 358). If girls, for example, "love adornment almost from birth" (*E,* IV, 703; 365) and love to play with dolls, they do so not because educators and parents box them into their assigned and socially constructed gender roles but because nature intends it. "The doll is the special entertainment of this sex. This is evidently its taste, determined by its purpose" (*E,* IV, 706; 367). Girls, long before puberty, love adornment because nature means for women to enchant men and make them fathers and providers. In support of the family, Rousseau argues that nature makes men and women complementary parts, so that the perfection of each, when combined with the perfection of the other, forms a perfect whole, the family. But is the family nature's end? Emile's governor has no family. In describing the life he would lead if he were rich, Rousseau includes friends but not family in his daydream (*E,* IV, 678–91; 344–55).[17] Though the governor does not necessarily have a more perfected nature than Emile has, his knowledge and abilities, along with Emile's ordinariness, lead us to wonder if Rousseau's account of nature's end is not misleading and exaggerated precisely where it seems most straightforwardly presented.

While *Emile* reveals, perhaps more clearly than any of Rousseau's other works, that the question of human nature cannot be separated from the question of human perfection, it cannot be said to offer a neat answer to either of those two questions. Even if one can argue, as I do in Chapter 2, that Rousseau understands his objective to consist in the natural perfection of a naturally disharmonious being, one cannot point to an altogether satisfactory achievement of that objective, even in the autobiographical works. For this reason, the study of Rousseau's rhetoric is not meant to decode the pat answers Rousseau deviously hid from the uninitiated but rather to reveal Rousseau's profound understanding of human problems behind the variety of striking provisional or experimental solutions he puts forward. I agree with Allan Bloom that one

is left with a sense of incompletion or imperfection in Rousseau's view of human life. Civil society does not satisfy much that is deepest in man. The dreamer cannot live well with his fellows. And, in the state of nature . . . man was not really man. But Rousseau resisted the temptations to which his successors succumbed. . . . All these possibilities are to be found in his thought, but each was given no more than its due. (1987, 578–79)

But, as Bloom recognized, revealing profound questions demands more from rhetoric than advancing simple solutions, however controversial or bold.

4

Rousseau and Charles Taylor

The last three chapters were part of an attempt to recover Rousseau. In the place of the Rousseau who slew nature for the sake of freedom, I have put a Rousseau for whom nature remains a guide and limit for human beings in their pursuit of the best way of life. In the place of the Rousseau whose expeditions led inevitably to the polar extremes of our discontent with modernity, to radical individualism and radical collectivism, I have put a Rousseau who endorses a middle way, in which one succeeds in combining, however warily, the goods the bourgeois seeks so unsuccessfully to combine. Rousseau's thought, on my reading, is a reflection on the natural perfection of a naturally disharmonious being.

Rousseau's legacy is often understood in two different but related ways. Contemporary defenders of community, usually known as communitarians, admit that Rousseau is a relative but only a kind of crazy uncle, from whom the family does well to distance itself.[1] Charles Taylor captures the most important sense in which Rousseau's assault on modernity is connected to contemporary defenses of community. Like many contemporary communitarians, Rousseau is concerned at one and the same time with community and authenticity, which at first appear to be opposed concerns.[2] Rousseau is "one of the points of origin of the modern discourse of authenticity" but he understood that complete independence from social opinion is impossible for individuals. Consequently, at the same time that he is a point of origin for the modern discourse on authenticity, he is "one of the originators of the discourse of recognition" (Taylor, 1994, 35, 44–49). Rousseau, then, is a trailblazer for all those who value authenticity but recognize that authenticity is grounded in community. However, Rousseau, who blazes so many trails, ultimately follows only one to its end, and it leads to a political community characterized by "a tight unity of purpose that seems to be incompatible with any kind of differentiation." That political community, described in the *Social Contract*, is in many ways a model for "the most terrible forms of homogenizing tyranny, starting with the Jacobins and extending to the totalitarian regimes of this century" (Ibid., 50–51). Rousseau, therefore, cannot be fully owned by contemporary defenders of community. However seriously they may take the threat that inequality of recognition poses to everyone's sense of identity and even freedom, they do not suppose that imposed equality of recognition and the suppression of difference is either desirable or likely to succeed. Rousseau, then, begins to perceive the importance of authenticity and its social preconditions, but it will be left up to others, including contemporary communitarians, to explain how strong communities and authentic individuals can coexist.

Some critics of communitarianism see Rousseau's legacy somewhat differently: Rousseau, though an extremist, is a realist about the requirements of community. Clifford Orwin argues that both contemporary liberals and contemporary communitarians have been far too optimistic about the possibility of alleviating the ills of modern life, as Rousseau describes them, without abandoning liberalism. He observes:

> While Rousseau viewed liberalism as necessarily inimical to community, our communitarians join our liberals in espousing a community of liberals, soft rather than hard, tolerant rather than austere, cosmopolitan rather than patriotic. (Orwin, 2000, 63)

Similarly, Steven Kautz thinks that both sides of the liberal–communitarian debate have incorporated soft-core versions of Rousseau's extremism. We long for both privacy and community, and both loves are marked by "a sort of fanaticism" that can be traced to Rousseau. At the same time, we cling to the bourgeois virtues and more or less liberal politics that Rousseau, a true radical, opposed. Insofar as Rousseau offers something to the contemporary debate between liberals and communitarians, it is to help us see the hard choices that contemporary liberals and communitarians alike tend to obscure, between the "sober liberal rationalism and moderation" of Locke and Montesquieu and the "respectable extremes" of Spartan republicanism and natural individualism championed by Rousseau; "perhaps it is time to take up the quarrel between Locke and Rousseau once again" (Kautz, 1997, 249–51, 268–69).

These critics of communitarianism are, I think, almost certainly right that Rousseau would have seen attempts to accommodate his criticisms of modernity within more or less liberal societies as, at best, ways of making bad societies somewhat gentler (Orwin, 2000, 63). In this respect, Rousseau's radicalism offers a challenge to contemporary liberals and communitarians, who hope for a good deal more. Oddly, Rousseau's radicalism, when considered in the contemporary context, encourages a kind of sobriety because it insists that the kinds of changes required to address the ills of modernity seriously are so difficult, dangerous, and contrary to liberal tastes and sensibilities that almost no one would be interested in making them. However, it is also important to notice that Rousseau's sobriety, which both understandings of Rousseau's legacy tend to neglect, encourages sobriety, too. Once we notice that Rousseau does not favor an all-or-nothing choice between individualism and collectivism, we are in a position to compare the balance between individual and social goods he looks to effect in his political and moral teachings, and the balance between authenticity and community that communitarians seek. Once we notice that Rousseau did not slay nature for the sake of freedom, we are in a position to compare his moral and political teachings, in which nature remains a standard, to the teachings of communitarians for whom nature has been, at best, dramatically compromised as a standard.[3] In contrast, the old charge that Rousseau is a totalitarian, which Taylor relies upon, and the more qualified and essentially correct observation that Rousseau is a radical, which certain critics of communitarianism emphasize, discourage such a comparison.

I must immediately qualify the objective of this chapter, since I intend to deal with just one communitarian, Charles Taylor, though Taylor's observation that individuals necessarily find themselves embedded in a social matrix and the related attack he launches against "atomism," with which this chapter is primarily concerned, is certainly common enough among communitarians.[4] Dealing with just one communitarian thinker, however influential, has the disadvantage of raising questions about the generalizability of the argument I am about to make, but it has the advantage of enabling me to compare Rousseau and at least one communitarian at more length and in greater depth than would be possible in a brief survey of communitarian thought. Taylor is an especially suitable candidate for comparison because Rousseau is a pivotal figure in his understanding of the history of modernity, one to whom he frequently refers and who arguably "had a major impact on his thinking" (Abbey, 2000, 5). Since Taylor interprets and, I will argue, misinterprets Rousseau, dealing with Taylor will also give me the opportunity to show that something rides on getting Rousseau right.

To repeat: Taylor attempts to do successfully what Rousseau merely pointed at and then emphatically failed to do, namely, to make peace between the demands of authentic individuality and the demands of community. In order to do so, Taylor must rescue the ideal of authenticity from its most extreme partisans. He attacks those partisans on their own chosen battlefield. That is, he accepts the premise that defining one's own identity is a worthy ideal but shows that it can be fulfilled only by those who participate in a common life and have due regard for their (not merely instrumental) ties with others. Taylor offers what he regards as at least the beginning of a satisfactory solution to one of the great tensions in modern life, and he does so without turning to extremism, as Rousseau allegedly does. However, in comparing Rousseau's "middle way" to Taylor's I will argue that the peace Taylor makes between the demands of authenticity and the demands of community, in fact, come at too high a cost to the individual, leaving him much more dependent on the community than Rousseau does. Although Taylor's political preferences are more or less liberal, he offers a theoretical attack on individualism and a foundation for social tyranny more powerful than any he finds in Rousseau's thought. Since Taylor begins with identity and authenticity, I will, too. Then, I will treat his defense of community and his explanation of our obligations to it more directly.

Since I have been writing about reconciling the demands of authenticity and the demands of community, let me say something about what I take authenticity to mean.[5] In *The Politics of Authenticity*, Marshall Berman begins by suggesting that authenticity is "a persistent and intense concern with being oneself" and that he could just as easily have used "autonomy" or "individuality" or "self-realization" to "designate a whole family of aspirations and ideals which are central to the cultural life of our age" (1970, xv). But leaving aside the stark differences with respect to how autonomy and authenticity are used by contemporary political theorists, Berman's definition obscures the important difference between being oneself understood as realizing one's nature and being oneself as the creation of an identity in the absence of such a nature.[6] While Berman does not understand authenticity in quite the latter way, he does claim that the search for authenticity comes into its own only when the self is perceived as a problem and when the self is not merely disclosed or discovered but created in the course of the search for it. Rousseau's autobiographical writing, for example, in Berman's estimate, is not merely or primarily an act of discovery by Rousseau but a way of "*bringing his authentic self into being*" (Ibid., 86). It seems worthwhile to keep the latter, distinctly modern, sense of authenticity apart from the less distinctive idea of being oneself.

Taylor does a better job of capturing the novelty of the idea of authenticity. He observes that the modern, or better the late modern, ideal of authenticity consists of a cluster of beliefs about how one goes about being oneself: that there "is a certain way of being human that is *my* way," that one is called to live one's life that way, that being oneself "involves creation and construction as well as discovery," and that it frequently requires "opposition to the rules of society and even potentially to what we recognize as morality" (Taylor, 1991, 28–29, 66). It also seems to me that Taylor is more careful to place Rousseau at a distance from the ideal of authenticity than Berman is; it hardly seems obvious that Rousseau is engaged in a work of self-creation in the *Confessions,* nor does it seem likely that Rousseau places sufficient emphasis on the value of being oneself in a unique or original way to count as a partisan of authenticity in the modern sense.[7] Indeed, if we neglect the emphasis in the contemporary ideal of authenticity on originality, opposition, and self-interpretation, we risk missing the challenge earlier understandings of being oneself, including Rousseau's, pose to the new ideal.

OUR BODIES, OUR SELVES? ROUSSEAU, TAYLOR, AND
THE SENTIMENT OF EXISTENCE

Consider Taylor's surprising but illuminating misreading of Rousseau's sentiment of existence. Taylor makes his mistake in describing Rousseau as the first articulator of a new form of inwardness that develops into the modern ideal of authenticity. For Rousseau, according to Taylor, the self we experience when we feel our existence, though more fundamental than any particular moral view, causes us to adhere to the rules of morality. "Our moral salvation comes from recovering authentic moral contact with ourselves," and this intimate contact with oneself is called "the sentiment of existence." "Le sentiment de l'existence would make me a perfectly moral creature if I were but in full contact with it," where morality is understood to be more or less in agreement with the rules regarding the right treatment of others imposed by most societies (Taylor, 1991, 27, 63). For Rousseau, then, self-definition and morality are held tightly together. But Taylor has conflated the sentiment of existence and conscience. In fact, for Rousseau, the sentiment of existence offers no moral guidance. Solitary, amoral, natural man enjoys "the sentiment of [his] present existence" (*SD*, III, 144; I, 21). Man's "first sentiment was that of his existence" (*SD*, III, 164; II, 2). The passage Taylor cites from the *Reveries* nowhere mentions morality and even suggests that a man who indulges himself in the sentiment of existence may develop a distaste for his duties; such indulgence is appropriate only for a man who "can do nothing more in this world to benefit himself or others" (*R*, I, 1047, 89).

From the very beginning, then, of his history of authenticity, Taylor writes out of it a deep conflict between the individual and society and prepares the way for the reconciliation he hopes to effect. If the senti-ment of existence is conscience, then it is at least plausible to claim that it depends on society, since conscience is manifestly something that de-velops and is needed only in society. But if the sentiment of existence is, as Rousseau says it is, a contentment whose source is "nothing external to us, nothing apart from ourselves and our own existence" (*R*, I, 1047, 89), then it is an obstacle to the argument Taylor wants to make – that we cannot be ourselves if we do not participate in a common life and acknowledge our ties with others.

It is especially useful to compare Rousseau to Taylor because he ini-tiates the argument that Taylor carries forward, that what is most recog-nizably human is social. He criticizes his predecessors who went back to the state of nature for including in it not only vices but also faculties, like reason and language, that develop only in or with society (*SD*, III, 132, 144–51; Exordium, 5; I, 21–32). Human beings who appear to be atomic individuals in Hobbes and Locke already exist in fact in a social matrix. But Rousseau does not move from this premise to the conclusion that community makes us what we are, or that we cannot be ourselves outside of communities. Instead, in works like the *Second Discourse* and *Reveries*, he asserts the opposite. He digs beneath language and reason to a natural man who enjoys a sentiment of existence that, though hardly distinctly human, though prerational and prelinguistic, puts us in con-tact with our existence – i.e., what we are – and sweetens it. To be sure, Rousseau's understanding of the sentiment of existence is more complex than I have indicated. For example, there is little question that the de-velopments human beings undergo in society, when they do not fatally undermine our capacity to enjoy the sentiment of existence, can enhance it. The uncivilized natural man enjoys the sentiment of his present exis-tence; the civilized Rousseau is enraptured.[8] Nonetheless, by conflating the sentiment of existence and conscience, Taylor understates the tension between individual and society.[9]

In the later stages of Taylor's history of authenticity, identity must be ar-ticulated in a struggle with at least some social rules. But identity remains a product of self-understanding, self-definition, and self-expression, or reason and art (1991, 33, 65). This feature is built in to Taylor's definition of identity, as in *Sources of the Self*:

> To know who I am is a species of knowing where I stand. My identity is defined by the commitments and identifications which provide the frame or horizon within which I can try to determine from case to case what is good, or valuable, or what ought to be done, or what I endorse or oppose. In other words, it is the horizon within which I am capable of taking a stand. (1989, 27)[10]

To see that this definition of identity is not the only obvious one, compare Rousseau's fanciful description of a man who has at his birth the strength and stature of a man:

> He would see nothing, hear nothing, know no one, would not be able to turn his eyes toward what he needed to see. Not only would he perceive no object outside of himself, he would not even relate any object to the sense organ which made him perceive it. . . . He would have only a single idea, that is, of the *I* to which he would relate all his sensations.

I bring up this odd passage for two reasons. First, it compels us to take note of the *I* that precedes our capacity to take any stand. Second, it ends by noting that this idea of the *I* is the only sentiment the man born full-grown would have that an ordinary baby would lack (*E*, IV, 281; 61). That is, the sentiment of the *I* is connected with the *body*. If the definition of identity is what Taylor says it is, then Rousseau and he are not far apart, for Rousseau, to repeat, prepares the way for Taylor's claim that reason, language, and most of the things that make us "full human agents" are social. But Rousseau, unlike Taylor, places great weight on the body, which, to be sure, does not make us full human agents but is no small part of "who we are." Taylor's more or less disembodied identity has the effect of drawing the individual and society closer together because it sets aside what we have without community and what emphatically distinguishes our interests and goods from those of the others.[11]

It is not that Taylor does not concede that the separateness of our bodies is likely to make us care more about ourselves than about others. Consider his amusing description of the way in which the sense of personhood, however much it may vary across times and cultures, is in at least one way the same all over:

> We can probably be confident that on one level human beings of all times and places have shared a very similar sense of 'me' and 'mine.' In those days when a paleolithic hunting group was closing in on a mammoth, when the plan went awry and the beast was lunging towards hunter A, something similar to the thought

'Now I'm for it' crossed A's mind. And when at the last moment, the terrifying animal lurched to the left and crushed B instead, a sense of relief mingled with grief for poor B was what A experienced. In other words, the members of the group must have had very much the same sense that we would in their place: here is one person, and there is another, and which one survives/flourishes depends on which person/body is run over by that mammoth.

But Taylor makes nothing of this admission of the way in which our having bodies limits rather than expands our attachments to the community, or of its moral and political ramifications, choosing to concern himself almost entirely with what he calls the "moral and spiritual dimension" of personhood (1989, 112–13).

To draw attention to the connection of identity to the body is, of course, not to deny Taylor's claim that we "become full human agents" only with the aid of a language we learn from others and learn to use for our own purposes in exchange with others (1991, 33). But as we take seriously Taylor's proposition that a "human being alone is an impossibility," a proposition directed not only against extreme partisans of authenticity or even Rawlsian liberals but against the liberal tradition from Locke on (1985, 8), we should also bear in mind that the extent to which we do find ourselves alone is humanly and politically important. Taylor's very definition of identity lulls us into forgetfulness on this score and, incidentally, loads the dice in favor of his argument for strong commitment to community. By contrast, as I observed in Chapter 2, Rousseau never loses sight of the most radical claims of the individual, even in his most apparently collectivist works.

LET YOUR CONSCIENCE BE YOUR GUIDE?
THE INNER VOICE AND NATURE

Most of the arguments I make in this chapter are meant to show that Taylor unintentionally makes individuals more dependent on community than Rousseau does. However, at times and equally unintentionally, he neglects the individual's dependence on community, or at least on others. Recall that Taylor is in a partisan of authenticity who wishes not so much to undermine that new ideal as to tame it by showing that we need community in order to be authentic individuals. Rousseau is, in fact, a good deal more anti-Romantic than that for the following reason: He is persuaded that, with the exception of rare individuals who "raise themselves in spite of what one does" (*E*, IV, 266; 52), people are bound to be led astray by their inner voices, unless they are subjected to a careful and extensive regime of voice training. It is not only the case that conscience develops only in the course of exchanges with others but also the case that it develops, at least in the sense we usually understand it, out of a difficult and well-planned education.

Taylor, who considers Rousseau's understanding of conscience at some length in *Sources of the Self*, does not notice this aspect of Rousseau's thought because he accepts the standard view according to which Rousseau thinks that "the original impulse of nature is right"; if we can only be made to ignore the clamor of artificial opinion, we will again be able to hearken to conscience, the voice of nature, and be true to our own, moral, selves (1989, 358–59). One can hardly fault Taylor for understanding this to be Rousseau's teaching. Rousseau himself, especially in the "Profession of Faith of a Savoyard Priest," a part of *Emile* that expounds a natural religion, appears to advance something like it, and any number of commentators have understood the teaching offered in the "Profession" to be part of Rousseau's considered thought.[12] Although Rousseau puts the "Profession" in a priest's mouth, rather than his own, the main elements of it appear elsewhere in Rousseau's own name.[13] On the other hand, as some commentators have noted, that priest's opinions appear to differ from Rousseau's on several crucial matters, including the source of wickedness, whether human beings are naturally social, the dualism of freedom and nature, and the existence of natural law – all of which would seem to have some bearing on the teaching concerning conscience (Melzer, 1996, 335; Orwin, 2000, 70).

However, I have no intention of trying to settle the question of the place of the "Profession" in Rousseau's thought. Instead, I want to make a more limited claim, using a promising source of evidence for Rousseau's understanding of conscience that has suffered surprising neglect, that is, the discussion of the development of Emile's own conscience in *Emile*. In Chapter 2, I observed that the impulse of one's given nature leads in the direction of unhealthy superstition and fear, which the governor forestalls in Emile only by instilling a certain prejudice in him about nature's goodness. It will therefore be no surprise to learn that I think a careful reading of Rousseau on conscience reveals that he can't possibly think, at least in the way that a "moral sense" interpretation of his thought implies, that "the original impulse of nature in us is right." I limit myself to Rousseau's account of the very first stages of the development of conscience because I think that account is adequate to demonstrate where he differs from how Taylor sees him and, ultimately, from Taylor.

In *Emile*, the voice of conscience is first raised in rebellious anger. Rousseau's Savoyard priest defines conscience as "an innate principle of justice and virtue according to which, in spite of our own maxims, we judge our actions and those of others as good or bad" (*E*, IV, 598; 289).[14] If that is what conscience is, then it is, at least at first, a problem. Consider its first appearance in *Emile*, when a crying child, who has just been struck by an impatient nurse, lets his conscience be his guide:

> The unfortunate was suffocating with anger; he had lost his breath; I saw him become violet. A moment after came sharp screams; all the signs of the resentment, fury, and despair of this age were in his accents. I feared he would expire in this agitation. *If I had doubted that the sentiment of the just and the unjust were innate in the heart of man*, this example alone would have convinced me. (*E*, IV, 286; 66; emphasis added)

One may be tempted to object that this is not the voice of conscience at all. After all, it is not a judgment but a sentiment and Rousseau explicitly says that "conscience, although independent of reason, cannot . . . be developed without it." He adds that "there is no morality" in a child's actions "before the age of reason." However, he makes an exception for "the sentiment of others' actions which have a relation to us" (*E*, IV, 288; 67), precisely the kind of sentiment the child in the example experiences. Moreover, while conscience cannot be fully developed where the capacity to judge between good and bad is undeveloped, it is, itself, arguably a sentiment, "the first sentiment of justice . . . innate in the human heart" (*E*, IV, 584; 279).[15] There is no good reason I can discern for refusing to call the child's "sentiment of the just and unjust" conscience, as long as we bear in mind that it is little developed in the child. Rousseau's usage authorizes us to do so.

But there is, as the description of the child's resentment suggests, trouble with that sentiment of the just and unjust. From the first tears of a child "is born man's first relation to all that surrounds him" (*E*, IV, 286; 65). One may begin by indulging children's tears. But if this indulgence is not carefully limited to real needs, then children will see adults as tools to satisfy their inclinations and "become difficult, tyrannical, imperious, wicked, unmanageable" (*E*, IV, 289; 68). And as a child grows accustomed to getting what he wants, "his desires grow constantly due to the ease of satisfying them"; "Without being God, how will you content him?" One must finally refuse, and

> [W]hen one is finally forced to refuse him something, he, believing that at his command everything is possible, takes this refusal for an act of rebellion. . . . He

sees ill will everywhere. The feeling of an alleged injustice souring his nature, he develops hatred toward everyone. (*E*, IV, 314; 87)

The child's hatred is not limited to his fellow human beings: "Of two spoiled children, one beats the table and the other has the sea whipped" (*E*, IV, 315; 88). The child populates his universe with hostile and arbitrary wills that must be either imperiously commanded or cravenly obeyed.

Stated simply, the problem is this: The voice of conscience, if circumstances are not carefully regulated, is a voice always raised in complaint and rebellion. The first stirrings of conscience do not oppose but instead support the selfish passions.[16] A child in whom conscience manifests itself this way is in grave danger of growing up to be a man who is bad for himself and bad for others. Rousseau therefore looks to avoid giving the child any target against which to rebel or complain. As we saw in Chapter 1, Rousseau begins by advising the governor to mimic natural necessity, on the grounds that "it is in the nature of man to endure patiently the necessity of things but not the ill will of others." As long as the child is unaware of wills, the moral universe is closed to him. But ultimately, the governor mimics natural necessity only in the sense of being immovable by pleas; he does not mimic natural necessity in the sense of being indifferent. He "grants with pleasure" and refuses "only with repugnance" (*E*, IV, 320; 91). Far from viewing the governor and others who surround him as indifferent natural forces, the child expects within limits that they will be benevolent, even though he cannot order them about (*E*, IV, 335; 101).

Why does the governor reveal any will at all, even a benevolent one, if there is some chance of restraining the child's tendency to see everything in terms of will? The evidence adduced in Chapter 1 suggests that even savages tend to fill the universe with wills, to turn natural forces into powerful gods (*E*, IV, 552–53; 256). Now, if Emile, like the savage, can be expected naturally to fill the universe with a will or wills, it matters a great deal for his own happiness and his morality how he thinks the universe is disposed toward him. If he thinks it is simply fearsome and arbitrary or, worse, actively unjust and hostile, he can be expected to be unhappy and, at least at heart, immoral. If, on the other hand, he thinks it bends to his will, he can be expected to be a tyrant with, since his expectations are bound to be thwarted, essentially the same results. We can think of this as an early manifestation of the problem of recognition since everything seems to depend on how the child thinks he ranks in the universe's estimation. Rousseau's response to the problem is a careful and delicate education. Even if Rousseau, who did not view *Emile* as an education manual, exaggerated the extent to which a child's education can go wrong without what seems like superhuman attentiveness and delicacy, he demonstrates himself to be a much more subtle student of the problem of recognition than Taylor supposes. Indeed, as Joseph Reisert has suggested, Taylor's account of the problem of recognition, which depends so much on his analysis of the ontological preconditions of agency, could stand at least to be considered alongside Rousseau's account of the psychological or emotional dimensions of the problem (Reisert, 2000, 327–28). The latter account is anti-romantic insofar as it suggests that unless being true to oneself is understood as achieving one's natural end or perfection in spite of the obstacles posed by one's given nature, being true to oneself cannot be expected to yield anything good or exalted. Rousseau, unlike Taylor, is not a partisan of authenticity. It is also anti-romantic insofar as it suggests that human health depends not upon our liberation from constraints and prejudices but, at least in most cases, on the imposition of new constraints and prejudices. Moreover, the source of those constraints and prejudices is neither oneself nor the current of nature but the artifice of those capable of distinguishing between health and illness, of discerning the sources of one and the other, and of devising cures.

Taylor, like any cultural critic, implicitly acknowledges that the diagnosis and resolution of our cultural ills requires, at least for the time being, the art of thinkers who have reflected on matters like the ontological preconditions of agency. However, he is himself evidently too much the egalitarian, too much committed to what he calls the affirmation of everyday life, to consider seriously the view that prejudices of the sort even Emile has may be worth having. Indeed, Taylor is so much the egalitarian that he wishes to share the problems experienced by contemporary philosophers with all contemporary human beings. After all, he claims again and again that certain options are no longer available to "us," especially, as we will see, the idea of a divine or natural order, whether orthodox or deist, that is not explored and in part defined by what he calls "personal resonance,"[17] and that is not, in some sense, a "horizon." Without wishing by any means to deny that Nietzsche, Heidegger, and others have had some broad cultural impact, it hardly seems likely that, for many, even the old idea of a providential order is simply foreclosed. Indeed, Taylor's understanding of the predicament of students of philosophy and its history, let alone "our" predicament, is debatable.[18]

The difference between Taylor and Rousseau on this score is most striking with respect to their treatments of religion. Although Rousseau is well aware of the objections that can be made by skeptics to natural religion and is even aware that those objections cannot be decisively answered, he nonetheless has his governor teach Emile natural religion and, in his letter to Voltaire on providence, obscures his full acknowledgment of the doubt surrounding religious questions, including the very existence of God with a poetic endorsement of the immortality of the soul and beneficent providence, both of which he promises to "defend...until [his] last breath" ("Letter on Providence," IV, 1070–1, 1075; 117, 121; *E*, IV, 635–6, 313). As Victor Gourevitch has argued, Rousseau takes on the role and cause of the nonintellectuals, or the "vulgar," in offering a loud endorsement of providence in the midst of a quieter and more qualified defense in which the only thing certain is Rousseau's opinion that belief in a kind of providence is consoling and useful (Gourevitch, 2001, 214–19).[19] Taylor, by contrast, though a theist, keeps his theism in the background, persuaded on the one hand that theism has greater potential than secularism to restore meaning to modern life and, on the other hand, that he does not yet have the arguments to back up that claim, let alone to prove that theism is the best available account of our situation (Taylor, 1989, 517–18; 1994a, 225–26). Moreover, the only religious account that Taylor seems to think genuinely open to moderns goes through the route opened up by thinkers close to the existentialist tradition, like Dostoyevsky, Kierkegaard, and Nietzsche, in which we find ourselves faced with the crisis of affirming a world that does not seem obviously worth affirming and meet it through a "transfiguration of our own vision, rather than simply through a recognition of some objective order of goodness."[20] From a Rousseauian perspective, the insistence that "we" must now come to religion, if we are to come to it at all, via existentialist despair is neither salutary nor true. That is to say both that the existentialist route may lead to more underground men than Alyoshas, and that Taylor's attempt to make his dilemma "our" dilemma is akin to the attempt of some Enlightenment thinkers to establish skepticism as the only available response to what was known about the natural and human worlds, even though skepticism had not obviously succeeded in dethroning religion; both attempts are dogmatic[21] and, however humanistic their intentions, inhumane in their consequences.[22]

AUTHENTICITY, NATURE, AND MISRECOGNITION

Taylor observes that concern about authenticity and identity, on the one hand, and social recognition, on the other, arose around the same time.

However, his understanding of the causes of this concern is not only debatable but also silently elevates the importance of community. According to Taylor, recognition and identity emerge as problems in modernity largely when social ranks and categories become questionable. I must quote Taylor's explanation at some length:

> The point is not that this dependence on others arose with the age of authenticity. A form of dependence was always there. The socially derived identity was by its very nature dependent on society. But in the earlier age recognition never arose as a problem. General recognition was built into the socially derived identity by virtue of the very fact that it was based on social categories that everyone took for granted. Yet inwardly derived, personal, original identity doesn't enjoy this recognition *a priori*. It has to win it through exchange, and the attempt can fail. . . . In premodern times, people didn't speak of "identity" and "recognition" – not because people didn't have (what we call) identities, or because these didn't depend on recognition, *but rather because these were then too unproblematic to be thematized as such.* (Taylor, 1994, 34–35; emphasis added)

I do not think that Taylor can be right about this. The claim that Thrasymachus makes early in Plato's *Republic*, that justice is the advantage of the stronger, is also, of course, a claim that conventional justice fails to recognize who is fit to rule. Conventional justice keeps the naturally best men down and fails to accord them due recognition, or honor. The problem of identity and recognition is here "thematized" as that of nature and convention. What we call failures of recognition are captured in countless stories in which the king, or the servant of God, or the true heir, or the best wife goes unnoticed or is taken for someone else.[23]

Failures of recognition and cases of "mistaken identity" are certainly exacerbated by what Tocqueville called equality of conditions, which dissolves dstinctions in rank and the more or less fixed understanding of one's place, possibilities, and deserts that went along with each rank (Tocqueville, 1969, 54, 452–53, 626). The democratic revolution Tocqueville described does, indeed, render social ranks and categories negligible. It universalizes ambition, makes people more sensitive to and anxious about inequalities, and dethrones every authority, aside from the unreliable majority, to which one might once have appealed to determine one's identity and worth (Ibid., 629, 538, 429–30, 435–36). The problem of being properly recognized has certainly been democratized, then, but it was just as certainly recognizable to thoughtful premoderns who were perfectly capable of noticing a difference between the natural or divine order, which entailed one order of rank or distribution of honors, and the conventional order, which entailed quite another. If the terms in which we speak about these problems have changed, so that, for example, we speak of identity rather than a nature or a calling, it is surely, in large part, because many of us can no longer appeal with confidence to any authority above society, be it nature or God's judgment, to define ourselves.[24] Community is the only arbiter left standing in disputes over recognition.

The problem is, again, well illustrated by a comparison. When he writes *Emile*, Rousseau understands that the *ancien regime* is deteriorating; he writes of the "unsettled and restless spirit of this age" and predicts that Europe is "approaching a state of crisis and the age of revolutions" (*E*, IV, 252, 468; 42, 194). The distinction between noble and commoner, which may once have provided a settled "script" for a young man's education, will not serve Emile. In other words, Rousseau understands that recognition and the establishment of identity can fail. For Rousseau, however, this failure of conventional scripts is, in part at least, a welcome opportunity to investigate what education best suits his fictional pupil's nature. *Emile* tells the story of a natural education, one that suits both what Emile has in common with other human beings and his particular talents and dispositions. Rousseau's response to the breakdown of those conventions that established identity is not to raise the question of how whatever new identities spring up, from whatever source, will get recognized but instead to raise the question of what identities best suit our natures. Proving that nature, according to Rousseau's argument, offers substantive guidance about how to live on the level of society was, of course, the burden of Chapter 1 of this book. Taylor does not consider Rousseau's move a possible one in our time, and this reflects his implicit admission that there is no court of appeal beyond community.

Now, in a way, the difference between Taylor and Rousseau on this point is one of emphasis. That is, Rousseau would be the last to deny that social recognition is important and that "identity can be formed or malformed through our contact with significant others"; it is for this reason that Emile is for a long time shielded from social opinion and confined to a single significant other, his governor. And Rousseau, as Taylor points out, is attentive to the problem of honor in his own politics (Taylor, 1994, 36, 46–51). But Rousseau, as Taylor also mentions, "often sounds like the Stoics" (Ibid., 46). He seems to encourage his readers to disdain social honor and instead to use their own powers of observation and discrimination, aided, to be sure, by Rousseau's own reflections, to make their own judgments about the nature of things and to distinguish between social opinions that are worthy of respect and social opinions that are not. Because Taylor dismisses this alternative, the difference between him and Rousseau proves, after all, more than one of emphasis. For Emile is an impressive human type, of whom Taylor can make little sense, one who gives "nothing to opinion," "nothing to authority," "who values nothing according to the price set by opinion" and cares "little about being esteemed" by others (*E*, IV, 486, 669; 207, 338). He will care about the opinions of some others, but

he will not precisely say to himself, "I rejoice because they approve of me," but rather, "I rejoice because they approve of what I have done that is good. I rejoice that the people who honor me are doing themselves honor. So long as they judge so soundly, it will be a fine thing to obtain their esteem. (*E*, IV, 671; 339)

Emile's spouse, Sophie, though more attentive to reputation than he, also has the capacity to judge her judges. "She has that noble pride based on merit which is conscious of itself, esteems itself, and wants to be honored as it honors itself" (*E*, IV, 809; 439). And

she becomes the judge of her judges; she decides when she ought to subject herself to them and when she ought to take exception to them. Before rejecting or accepting their prejudices, she weighs them. (*E*, IV, 731–2; 383)

Taylor emphasizes, in contrast, how the making of one's identity remains dependent on others throughout our whole lives, absent a "heroic effort to break out of ordinary existence," and that preventing our identity from being formed by the people we love "would take a great deal of effort, and probably many wrenching break-ups" (Taylor, 1991, 34–35). Taylor is so alive to the extent to which the denial of recognition "can inflict damage on those who are denied it," so emphatic about the dependence of individual identity on others, that he rejects out of hand as unrealistic the independence Rousseau grants to middling, though well-educated, souls (Taylor, 1994, 36).[25]

Moreover, for all Taylor's concern about the absence of recognition or misrecognition, either of which can imprison "someone in a false, distorted, and reduced mode of being," it is hard to see how he can distinguish between true and false recognition (Taylor, 1994, 25). For Taylor, it would seem as if the standard is "my own original way of being"; this standard, which Taylor derives from Herder, is after all what distinguishes authentic from inauthentic being (Taylor, 1991, 47). Yet, for Herder, our original way of being is an expression of "the impulse in us of nature"; further, Herder "held views about the natural order as harmonious and providentially created" (Taylor, 1989, 370). Now, Herder's understanding is not ours. Taylor observes in a somewhat different context that even as we have maintained certain Romantic aspirations, the understanding of nature behind those aspirations has no currency:

The idea of nature as a source no longer refers to a God or cosmic spirit in the world, but the demand remains very much alive that we be open to or in tune with nature in ourselves. . . . The loss of belief in a spirit in nature has itself, of course, been the occasion of crisis and doubt, but the understanding of nature as a source still survives, although what underlies it is very uncertain and problematic. (Taylor, 1989, 384)

Here is the problem. For Herder, nature is a standard that allows us in principle, if not from the outside, to distinguish between distorted and undistorted identities. For Taylor, nature is just one of a number of "conditions of significance," or "candidates for what matters," like solidarity, or history, or society, or God, in terms of which I define my identity (Taylor, 1991, 40). Taylor is left without a standard by which to distinguish cases in which social horizons distort my identity and cases in which they leave it undistorted, or even support it.

A similar problem emerges when we consider another illuminating error Taylor commits about Rousseau. According to Taylor, Rousseau criticized hierarchical honor or preferences and dreamed of a society in which all "would share equally in the light of public attention"; Rousseau understood that when we began to desire preferential esteem, society took a turn for the worse.[26] Taylor implies that Rousseau sees the unequal granting of esteem as in itself a problem to be resolved, but Rousseau understood the problem of unequal recognition somewhat differently. Consider the passage that immediately follows the one Taylor cites to demonstrate Rousseau's worries about preferential esteem. In that passage, trouble arises when *everyone* claims a right to esteem:

As soon as men had begun to appreciate one another and the idea of regard had taken shape in their mind, everyone claimed a right to it, and one no longer could with impunity fail to show it toward anyone. (*SD*, III, 170; II, 17)

The problem is not that society oppresses or distorts when it judges that one person sings, dances, or looks better than another. Rather, it is that human beings, who desire preferential esteem, will demand to be recognized, not for what they are, but for what they are not, or that they will wish to have an identity that is not in conformity to their natures – that is, they will wish to have a distorted, if not oppressive, identity. That is surely what it means, at least for Rousseau, to claim a *right* to esteem.

Rousseau, in a way, anticipates a political trend that Taylor criticizes. Both argue that the demand for unconditional equal esteem is unfounded. Taylor, writing of the recognition of difference, claims that the fact that people choose to be different or find themselves in different races, sexes, or cultures does not in itself mean that they are all entitled to esteem. "Mere difference can't itself be the ground of equal value" (Taylor, 1991, 51). But the basis of Taylor's objection is quite different from Rousseau's. Human beings, on Rousseau's account, can be observed to have "a prodigious diversity of minds" by nature, and to bring into the world with them "a particular temperament" and particular capacities that determine "genius and character" for each (*J*, II, 562–66; 461–65).[27] For Rousseau, a man with no artistic ability who wishes to be and to be recognized as a great artist closes his eyes to nature. For Taylor, a person who is "different," good or bad, and demands unquestioned esteem closes his eyes to the very communal standards in terms of which even he defines his identity:

> To come together on a mutual recognition of difference – that is, of the equal value of different identities – requires that we share more than a belief in this principle; we have to share also some standards of value on which the identities concerned check out as equal. There must be some substantive agreement on value, or else the formal principle of equality will be empty and a sham.... Recognizing difference, like self-choosing, requires a horizon of significance, in this case a shared one. (Taylor, 1991, 52)

Taylor's argument is laudable, for it requires that we not only promise to esteem those who are different from us but actually open ourselves to the possibility of having our "horizons" expanded. Nonetheless, there is something strange about appealing to a "shared horizon of significance," which is not obviously more likely to recognize us for what we are than any other horizon, to determine when an unwarranted claim to recognition is being made or when someone is attempting to establish a distorted identity for himself.[28]

Now, it is true that, inasmuch as Taylor claims only that selves are "partly" (1989, 34) constituted by self-interpretations, there may be a basis for distinguishing between recognition and misrecognition in that part of the self that is not constituted by self-interpretation. Ruth Abbey has argued that, for Taylor, of course, "just thinking about myself in a particular way does not necessarily or automatically make me that: I can have a deluded or exaggerated interpretation of my own prowess or of my intellectual acumen, for example" (Abbey, 2000, 59). Taylor, then, like Rousseau, should be entitled to the appeal to nature. However, here

Taylor's admission parallels his admission that we inhabit separate bodies; it may be made in passing but it plays no role in his argument. One reason it plays no role in his argument is that Taylor has not decided how far his "partly" goes. As Frederick Olafson has argued:

Taylor never successfully explains just what this "partly" takes in and what it does not. It seems to me that this is because he is really quite uncertain about how radically historical he is prepared to make this self that supposedly constitutes itself by its interpretations of itself. (Olafson, 1994, 192, 193)

For this reason, among others, it is "not at all easy to say what general concept of human being really serves as the cornerstone of Taylor's thinking." Taylor, while he scores any number of points against Olafson in his response, concedes that he has not said enough about the "huge question" of "how radically historical [we should] be in understanding the different constructions of human identity in different cultures," and insofar as he appeals to a transhistorical standard, he appeals only to the idea that an "agent" inescapably finds herself in a "space of moral issues" (Taylor, 1994a, 207–208).[29] This claim, while important for establishing that natural science is insufficient for the study of human things, is not the kind of claim that will help us distinguish between recognition and misrecognition in most cases. To make such a distinction Taylor appears to have no recourse other than the community.

The difference between Taylor and Rousseau may be put in another way. For Rousseau, the question of whether my identity is distorting may be formulated like this: Does my identity accurately reflect my nature? For Taylor, the question of whether my identity is distorting must be framed as follows: Is my identity in accordance with the horizons of significance I share with my community? The trouble is not necessarily that the latter question admits only a politically or culturally conservative answer, for it may be that a community's failure of recognition is based on a misunderstanding of its own values, or their consequences, or their range of possible interpretations. The trouble is instead that Taylor's approach appears to minimize, at the very least, the potential for distortion. For there is no reason to believe that a self-image in accord with shared horizons is more accurate, even if it is more gratifying, than one that fails for the most part to be in accord with shared horizons. Members of a society or culture may come to value women because they think women conciliators and because their shared self-understanding demands that they value conciliators. But none of this is to say that the image of women in question does not distort and limit them; one could draw that conclusion from the premises only if there is no "text" of women at all to which to compare an interpretation, however widely shared. But if that were so, and Taylor does not seem to wish to say that it is, it would be hard to make sense at all of the idea of "misrecognition."

The account I have given of Taylor's thought is, of course oversimplified, since Taylor is eager to get beyond the notion that our understanding of the good is merely either an individual or communal creation. Although he insists that human beings are incapable of an interpretation-free understanding of the good, he also opposes himself to projectivism, according to which understandings of the good are simply matters of human beings imposing meaning on a meaningless world. Taylor seeks an alternative that acknowledges both that the human world is shaped "by one's form of life, or history, or bodily existence" and that human beings cannot avoid supposing that their moral lives are anchored in "the features of some reality – it can be God, or the universe, or human nature – which make sense of the goodness of the goals and norms we adopt, and the better understanding of which may inspire us to encompass these goals, or fulfill these norms, more fully and heartily" (Taylor, 1994a, 211–12). Taylor offers as one model of such an alternative the "interweaving of the subjective and transcendent" practiced by modernist poets, from whom a "metaphysics or theology" comes "indexed to a personal vision, or refracted through a particular sensibility" (Taylor, 1989a, 491, 492). What such poets express may be inseparable from their work – "We cannot just detach the nugget of transcendent truth" – but far from being purely subjective, it reflects a demand that "emanates from the world" (Ibid., 492, 513). Taylor is consequently some kind of moral realist for whom a demand issues from a source that transcends the individual and the community.

However, Taylor's appeal to a standard beyond individuals and communities is too uncertain and vague to function as a genuine check on the power of community. That it is too uncertain is demonstrated by Taylor's own language. We have already noted one instance, in which he concedes that whatever might replace the discredited Herderian understanding of nature is "very uncertain and problematic." Here is another: In responding to Rorty's suggestion that he embrace a more thoroughgoing anti-foundationalism than he does, Taylor does little more than gesture at his own commitments to theism and "deep ecology," adding that "I am now far out on a limb and cannot hope to do justice to the penetrating questions which Richard Rorty has raised" (Rorty, 1994, 200–201; Taylor, 1994a, 213). Yet doing justice to the questions Richard Rorty has raised is the only way of preventing a slide into the view that "the social creative imagination" is that in which our moral judgments are anchored (Rorty, 1994, 199).[30]

As Rorty points out, Taylor, in a remarkable passage, describes *Sources of the Self* as in the ephiphanic tradition:

> The only way we can explore the order in which we are set with an aim to defining moral sources is through this part of personal resonance. This is true not only of epiphanic art but of other efforts, in philosophy, in criticism, which attempt the same search. This work, though it obviously fails of any epiphanic quality, falls into the same category. I have throughout sought language to clarify the issues and I have found this in images of profound personal resonance.... They could, I believe, be the animating ideas of an epiphanic work.... The great epiphanic work actually can put us in contact with the sources it taps. It can *realize* the contact. The philosopher or critic tinkers around and shapes images through which he or another *might* one day do so. The artist is like the race-car driver, and we are the mechanics in the pit; except that in this case, the mechanics usually have four thumbs, and they have only a hazy grasp of the wiring, much less than the drivers have. The point of this analogy is that we delude ourselves if we think that philosophical or critical language for these matters is somehow more hard-edged and more free from personal index than that of poets or novelists. The subject doesn't permit language which escapes personal resonance. (Taylor, 1989a, 342, 512, 513)

Elsewhere, Taylor describes his claim that our best self-interpretation cannot be "purely immanent-human" but requires a nature, cosmos, or God as "my hunch." When we seek to explain what it means for a demand to emanate from the world, "it is hard to be clear... because we are deep into a language of personal resonance." Taylor's endorsement of the superiority of poetry to philosophy makes us wonder to what extent Taylor's denial that we are left with community as the ultimate arbiter of morality can be rationally defended. It may be for this reason that Taylor doesn't even attempt to argue that questions of recognition and misrecognition can be settled by appealing beyond the community.

For Taylor, the ultimate source of appeal on the question of whether one's identity has been distorted is unavoidably the community itself. To argue that Rousseau endorses homogeneous and coercive communities is plausible enough, though debatable, but it is also important to point out that Taylor is in danger of endorsing, however unintentionally, virtually unlimited claims of the community on the individual. For Rousseau, there are, as we noticed in Chapter 2, "private persons... whose life and freedom are naturally independent" of the public person (*SC*, III, 373; 62). There is, as we have discussed at length, a sentiment of existence that is impervious, or almost impervious, to the claims of the community. One might add, drawing on *Emile,* that there is a natural "génie," a "germ of... character"; "each mind has its own form" (*E,* IV, 324; 94; cf. IV, 465; 192; IV, 478; 201), which an education can develop or suppress.[31] In Rousseau, then, there are points of resistance to society's claims that are unavailable for Taylor. To be sure, Taylor himself points out this problem when he admits that the idea of authenticity is related to an understanding of nature that is no longer ours. But he does not point out the extent to which the problem undermines his own hopes that the power of the community he wishes to release can be contained. My point here is not to endorse Rousseau's understanding of nature and condemn Taylor's but to expose a problem that Taylor does not face squarely; either his argument is parasitic on an understanding of nature he rejects, or it leaves community unrestrained.

It is true that the practical threat that modern communities pose is mitigated by the disagreements that typically characterize them. Even if shared horizons are the last appeal in questions of recognition and misrecognition, the citizen of a modern liberal democracy, at least, has a variety of such shared horizons from which to choose.[32] Indeed, modernity is characterized by the availability of a plurality of what Taylor calls moral sources, the ideas about the good that underlie our other moral judgments, and by the absence of "publicly available orders of meaning" (Taylor, 1991, 84; 1989a, 312–13, 512). In this sense, the spectre of an unrestrained community seeking to form all of its citizens in the same way is not the spectre most to be feared in this moment in the history of the West. But first, this pluralism, as Taylor acknowledges, is both historically contingent and fragile. It is historically contingent because, in Taylor's view, it may be possible to reconcile values that today seem irreconcilable. It is fragile because, among other reasons, pluralism is not easy to live with, and we can expect to be tempted by specious solutions, which "can wreak terrible destruction, as the sad story of Bolshevism shows beyond question" (Taylor, 1994b, 214).[33] Arguments concerning the end of history notwithstanding, it seems too early to let down one's guard about the homogenizing and coercive possibilities of modern communities.

Second, however plural modern moral sources may be, modern societies are nonetheless characterized by "general agreement" about many of the specifics of morality, especially about "the demand for universal justice and beneficence," "the claims of equality," "the demands to freedom and self-rule as axiomatically justified," and the priority of avoiding death and suffering (Taylor, 1989a, 495).[34] I do not mean to argue that this general agreement is oppressive, though Tocqueville has argued that unobjectionable beliefs about equality, which on their surface seem to support individualism, can lead to a kind of tyranny (Tocqueville, 1969, 246–61, 429–36). I mean to argue only that we ought not confuse pluralism with respect to the frameworks within which we make moral judgments, say that there are Christian and non-Christian defenses of equality, and pluralism with respect to the more specific moral positions we feel compelled to defend. The pervasiveness and uniformity of these positions cannot fail to have some impact on what identities are possible for us. Communities, even when they are not directly coercive, may suffocate us, and Taylor's understanding of community tends to make them potentially more suffocating.

COMMUNITY AND IDENTITY

I now turn directly to Taylor's defense of community, which has been in the background of the preceding sections. That defense consists above all in the claim that, without community, we have no identity. There "is no such thing as inward generation, monologically understood. . . . My own identity crucially depends on my dialogical relations with others" (Taylor, 1991, 47–48). Our identities are generated and maintained not alone but through interaction and exchange with others. Taylor's argument is not merely that we need the resources of society to generate our own identities, as we need them to protect our life, liberty, and property, but that it is senseless to try to abstract individuals from their social circumstances:

A human being alone is an impossibility, not just de facto, but as it were de jure. Outside of the continuing conversation of a community . . . human agency . . . would be not just impossible but inconceivable. (Taylor, 1985, 8)

The self is constituted, not merely assisted, by community.[35] Taylor grants that, for various reasons, "more needs to be filled in," but

we can already see how the argument might go: how developing and nursing the commonalities of value between us become important, and one of the crucial ways we do this is sharing a participatory political life. (Taylor, 1991, 52)

That is to say, although Taylor's initial argument merely proposes that the self is constituted by community, without arguing that the political community, in particular, is crucial, Taylor plainly thinks his argument can be expanded to justify a certain kind of politics. He leaves open the precise political consequences of his argument, but there is no question that it is meant at least to supplement both Lockean and Rawlsian or procedural liberalism by putting greater weight on obligation, a sense of belonging, cultural survival, and collective ends.[36] Broadly speaking, Taylor's argument about community and identity is designed to get individualists to combat a regrettable self-centeredness connected to authenticity in particular and individualism in general and to compel even the individualist to admit the "demands of our ties with others" (Taylor, 1991, 4, 35).

In noting that Taylor's argument has certain distinct political consequences, I do not mean to deny the distinction Taylor makes between the ontological issues in the debate between liberals and communitarians and the advocacy issues that arise in connection with that debate (Taylor, 1989b, 159–60). That is to say, I will not claim that there is an inevitable slide from the claim that identities are constructed in social matrices and the abandonment of liberalism in favor of collectivism.[37] Far from it: I will be arguing that the moral and political conclusions Taylor *does* draw from his ontological argument are unwarranted. I agree with Taylor that "we need some normative, deliberative arguments" to determine if we should advocate one or another of the range of moral and political possibilities an argument about how our identities are constituted leaves open to us (1989b, 161). Indeed, I wish to hold Taylor responsible for explaining why he draws more or less liberal conclusions from "normative, deliberative" arguments that seem to have illiberal implications.

Taylor, then, finds our obligation to community above all in what it does to shape our identities or make us what we are. Rousseau may be credited with one of the most powerful formulations of this claim, which I quoted in part in Chapter 1:

This passage from the state of nature to the civil state produces a remarkable change in man, by substituting justice for instinct in his behavior and giving his actions the morality they previously lacked. . . . Although in this state he deprives himself of several advantages given him by nature, he gains such great ones, his faculties are exercised and developed, his ideas broadened, his feelings ennobled, and his whole soul elevated to such a point that if the abuses of this new condition did not often degrade him beneath the condition he left, he ought ceaselessly to bless the happy moment that tore him away from it forever, and that changed him from a stupid and limited animal into an intelligent being and a man. (*SC*, III, 364; 55–56)

Natural man is devoid of self-consciousness, let alone the capacity for self-interpretation. Only the act of association that forms the civil state forces man to step outside of and impose order on himself. It is in this sense that there is real truth to the idea, which a legislator must somehow make true for those for whom he legislates, that "each citizen is nothing . . . except with all the others" (*SC*, III, 382; 68).[38] Rousseau, then, seems to agree, first, that community is the crucial precondition of identity and, second, that it is in large measure for this reason that we should be willing to cede our natural freedom or to meet our obligations to society.[39]

But it is not so much the formation of identity as the formation of a particular kind of identity, that of the citizen, that justifies society in the passage in question, in which we are not merely turned into beings capable of nobility and ignobility but actually ennobled. The citizen is the man who acts justly or morally, who orders his appetites and faculties so that he acts in accordance with the general will of the community as expressed in its laws. To have an identity is to have a self-interpretation. To be a citizen is to interpret oneself as a member of the polity. "A citizen of Rome was neither a Caius or Lucius; he was a Roman" (*E*, IV, 249; 40). This striking formulation shows that Rousseau argues in favor of obligation to the community not on the grounds that it confers an identity on us, for to be a Caius or Lucius is to have an identity, but on the grounds that entering into a certain kind of community makes us into moral beings.[40] By moral beings, Rousseau means not beings capable of acting morally, or of thinking in moral terms, but beings who actually do act morally, men of virtue, citizens.[41]

It almost goes without saying that, for Rousseau, who sets the bar for political legitimacy notoriously high, very few communities can be justified in this way. The fact is, as the passage above says, and as the sad history narrated in the *Second Discourse* shows in detail, the abuses of the new human condition almost invariably degrade man beneath the condition he left. Few if any polities fail to be, in effect, the rule of the few over an exploited and unfree many. For that reason, among others, the "two words, *fatherland* and *citizen*, should be effaced from modern languages" (*E*, IV, 250; 40). We may provisionally formulate at least one serious difference between Rousseau and Taylor as follows: Whereas the latter justifies community in terms of identity, Rousseau justifies it in terms of moral identity or citizenship; and whereas Taylor's defense is therefore potentially quite broad with respect to the range of communities it could justify, Rousseau's seems quite narrow. But this provisional formulation is too simplistic. I now turn to some plausible objections to it.

Here is a first objection. Taylor well understands his differences with Rousseau and celebrates them. As I noted at the outset, Taylor actively resists what he regards as the dangerous tendencies of Rousseau's political thought, which follow directly from Rousseau's too narrow conception of identity. Rousseau's model of the polity is characterized by "the absence of differentiated roles . . . and a very tight common purpose," which "has been the formula for the most terrible forms of homogenizing tyranny" (Taylor, 1994a, 51). Simply put, Taylor thinks that we are obliged to community for forming our identities but that a community is at fault when it discourages its citizens from forming differentiated identities. So it is true that Rousseau justifies fewer communities than Taylor does, but Rousseau justifies only bad communities while excluding many good ones.

But if Rousseau's understanding of obligation to community is too exclusionary, it may point out one sense in which Taylor has too inclusive an understanding of such obligation. For if the community earns a citizen's loyalty by providing him with an identity rather than moral citizenship, with moral depth rather than morality, it is difficult to see how one avoids obligations to very bad communities.[42] The assertion "I now know that I am a Karamazov" or "in spite of everything, I retain the prejudices of my anti-Semitic and racist community" may point to a much thicker identity than liberalism offers. But it is hard to see why such an assertion should make one grateful or obliged to the communities in question. Similarly, the experience of being persecuted may provide one with a strong sense of identity that one would otherwise lack. Taylor recognizes defining oneself in opposition to a community as one way of forging an identity (Taylor, 1991, 33). But, of course, the one persecuted may not even be a member of the community, let alone required to regard himself as indebted to it. To understand our obligation to community in terms of identity renders the legitimacy or goodness of polities a secondary consideration, at best, in determining whether we should regard ourselves as members in them.[43]

To put it another way, our dependence on a community establishes neither our membership in it nor our obligation to it. If the test for our obligation to a community is whether we need it to establish our identity, there is virtually no community that could fail to meet the test, since even very corrupt or oppressive communities are matrices in which language and reason are "available" to form a character of one kind or another. Taylor does not distinguish adequately between legitimate communities and communities that are merely necessary or inescapable. This inadequacy is especially dangerous if one wishes to argue, as Taylor does, for even stronger attachments to community than Rawlsian or Lockean liberalism seem to foster.

To be fair, Taylor does not, of course, think that the provision for just any identity generates obligations to communities. As we have already observed, for Taylor, the demand for "recognition" takes off from the idea that "the projecting of an inferior or demeaning image on another can actually distort or oppress, to the extent that it is interiorized." But this argument does more than soften the consequences of justifying community in terms of identity; it undermines the justification. Consider again how one is supposed to distinguish between distorted and oppressive images and accurate and liberating ones, the Herderian idea that "there is a certain way of being human that is my way. I am called upon to live my life in this way, and not in imitation of anyone else's (Taylor, 1991, 28–29). A distorted image is one that does not reflect one's original way of being human. But this argument poses an obvious challenge to the assertion that community constitutes the self, for if the community provides the space in and materials with which we pursue our original way of being, there is a sense in which our orientation or perfection is determined in spite of the community and may ultimately demand that we abandon it. Although part of the purpose of Taylor's *Ethics of Authenticity* is to demonstrate that authenticity and community are compatible, his argument does not warrant very strong ties to the community at all. Thus, in response to the example of the hermit or the solitary artist, who appears to have overcome his initial dependence on community and to have established an identity quite apart from it, Taylor argues that each type aspires

to a certain kind of dialogicity. In the case of the hermit, the interlocutor is God. In the case of the solitary artist, the work is addressed to a future audience, perhaps still to be created by the work itself. (Ibid., 35)[44]

While this argument may silence a solipsist, it certainly fails to justify thicker or stronger ties to community than the atomism Taylor opposes. Taylor's argument for community, then, proves either too much, because it justifies bonds to almost any community, or too little, because the bonds it justifies are extremely weak (and may not even be to any existing community).

Here is a second objection. In *Emile*, Rousseau's book about the education of a natural man fit to live in society, Rousseau himself seems to justify allegiance to a much wider range of polities than the demanding criteria of the *Social Contract* would seem to allow. After Emile has completed his political education, he decides that he does not want or need to attach himself to any political community, for such attachment, especially in a

Europe devoid of legitimate polities, would decrease his freedom. But his governor convinces him otherwise. And among the arguments he uses is this:

> If I were speaking to you of the duties of the citizen, you would perhaps ask me where the fatherland is, and you would believe you had confounded me.... O Emile, where is the good man who owes nothing to his country? *Whatever country it is,* he owes it what is most precious to man – the morality of his actions and his love of virtue.... The mere appearance of order brings him to know order and to love it. The public good, which serves others only as a pretext, is a real motive for him alone. He learns to struggle with himself, to conquer himself, to sacrifice his interest to the common interest. It is not true that he draws no profit from the laws. They give him the courage to be just even among wicked men. (*E*, IV, 858; 473)

While this argument is about moral being rather than identity simply, it is much more permissive than the argument of the *Social Contract* and much closer to Taylor's. Emile's governor seems to argue as follows. All polities have some semblance of law and justice. But the appearance or pretense of justice points one toward real justice; the tyrant's false claim that he does what he does not for himself but for the common good points one toward the idea of genuine virtue or sacrifice for the common good. The fraudulent proposal the rich make in the *Second Discourse* more or less captures the formal conditions of the legitimate social contract, even if the plan is to undermine that contract (*SD*, III, 177; II, 31). Therefore, the good man, who discerns true justice behind its semblance, is, however indirectly, indebted to the polity for what he is. So Rousseau has no real advantage over contemporary defenders of community; his defense justifies bad regimes, too. This objection is, in a way, beside the point; that is, the danger of the contemporary defense of community is not diminished in any way if Rousseau's argument is also dangerous. Nonetheless, it is worth responding to, if only because the case of Emile strongly suggests, again, that a very limited obligation to community, at most, follows from the recognition that it has made me what I am.

Rousseau's argument for duty even to bad political communities is very qualified. Emile is an outsider in his political community. He does not share his community's values. He despises his agemates in Paris who, corrupted by the scandalous morals of the age, are incapable of noble feelings. Emile could crush them like insects and become their master, but "he would despise these young men too much to deign to enslave them" (*E*, IV, 665; 335). As for his countrymen in general, Emile does not share their opinions either. He hides his contempt for them only because "he pities them." "Unable to give them the taste for things that are really good, he leaves them with the things that are good according to popular opinion" (*E*, IV, 336; 666). To the others, Emile seems not a countryman but a "likable foreigner" (*E*, IV, 670; 339). Plainly, even if Emile is obliged to the community, he is a member of it in only a very qualified sense. If his moral being is indirectly owed to France, being French has very little to do with his self-understanding or self-interpretation. It may be true, as the governor tries to persuade him, that Emile owes what he is to his country, but his identity is not distinctly French. The case of Emile, then, illuminates the distinction between owing one's identity to a community and *identifying* with a community; in fact, Emile's duty to France has nothing to do with being in any strong sense a member of the French community. Taylor does not take this difference seriously enough, for he does not observe that his argument in favor of obligation to community is perfectly consistent with the individual's estrangement from the community, or with *weaker* social bonds than one might expect in a Lockean or Rawlsian liberal society.

However, the evidence cited so far concerns only Emile's visit to Paris. What about the provinces, where Emile makes his home? There, far from urban corruption, perhaps he really is a member of the community. Yet Emile is an outsider in the provinces, too. He cannot possibly share the tastes of the provincials because his taste has been cultivated in Paris. Indeed, Rousseau argues that good taste cannot be cultivated in the provinces because one learns about taste only in places where it is already corrupted:

Taste is corrupted by an excessive delicacy which creates a sensitivity to things that the bulk of men do not perceive. This delicacy leads to a spirit of discussion. . . . In the disputes about preference, philosophy and enlightenment are extended, and it is in this way that one learns to think. (*E*, IV, 674; 342)

Rousseau implies that provincials, unless they visit Paris, are insensitive in matters of taste. To be sure, Emile begins with only the taste that concerns trivial things, "things which are neutral or which are at most of interest as entertainment" (*E*, IV, 671; 340). But Rousseau soon reveals that there is a related taste in moral things as well. "By means of taste the mind is imperceptibly opened up to ideas of the beautiful of every sort and finally to the moral notions related to them (*E*, IV, 718; 375).[45] What Emile does not share with the provincials, then, is of the highest importance. He is not one of them. We may tentatively characterize the difference this way: Whereas provincials are not corrupted and consequently act less immorally than Parisians, Emile has a self-conscious taste for morality; whereas the provincials are, on the whole, not immoral, Emile has "moral values." If a community lives within certain horizons, Emile looks at the community within which he resides from outside of its horizons, and in this sense he is more a stranger than a member.

All this presents a problem for Taylor, who appears to want members of a community to have a sense of belonging that Emile lacks even though he recognizes that he owes his identity to his country. Nonetheless, there remains the matter of obligation, where Emile seems to prove the case for Taylor. Does the governor, after all, not convince Emile that he must serve the community because he is constituted by it, even if not in the same way as the other members are? Even here, it is important to notice some qualifications. First, the governor makes Emile's service rather easy by telling him that his primary task is to lead a patriarchal and rustic life (*E*, IV, 859; 474), a life, that is, that he would have led anyway. He will benefit his neighbors, but doing so in no way cuts against the grain of his compassion for humanity, which only incidentally knows any communal bounds. Second, although the governor does insist that Emile is obliged to leave his rustic life if the country calls him to serve, he also softens the blow by observing that such a call will probably never come: "[Y]ou need have little fear of being burdened with such a responsibility. As long as there are men who belong to the present age, you are not the man who will be sought out to serve the state" (*E*, IV, 860; 475). In the highly unlikely event that Emile is called upon, the governor advises him to fulfill his duty "with enough integrity so that it will not be left to [him] for long" (*E*, IV, 860; 474-5). Emile's duty to his political community is so qualified that certain questions are avoided. What if Emile is asked to serve in an unjust war? Does serving with integrity mean being true to humanity or true to his country? Does service to his country mean service to the principles to which its bad laws point or obedience to the bad laws themselves? Finally, while Emile may or may not be a good citizen when called, there is never any question of his volunteering his services, except in the neighborhood and in the context of his rustic and patriarchal life. Thus, while Rousseau does make an argument for obligation to political communities on the grounds that they confer (moral) identity, this obligation does not go very far at all, certainly not so far as contemporary defenders of community might hope, given that Emile recognizes precisely what Taylor wants citizens to recognize.[46]

One should note, too, that the governor's argument is not necessarily Rousseau's. Emile, after a long and careful education, concludes initially that he should not be a member of any political community.[47] He wants instead to minimize his dependence in order to maintain his freedom, although he has already learned about the benefits of freedom within a political community (*E*, IV, 841, 855–57; 461, 471–3). While the governor persuades Emile otherwise, the many qualifications we have been compelled to make to his argument, which we have drawn from *Emile* itself, suggest that there are problems with it. In particular, the governor goes to great lengths to disguise the tension between Emile as man of nature and Emile as potential citizen, a tension that is the point of departure of the whole *Emile*. That tension, which may be reformulated as the tension between the identity conferred on us by our communities and our natures, may not admit to a full resolution, at least within a political community. For Rousseau, the importance of identity is qualified not only by the importance of moral being but also by the importance of nature.

CONCLUSION

The apparent advantages of defending community in terms of identity are these. First, it satisfies a craving for depth that Rawlsian and Lockean liberalism fail to satisfy. But it does so without hemming us in with potentially restrictive and seemingly indefensible ideas of virtue or nature. Second, it renders our obligation to community ironclad, for it relies not on an instrumental argument, from which the individual may sometimes conclude that the cost of society outweighs its benefits, but instead on an argument that seems to cover all contingencies – that human beings come to be and remain human beings in an atmosphere and especially in a language that they do not individually invent. But when the craving for depth becomes a matter of political concern, the power of the community is increased while the bounds of that power become less well defined. When the grounds for the obligation to community become ironclad, there is no escape from it. Rousseau, whose politics are justly understood as basically illiberal, whatever its liberal aspects, never offered so broad and extensive a justification for community as the more or less liberal Taylor does. Communitarians like Taylor, who wish to supplement liberalism with a sense of belonging, cannot afford to dismiss as philosophically naïve the claim that seventeenth-century "atomists" and Rousseau have in common, that "man is born free."

Conclusion

Rousseau's Challenge to Classical Liberals

In Chapter 4, I compared Rousseau to Charles Taylor and showed that Rousseau, who is so often regarded as a powerful but unsound advance guard for communitarianism, can be effectively deployed against at least one important and influential version of it. But, of course, Rousseau is best known as a critic of liberalism, or at least of liberal political theory.[1] The more moderate Rousseau who has emerged in this book presents at least a somewhat different problem for liberals than the bipolar extremist he seeks to replace. As I have already noted, there is a way in which the extremist Rousseau buttresses the case for liberalism by showing that the case against it, when it is thought through by a great thinker, has consequences that today's critics of liberalism cannot stomach. It seems to me that the liberal reader of Rousseau is in part right to see Rousseau's thought as a weapon to wield against today's soft anti-liberals. Even the Rousseau described in these pages is too radical for them and makes the project of resolving the problems he identifies seem all but impossibly difficult and, within the context of large, modern states, plain impossibly difficult. However, even if it were true that Rousseau has nothing useful to say to residents – he does not usually let us say citizens – of such states, defenders of liberalism would need to respond to his assault on their way of life. They can hardly concede that liberal polities are illegitimate and that they make their citizens miserable, even if their opponents have nothing constructive to say.

For that reason, it seems to me that Steven Kautz is right that "perhaps it is time to take up the quarrel between Locke and Rousseau once again." Another way of putting this is that the debate between liberals and communitarians will benefit from a recovery of the conflict between liberalism and anti-liberalism, of which that debate is a distant echo. Classical liberals have been attentive to distinguishing the liberalism of Locke and Montesquieu from the liberalism of Rawls; one must also be attentive to distinguishing Rousseau's attack on liberalism from its successors. Yet it is the almost universal tendency, even among Rousseau's finest readers, to absorb Rousseau's thought into that of his successors. For example, there is the tendency I have already identified to understand Rousseau as beginning an emptying our of nature's normative content that is brought to completion by Nietzsche and *his* successors. I have already noted, too, that Kautz himself, who thinks about taking up the quarrel between Locke and Rousseau once again, follows this line of interpretation. If my interpretation is correct, then there are two errors we should be concerned about. First, if Rousseau did not in fact return to nature only in order to kill it, then reading Rousseau as a proto-Nietzschean conflates two distinct anti-liberalisms, one flowing from Rousseau and grounded in nature, another from Nietzsche and beginning from radical skepticism about, if not the complete rejection of, nature. Second, reading Rousseau as a proto-Nietzschean contributes, however unintentionally, to the cruder argument that "Hitler is an outcome of Rousseau." Any quarrel between Locke and Rousseau in which Hitler is really on Rousseau's team is at best a classroom exercise and unlikely to inspire much interest even at that level. The interpretation I have offered, then, potentially makes for a more fruitful quarrel.

Rousseau's attack on emerging liberalism is fairly well known, but let us rehearse at least a few of his charges against it, in order to get a better idea of what the proposed quarrel might look like. Perhaps most famously, Rousseau attacks liberalism on the grounds that it promotes the exploitation of the poor by the rich. In particular, the social contract, which proposes equality before the law, is a scam. As Rousseau tells it in the *Second Discourse*, there comes a time in human history when land becomes scarce and the poor, however industrious they may be, are compelled "to receive or to seize their subsistence from the hands of the rich" (*SD*, III, 175; II, 28). The poor who decide to receive from the rich are dominated and exploited by them; the poor who decide to steal from the rich instead learn to be thieves and resort to violence. The result is what Rousseau calls the state of war. In this state everybody suffers, but the rich, who have property to protect, have the most to lose. They therefore conceive "the most well-considered project ever to enter man's mind" (*SD*, III, 177; II, 30). That project is to propose a social arrangement that, as has often been noted, closely resembles the legitimate arrangement proposed in the *Social Contract*. In particular, the arrangement specifies that the laws will protect everyone and apply to everyone equally (SD, III, 177; II, 31). And yet, in rushing to agree to this proposal, the poor are rushing to meet their chains.

Here is why. First, the rich have much more to gain by laws that protect everybody's lives and possession, since they are the only ones who have any possessions. Through the social contract, the rich, who had been hard pressed to defend themselves against the poor both practically and morally speaking, get a legitimate claim to their property, their often ill-gotten gains. The social contract "transformed a skillful usurpation into an irrevocable right" (*SD*, III, 178; II, 33). Second, the provisions of the social contract, which the poor can be forced to obey, are easily dodged by the rich. "The same vices that make social institutions necessary, make their abuse inevitable" (*SD*, III, 187; II, 50). The disparities of wealth that the social contract sanctions make a mockery of the idea of equality under the law because the wealthy can circumvent the law by, we would say today, hiring skillful attorneys and accounting firms or by putting influential politicians in their deep pockets. While one can disagree with Rousseau about the extent to which the property of the rich comes to them through fortune and crime rather than merit and also about the extent to which it is sensible to speak of "the rich" and "the poor" in a society with a large middle class and considerable social and economic mobility, it is hard to dismiss his basic complaint.

While Rousseau's attack on liberal inequality denies the legitimacy of modern societies, his attack on the bourgeois, the human type who is the outcome of liberal theory, denies that such societies succeed even in making people happier. First, the man who devotes himself to the Lockean end of comfortable self-preservation simply gives in to the historical tendency, first appearing among savages, toward infinite neediness. As Rousseau tells it, when human beings unite and, to however limited an extent, cooperate, they find it easy to satisfy their needs and enjoy leisure. They use this leisure to "acquire several sorts of conveniences unknown to their Fathers; and that was the first yoke which, without thinking of it, they imposed on themselves." These new conveniences have the following perverse character: "[I]t [is] much more cruel to be deprived of them than to possess them [is] sweet" (*SD*, III, 168; II, 13). One imagines and longs for new things intensely, but the habit of possession quickly dulls the pleasure of possession at the same time that it makes one dependent on what he possesses. The perversity does not stop there: Presumably because the imagination is freest to stoke our passions when those passions are least circumscribed by practical and immediate considerations, "the less natural and urgent the needs, the more the passions increase" (*SD*, III, 203; note ix, 3). Under these circumstances, happiness is an ever-demanding and receding goal. One recognizes here more than a germ of the now-familiar attack on the materialism and "consumerism" of liberal societies.[2]

Second, modern liberal societies inflame *amour-propre*, or other-regarding self-love. Liberal societies tend to be urban and commercial. They tend to be urban and commercial because their residents are unapologetically devoted to the pursuit of material well-being.[3] One outcome of this unapologetic pursuit is the division of labor, and one outcome of the division of labor is specialization. Specialists depend on other specialists for the provision of their needs. Consequently, they are drawn to cities and towns. Now, even before human beings are drawn into cities and towns, *amour-propre* is at work in the soul. Almost as soon as people gather together at all, each wishes to be esteemed by the others and to be esteemed more than the others (*SD*, III, 169–70; II, 16). When they gather together into cities and live cheek to jowl with a multitude of strangers on whom they depend for their everyday needs, they find themselves constantly under the gaze of others and acquire additional reasons to be concerned about what others think of them. If savages were deeply concerned about how they appeared in the eyes of others, urban moderns are obsessed, a remarkable result when one considers that liberal modernity defines itself in part against an aristocratic honor ethic. Nonetheless, concern with one's standing with respect to and in the eyes of others is pervasive in the bourgeois offspring of the liberal idea, so much so that the bourgeois is not only a calculating hypocrite who consciously seeks to appear so as to curry the favor of others but more deeply an uncalculating crowd-pleaser who stakes so much on the opinion of others that he finally, from his own perspective, ceases to exist except as others see him:

[S]ociable man, always outside himself, is capable of living only in the opinion of others and, so to speak, derives the sentiment of his own existence solely from their judgement. (*SD*, III, 193; II, 57)

Liberal man's material and psychological neediness leaves him scurrying and forever anxious: "[H]e has not a moment's respite" from the pursuit of wealth and is in a "frenzy"[4] to distinguish himself (*SD*, III, 203, 189; note ix, 3, II, 52). Such a man, of course, has no time for politics and is, is any case, led by *amour-propre* to favor whatever leader, however tyrannical, will raise him above the others (*SD*, III, 188; II, 51; *SC*, III, 428–31; 101–104). The bourgeois is not only unhappy but also unfree, representatives notwithstanding, because he has no real say in the decisions that ultimately determine what he may or may not do and that can make or break him.

Third, modern liberal societies, which found social ties on the selfish passions, leave the bourgeois in an unlivable halfway house, in which he lives divided between inclination and duty. The bourgeois is characterized by what Arthur Melzer calls "selfish selflessness," and, as Allan Bloom has observed, he is the "man who, when dealing with others, thinks only of himself, and, on the other hand, in his understanding of himself, thinks only of others" (Bloom, 1979, 5; Melzer, 1990, 80). The result of the liberal experiment of founding confessedly artificial social ties on confessedly selfish natural inclinations is a man who succeeds in being good neither for others nor for himself:

Swept along in contrary routes by nature and by men, forced to divide ourselves between these different impulses, we follow a composite impulse which leads us to neither one goal nor the other. Thus, in conflict and floating during the whole course of our life, we end it without having been able to put ourselves in harmony with ourselves and without having been good either for ourselves or for others. (*E*, IV, 251; 41)

Those who wish simply to deny that there is anything to Rousseau's charges have an uphill battle. They are so recognizable, in part, because they anticipate not only radical but also perfectly mainstream criticisms and anxieties about the liberal order that emerge from the right, the left, and the uncommitted. Those who concede that Rousseau has identified real defects of liberalism but find the alternatives he offers unattractive or impossible face two main alternatives.

The first is to defend the sober liberalism of Locke and Montesquieu, which reached theoretical maturity without the benefit of Rousseau's reflections. The sober liberal may deny that the bourgeois is as small, petty, and unappealing as Rousseau suggests. The classical liberals, after all, were not blind to the importance of virtue and were hardly inattentive to the problem of reconciling inclination and duty through a certain education, however much less demanding than Spartan or even Genevan education it may have been. But, ultimately, the sober liberal is willing to concede that liberal politics is not even *about* the happiness that the bourgeois lacks or the justice that certain economic inequalities violate, and that liberals are concerned above all with defending a peace treaty among free, sometimes rational, individuals who are naturally all too inclined toward partisan violence and fanaticism. Rousseau promises to invigorate our collective lives by making justice and happiness the central and public objects of our concern, but was it not the intention of classical liberals to push these controversial matters into the private sphere with a view to serving the prime liberal directive: seek peace?[5] In short, the sober liberal is compelled to defend liberalism like one defends an unpromising date: He is not very interesting or handsome; he won't make you very happy, but he is a reliable sort and a good earner. In this picture, Rousseau is the long haired bohemian-philosopher who offers a freedom, happiness, and ideals of which one had scarcely dreamed but whose incapacity to get by in the real world may have painful and even disastrous consequences.

The second alternative is to accommodate Rousseauian concerns within a liberal context. While one does not wish to exaggerate Rousseau's direct influence in these matters, it seems fair to say that a good deal of contemporary political theory can be understood as attempting just such an accommodation. Rousseau denied that genuine democracy was possible in modern polities, but democratic theorists like Benjamin Barber, who agree with Rousseau that modern polities are desperately defective with respect to democracy, argue that it can and must be achieved without abandoning liberalism.[6] Rousseau denied that genuine community was possible in modern polities, but communitarians like Charles Taylor, who agree that liberalism has been defective concerning community, argue that it can and must be achieved without abandoning liberalism.[7] Rousseau denied that the modern state could secure dignity, autonomy, or justice; contemporary liberals like John Rawls seek to reform the liberal tradition so that it can do a great deal better than classical liberalism at securing them.

This second strategy, to be sure, flies in the face of Rousseau's acute pessimism. Nations, once corrupt, are all but impossible to reform, and in deeply corrupt Europe there is precisely one country, Corsica, capable of receiving legislation (*SC*, III, 385, 391; 70, 75). Rousseau goes still further in *Emile*, asserting that "these two words, *fatherland* and *citizen*, should be effaced from modern languages" (*E*, IV, 250; 40). What is more, Rousseau once claimed that if legitimate politics could not be established, then the alternative was not to make compromises and seek modest improvements within existing states, but to establish a perfect despotism:

If unfortunately this form cannot be found, and I frankly admit that it cannot be, then I am of the opinion that one has to go to the other extreme and all at once place man as much above the law as he can be, consequently to establish a despotism that is arbitrary and indeed the most arbitrary possible.... I see no tolerable mean between the most austere Democracy and the most perfect Hobbism. ("Letter to Mirabeau," 270)

Rousseau, for all that, did not think it pointless to advise corrupt states. For example, he wrote *Considerations on the Government of Poland* in spite of the numerous obstacles to freedom in Poland, including great disparities of fortune between high and low nobility, not to speak of serfdom. Rousseau was willing to compromise, too, in the institutions he proposed for Poland, most notably in proposing a system of representation, even though he rejected representation in the *Social Contract*.[8] In irredeemably corrupt France, it seems as if Rousseau seriously intended, through *La Nouvelle Heloise*, to effect a reconciliation between the partisans of the Enlightenment and the partisans of the Church (*Confessions*, I, 435–36; 405–406). In addition, however politically pessimistic Rousseau may have been, his cultural ambitions were evidently considerable. He did after all seek to change "the objects of [men's] esteem" so that they no longer believe in the deep-rooted doctrine of progress and civilization his Enlightenment contemporaries were the latest to champion (*D*, I, 934–35; 213). He sought to "give men the love of a regular and simple life; cure them of the whims of opinion; restore their taste for true pleasures; make them love solitude and peace" (*J*, II, 21; 15). Rousseau is justly understood to be the bearer of a new table of virtues, including sincerity and compassion, that characterize the kind of life to which he seeks to attach at least some of his readers (Orwin and Tarcov, 1997, xi–xiii).[9]

Still, it is fair to say that Rousseau was deeply pessimistic about political change and aware of the limits of the cultural changes he attempted with remarkable success to set in motion. The note he sounds at the end of the Exordium of the *Second Discourse* is an exaggerated but true representation of his stance with respect to dramatic and widespread improvement in modern states:

There is, I sense, an age at which the individual human being would want to stop; you will seek the age at which you would wish your Species had stopped. Discontent with your present state for reasons that herald even greater discontents for your unhappy Posterity, you might perhaps wish to be able to go back; And this sentiment must serve as the Praise of your first ancestors, the criticism of your contemporaries, and the dread of those who will have the misfortune to live after you. (*SD*, III, 133; Exordium, 7)

Rousseau can hope for reform in a few societies and for a softening of the mores of others, but not for more than that. There is no reason to suppose, in light of his familiarity with English institutions and his apparently complete indifference to the American struggle for independence, that the practical outcome of liberal theory would have made him more optimistic about remedying the grave deficiencies of modernity in a liberal context. In this respect, he is properly used by proponents of the first strategy against proponents of the second.

However, it is hardly obvious that Rousseau is right to be so pessimistic. As Allan Bloom observed, taking Rousseau seriously does not entail despising liberalism, "and men of Rousseauean sensibilities" in many respects may think, as Rousseau probably would not have, that liberalism could be reinterpreted to accommodate such sensibilities, at least in part. Bloom's example is Alexis de Tocqueville (1997, 165–66).[10] Tocqueville remarked, famously, that Rousseau was among the three authors he read each day as he prepared the second part of *Democracy in America*.[11] While the precise character of Rousseau's influence on Tocqueville cannot, unless new evidence emerges, be pinned down, there are numerous and obvious affinities between the two authors. Like Rousseau's bourgeois, Tocqueville's democratic man is a restless hunter after an infinity of possible pleasures and obsessed with his relative position (Tocqueville, 1969, 535–38). While Tocqueville's Americans are engaged in politics, they are prone, like Rousseau's bourgeois, to become so engaged in self-interested pursuits that they will cede power to whoever will take it; they are potentially men without fatherlands. Like Rousseau's bourgeois, they are selfishly sociable, even if Tocqueville is relatively optimistic about the capacity of the myth of self-interest rightly understood to promote modest virtues among such men (Ibid., 691–92, 525–28). Tocqueville, while he agrees with Rousseau about several of the defects of the emerging modern human type, nonetheless takes the side of modernity and of liberalism.[12]

Yet Tocqueville does not sound like one of our sober liberals. The emerging democratic order is not only inevitable, if indeed Tocqueville really views it that way, but also potentially revealing of the "natural greatness of man." His description of the possibilities of democratic poetry, which seems to anticipate Whitman, is grand enough to satisfy a fervent romantic, while his depiction of the New England township has been an inspiration for communitarian and democratic critics of liberalism, however much Tocqueville's own endorsement of participatory democracy may have been hedged (Tocqueville, 1969, 62–70, 482–87). Tocqueville, as Bloom's comment suggests, is a weighty proponent of the second strategy for defending liberal democracy against Rousseau's charges and one much less easy to dismiss for defenders of the liberal tradition than contemporary theorists – for while Tocqueville undoubtedly departed from the liberalism of Locke and Montesquieu, I do not know of a defender of the classical liberal tradition who does not regard Tocqueville as, in important respects, one of his own.

If Tocqueville is right, and Rousseau is wrong, many of Rousseau's concerns can be accommodated in the context of a new and newly spirited liberalism. It is therefore not only time to take up the quarrel between Locke and Rousseau again but also time to take up the quarrel between Rousseau and Tocqueville.

Notes

Introduction: The Natural Perfection of a Naturally Disharmonious Being

Rousseau references are, in most cases, first to the Pléiade and then to an English translation. *Letter to Malesherbes* references are solely to the Pléiade. Editions are as follows: Jean-Jacques Rousseau, *Considerations on the Government of Poland*, in *Political Writings*, translated and edited by Frederick Watkins (Madison: University of Wisconsin Press, 1953); *Constitutional Project for Corsica*, in *Political Writings*; *Discourse on Political Economy*, in *On the Social Contract with Geneva Manusript and Political Economy*, edited by Roger D. Masters and translated by Judith R. Masters (New York: St. Martin's Press, 1978); *Emile, or on Education*, translated by Allan Bloom (New York: Basic Books, 1979); *The First and Second Discourses Together with the Replies to Critics and Essay on the Origin of Languages*, translated by Victor Gourevitch (New York: Harper & Row, 1986); *Letter to D'Alembert*, translated by Allan Bloom, in *Politics and the Arts* (Ithaca: Cornell University Press, Agora Editions, 1960); *Oeuvres Complètes*, edited by Bernard Gagnebin and Marcel Raymond (Paris: Gallimard, Bibliothèque de la Pléiade, 1959); *Rousseau, Judge of Jean-Jacques*, translated by Judith Bush, Roger D. Masters, and Christopher Kelly, *Collected Writings of Rousseau*, Vol. 1, edited by Roger D. Masters and Christopher Kelly (Hanover, NH: University Press of New England, 1990); *Reveries of the Solitary Walker*, translated by Peter France (London: Penguin Books, 1979); *Social Contract*, in *On the Social Contract.* I have used Gourevitch, 1986 (*The First and Second Discourses Together with Replies to Critics and Essays on the Origin of Languages* (New York: Harper & Row), for the "Letter to Philopolis," the "Preface to Narcisse," the "Last Reply," and "Preface of a Second Letter to Bordes." References to Gourevitch, 1986 are by paragraph number. For the "Letter to Mirabeau, I have used *The Social Contract and Other Later Political Writings*, translated and edited by Victor Gourevitch (Cambridge: Cambridge University Press, 1997) and have referred only to the English translation. For "Letter on Providence," I have used *Discourse on the Origins of Inequality (Second Discourse), Polemics, and Political Economy*, translated by Judith R. Bush, Roger D. Masters, Christopher Kelly, and Terence Marshall,

Collected Writings of Rousseau Vol. 3, edited by Roger D. Masters and Christopher Kelly (Hanover, NH: University Press of New England, 1992).

1. For a good account of the reasons Rousseau's thought has been subject to so much misinterpretation, see Melzer (1990, 1–12).
2. See, for example, Cassirer (1963, 51–55; 1989, 104–105, 108, 114–15).
3. See, for example, Melzer (1990, 41–42) and Babbitt (1968, 49, 233).
4. Quoted in Starobinski (1988, 115). See Weil (1952, 11).
5. It is odd that Rousseau says of happiness *or* of perfection, which leaves open the possibility that happiness has nothing to do with perfection. This ambiguity is especially important because Rousseau's original man, who seems to enjoy at least a measure of happiness, also seems to be not in the least perfected (*SD*, III, 142; I, 17). It also leaves open the possibility that one could be perfected, say perfectly virtuous, and not at all happy, which is, arguably, the situation of the citizen of an ancient republic like Sparta. The chapters to come, especially the first, will show that happiness is closely connected, for Rousseau, to flourishing and the perfection of our faculties. The second chapter will show that Rousseau remains concerned with happiness even when it comes to the ancient republic, so that even if it is possible to be virtuous and unhappy, Rousseau does not propose that such an outcome is the end of human striving.
6. See, for example, Schwartz (1984, 11) and Cooper (1999, xiii–xiv, 10–11, 62–63). Cooper argues that the *Second Discourse* conception is primary, though he thinks that the *Emile* conception is seriously meant and usually neglected. N. J. H. Dent is the most noteworthy exception I know of to this rule of Rousseau interpretation; he considers the conception in *Emile* to be straightforwardly and rather obviously Rousseau's primary understanding, so much so that he suggests Rousseau may have changed his mind between the two writings (Dent, 1988, 74–75; 80–81). Dent, however, takes this point to be so obvious that it is underargued in his book. I disagree with Dent's claim that we should not trouble ourselves with reconciling the *Second Discourse* and *Emile*. Rousseau, who had ample opportunity to make us aware of so vast a change in his understanding of nature as we would have to suppose takes place between the two works, does not do so, even in those works like the *Dialogues*, in which he reflects on his corpus and how it is to be read.
7. See also Strauss (1953, 265–66) and Bloom (1979, 15–16). No one has insisted on Rousseau's adherence to modern natural science and looked into its implications more than Roger Masters. For a recent statement, see Masters (1997).
8. The claim that Rousseau is an adherent of modern natural science is also complicated by the tensions within the science of the eighteenth century. What Cassirer describes as an emerging dynamic and organic conception of nature, which owes much to Leibniz, appears to leave more room for the possibility that nature can be understood in terms of ends or perfections than either Cartesian or Newtonian physics (Cassirer, 1979, 27–73; on Leibniz's distinctiveness, see also Taylor, 1989, 275–77). There is much work yet to be done on Rousseau's understanding of and relationship to the science of his century.

9. Not so Victor Gourevitch, who convincingly argues that the separation between original man and the developments that take him out of the original state is not only implausible as a matter of empirical fact but inconceivable as a matter of logic (Gourevitch, 1988).

10. See Velkley (2002, 40–48) and Horowitz (1987, 61). Neither Velkley nor Horowitz draws the conclusion that the conception of nature in *Emile* deserves closer scrutiny once the *Second Discourse* conception is shown to be incoherent.

11. I hasten to add that I have returned, for the moment, to using the term "nature" in contradistinction to the historical or artificial. Using the term in this sense cannot be avoided in a discussion of a secondary literature that typically uses it that way, nor can it be avoided, period, without departing radically from ordinary usage. Even Aristotle uses "nature" or "physis" to mean both the completion of a thing, which is not always or even often achieved, and its actual constitution.

12. Of course, unity (Melzer), transparency (Starobinski), and autonomy (Cassirer) are three different objectives, the latter of which is certainly not to be found in nature. I wish only to claim that Melzer, Cassirer, and Starobinski recognize one of the central problems to which Rousseau responds as loss of wholeness and that they think that Rousseau, *at least at first*, finds wholeness in or projects wholeness into the state of nature.

13. This outlook is not far from Mira Morgenstern's. She thinks that Rousseau's thought centers around what she calls "ambiguity." However, there is very little overlap between the arguments I make in this book and the ones Morgenstern makes in hers, perhaps because she thinks, as I do not, that Rousseau's ultimate end is authenticity and because she emphasizes the ambiguity of modern life more than she emphasizes the ambiguity of nature. That said, her chapter on "Pity, Imagination, and Love" adeptly demonstrates some of the predicaments nature itself presents to human beings. I also share Morgenstern's view that a Rousseau who recognizes the ambiguities or complexities in nature is wont to be a more moderate Rousseau than the Rousseaus usually encountered in the literature (Morgenstern, 1996, 4–6).

14. It is true that the claim is also supported by Rousseau's arguments that human beings would have been capable of living outside of society – for example, that even the family is an unnecessary institution. However, it is one thing to claim that solitude is a human possibility and another to claim that it is natural while sociality, which Rousseau shows developing in the course of human history, is not. The latter claim apparently depends on the premise that only the original state is natural.

15. This aspect of Rousseau's thought has received more critical attention than the other topics I cover. Todorov has argued that Rousseau favors neither solitude nor Sparta but a "third way" exemplified in *Emile* (Todorov, 2001). George Armstrong Kelly favors an interpretation that notes a pattern of "triplicity" (sensual-physical, moral-spiritual, and legal-political), which he contrasts with the "frequently noted" pattern of bipolarity. He suggests that Rousseau favors Emile, who is "neither a solitary hedonist fleeing social pain"

nor a "denatured" Gaius or Lucius, but will somehow bestride both positions" (Kelly, 2001, 23–27) N. J. H. Dent has also set himself against the bipolar interpretation of Rousseau's thought (Dent, 1988). Thus, this part of my argument can claim only to offer additional reasons for accepting an emerging but still minority understanding of Rousseau. See also Gourevitch (1993, 28), who, like Dent, offers some anticipation of the arguments of both of the first two chapters.

16. Werner Dannhauser (1997, 5) uses this phrase to characterize the bourgeois.

17. Though they already sing and dance together, each savage remains capable of "spending his life alone in the depths of the forests" (*SD*, III, 220, note xvi). The note from which I take this comment is appended to the section of the *Discourse* in which Rousseau calls the savage nation best for man and is a discussion of why savages self-consciously refuse to be civilized. We therefore have good reason to believe that Rousseau is referring to the savage in the savage nation and not to original man when he writes about the pleasure the savage takes in prolonged solitude.

18. Throughout this work, I will be using classical liberalism in this somewhat artificial sense. Of course, classical liberalism is sometimes taken primarily to denote defenses of the free market and it is often taken to include nineteenth-century liberals like Mill and Tocqueville. I use classical liberalism the way I do because it is difficult to understand the debate between Rousseau and liberalism without beginning with a liberalism that has not yet been infected by, or enjoyed the benefits of, Rousseau's reflections.

19. For two accounts that see Rousseau as offering an alternative between liberalism and communitarianism, see Parry (1995) and, in the same volume, Hampsher-Monk (1995). That said, interpretations of Rousseau that view him as having something to add to the liberal-communitarian debate, aside from a stern and unintended warning about the consequences of pursuing the Rousseauian alternative, are rare.

20. However, one need not be troubled by anti-foundationalism to view Rousseau as an anti-foundationalist. Penny Weiss, for example, thinks that Rousseau's questioning of the "notion of a fixed human nature" makes him useful to feminists (Weiss, 1993, 91). So also Elizabeth Wingrove, who finds Rousseau's treatment of nature consistent with her own "antifoundationalist commitment" (Wingrove, 2000, 9, 22–3).

Chapter 1: Natural Perfection

1. It may seem peculiar to discuss Rousseau on theodicy without discussing directly theological works like the "Letter on Providence" and the section of *Emile* entitled the "Profession of Faith of the Savoyard Priest." However, I agree with John Scott, among others, that these theological works, to the extent that they depart from "a strictly natural justification of nature and providence," are not reliable guides to Rousseau's real understanding of the theodicy problem (Scott, 1992, 706). In Chapter 3, I will draw attention to some of the reasons Rousseau had for exaggerating nature's innocence; these reasons also apply to Rousseau's theodicy and especially to the theological

works. For a remarkable treatment of the rhetoric of Rousseau's argument for providence, see Gourevitch (2001).

2. Here I differ from Laurence Cooper, who argues, contrary to most of the interpreters I treat, that nature is a substantive moral, political, and psychological guide for Rousseau. He insists, however, that Rousseau's nature "refers not to ends but to origins" and that "only those parts of man extant during [the] earliest period can be considered natural in the strict or pure sense (Cooper, 1999, 39). I reject the argument, which Joel Schwartz makes, too, that the understanding of nature advanced in the First Part of the *Second Discourse* is Rousseau's primary or strict understanding (Schwartz, 1984, 11). If, as I will argue, Rousseau is aware that the equation of the original and natural borders on incoherence, then one can go further than Cooper does in insisting on the substantive and teleological character of Rousseau's understanding of nature. Jeffrey A. Smith (2002) has begun to do so. See also an abridged version of this chapter (Marks, 2002).

3. Cf. Cassirer (1989, 75). Starobinski follows Cassirer (1988, 20–21).

4. Lovejoy is a noteworthy dissenter from the view that Rousseau intended the state of nature as a standard, formal or otherwise, for civilized human beings (Lovejoy, 1948).

5. Irving Babbitt (1968) makes this aspect of Rousseau's thought and legacy the basis of his polemic against "Rousseauism."

6. For another more or less Kantian interpretation of Rousseau's thought that explicitly discusses the depreciation of nature Strauss describes, see Rapaczynski (1987, especially p. 230).

7. Similarly, Ernest Wright, though he says that Rousseau's "natural man is not our first brute forbear but the last man whom we are travelling on to be" never rules out and sometimes seems to offer a Kantian Rousseau (Wright, 1929, 164). So also John W. Chapman, who thinks that there is "an inherent directedness to the growth of our capacities which we may either thwart or follow. Man either distorts or perfects himself" (Chapman, 1956, 7). For Chapman, though, perfection means, as it does for Cassirer, the emergence of "moral autonomy" or the "moral self" (Ibid., 28–29). Natural man, in spite of Rousseau's portrayal of him in the *Second Discourse*, is indistinguishable from morally autonomous and responsible man (Ibid., 26–27).

8. In my use of the term "history" I draw no distinction between nonhuman history (e.g., the evolution of the butterfly) and exclusively human history (e.g., a recollection or story of not only the accidents but also the deliberate human acts that have brought about the arrangements and circumstances in which a people lives). In this, I merely follow Rousseau's lead. Rousseau's account of human history includes strictly physical developments and could in principle draw on the observations of comparative anatomists and naturalists (*SD*, III, 134; I, 1).

9. I have changed Gourevitch's "to disentangle" to "in disentangling."

10. While the following two sections are about the dubiousness and even absurdity of distinguishing between nature and circumstances, one can also question Rousseau's attempt to exclude artifice or convention from the state of nature. Victor Gourevitch, in arguing that Rousseau understands his pure

state of nature to be necessarily conjectural, observes: "Human life may always, everywhere, necessarily be a mixture of the natural and the artificial or conventional, and it may be perfectly 'natural' that this be so" (Gourevitch, 1988, 34). In arguing that the premise on which Rousseau bases his description of natural man is false and known by him to be false, I join Gourevitch, as well as Francis Moran III (1995), in disputing the reading according to which Rousseau intends his description of the state of nature to be factual.

11. Rousseau concedes the existence of "natural or Physical" inequalities just paragraphs later, including not only inequalities of strength but also "inequalities of Mind" (*SD*, III, 131, Exordium, 2). The argument is presumably that these inequalities only develop and become significant with the aid of circumstances.

12. As Plattner observes (Plattner, 1979, 37), note iii does not take into account the very possibility Rousseau has just suggested – that the human body may, at one time, have been quite different from what it is today. Rousseau's arguments are based on the incompatibility of man's anatomy, *as it is today*, with the anatomy of quadrupeds.

13. Plattner (Ibid.) makes this same point.

14. There is not enough evidence to conclude that Rousseau thinks that new species come into being in the course of history, but he certainly recognizes a very wide range of variation within species, set in motion by external pressures, so much so that Rousseau is famous for the suggestion that orangutans may be humans, relatively unaffected by such pressures. Masters asserts that Rousseau "could be seen as a precursor of the historical or evolutionary approach" (Masters, 1997, 110–111; see also Horowitz, 1987, 53–62).

15. Alessandro Ferrara makes a parallel argument, which is weakened by his somewhat peculiar and counterintuitive conclusion from that argument, that freedom and not human nature must be responsible for removing man from the state of nature (Ferrara, 1993, 29–47).

16. Masters (1968, 150) makes essentially the same observation and concludes that perfectibility, a kind of free will, if not "in the fullest moral sense" (Ibid., 151), operates in the state of nature. He insists, contrary to the argument I am about to make, that Rousseau's conception of nature is "consistent with the most thoroughgoing or nonteleological physics" (Ibid., 414).

17. For a related argument, see Horowitz (1987, 50–85).

18. I have altered Gourevitch's translation, which omits some important words.

19. In the case of language, Rousseau's solution, presented in *SD* (III, 168–69; II, 14), accounts for one problem raised in *SD* (III, 146–47; I, 25) but not for more fundamental problems raised in *SD*, III, 147–51; I, 26–30. As for metallurgy, Rousseau explicitly denies that the accident of a volcano could have induced human beings as limited as those he has described to pursue metallurgy (*SD*, III, 172; II, 21).

20. In a note to the Pléiade edition of the *Second Discourse*, Starobinski also draws attention to the fact that the love of well-being is a force within human nature that pulls human beings out of or turns men against nature (*SD*, III, 1341, note 1).

21. Aubrey Rosenberg (1992, 280) makes a similar point about the emergence of *amour-propre* in *Emile*.

22. Laurence Cooper has also drawn attention to the fact that human beings seem to have by nature a latent taste for domination. He also observes, as I have above, that *amour-propre* seems not just latent but *barely* latent. Finally, he is also aware of the extent to which the departure of human beings from the state of nature may be driven by natural causes. He does not, however, think these observations add up to a serious problem for Rousseau's physiodicy (Cooper, 1999, 46, 121, 189 n.6).

23. Jacques Derrida's treatment of the *Essay on the Origin of Languages* parallels in many ways my treatment of the *Second Discourse*. For example, Derrida argues that articulation, which on Rousseau's account corrupts speech, is also, for Rousseau, the precondition of speech. "Rousseau wants us to think this move-ment [of the corruption of speech] is an accident. He describes it, however, in its originary necessity. This unhappy accident is also a 'natural progress.' It does not come unexpectedly upon a constituted song, nor does it surprise a full music. Before articulation, therefore, we now know, there is no speech, no song, and thus no music. . . . Thus language is born out of the process of its own degeneration" (Derrida, 1998, 242). Derrida takes this problem to in-dicate, however, a kind of confusion on Rousseau's part, though one locked into the history of metaphysics and, apparently, into meaning and discourse altogether (Ibid., 246). However, to insist, as Derrida does, that Rousseau is compelled, in spite of himself, to describe the penetration of nature by his-tory, song by articulation, and so on, is to insist, too, that Rousseau wishes to equate the original and the natural, even if it is impossible to do so. In what follows, I hope to suggest that there are no good grounds for such a claim.

24. I leave for Chapter 3 the knotty problem of why *Emile* differs from the *Second Discourse* in this regard. For the purposes of the argument here, it is enough to show that Rousseau, whatever reasons he may have had for proposing so sharp a distinction between nature and history, did not, ultimately, maintain that distinction.

25. For the proof that natural man is rare simply, not just rare in society, see the section of this chapter entitled "Beyond the Necessities of the Age."

26. However, I think that Rosenberg exaggerates when he claims that "the whole of Emile's education consists of a series of devices whereby certain natural and innate faculties are, as it were, neutralized before they can begin to develop" (Rosenberg, 1992, 280). In addition, it seems to me that Rosenberg does not give Rousseau sufficient credit for undertsanding the tension be-tween the resistance to nature that guides Emile's education and his asser-tions about nature's goodness.

27. Once, at least, Rousseau writes, only partially tongue in cheek, of "nature's mistake" (*E*, IV, 476; 200) in creating effeminate men and urges its correc-tion. While one may incline toward dismissing this evidence on the grounds that it is part of a highly rhetorical defense of the family, Rousseau also writes of "delicate, sensitive" natures, of "violent natures," and of children with "an inclination to stagnate in laziness" (*E*, IV, 299, 329, 377; 77, 97, 130), all of

which are troublesome and require regulation and outright resistance from the governor.

28. Cf. *SD* (III, 136; I, 6).

29. See also Emile's training against fear of sudden, loud noises: "[W]ith a slow and carefully arranged gradation man and child are made intrepid in everything" (*E*, IV, 284; 64).

30. Emile does not confound love of God with love of self merely because he expects rewards from God. The passage just cited goes on to treat the hope of reward as a separate reason Emile is inclined to be virtuous.

31. None of this is to say that Emile's prejudice is simply preposterous. Even if necessity operates, as in the *Second Discourse*, like the law of Sparta, by doing away with the unfit, nature's law must be judged good on balance, especially when compared to most human laws, which, according to Rousseau, entertain less defensible reasons for doing away with children (*SD*, III, 135; I, 4). Emile's prejudice is evidently a distortion but not the opposite of the truth about nature.

32. That is not to say that Rousseau sacrifices all to freedom and diversity of experience. There is a contrary emphasis in *Emile* on "keeping in place." We have seen an example of Emile's restraint with respect to judging the unknown; that restraint is crucial for keeping him in his place and enabling him to distinguish among worthwhile, indifferent, and harmful experiences.

33. Of course, one could argue that precisely because warm climates present fewer of the needs that drive human beings in society, the early onset of puberty presents as few difficulties as it would have presented in the state of nature. But first, it is not obvious how that objection applies to individuals – i.e., those of ardent temperament. Second, inasmuch as it is precisely love and not need that drives Southern human beings into society, according to the famous argument of the *Essay*, the failure of reason's development to keep pace with that of the passions is bound to lead human beings into dangerous errors.

34. When Rousseau argues that the well-raised young man is capable of friendship, he includes humanity. Here are the sentences that immediately follow the one I quoted on love and friendship: "The first act of his nascent imagination is to teach him that he has fellows; and the species affects him before the female sex. Here is another advantage of prolonged innocence – that of profiting from nascent sensibility to sow . . . the first seeds of humanity "(*E*, IV, 502; 220).

35. Talk of natural genius implies that there is more than one end or perfection for human beings. But we should not conclude that there is no substantive end or perfection for Rousseau, any more than we should conclude that Aristotle is not a teleological thinker because he thinks that some are suited to be slaves and others are fit to be free. For the inegalitarian implications of Rousseau's idea of natural genius, see *J* (II, 565–66; 463–65). One might add that even if Rousseau thought there were a plurality of natural human ends, we would still have to reject the view that he emptied nature to make room for freedom.

36. Quoted in Starobinski (1988, 50).
37. See Kelly (2003, 16).
38. Starobinski (1988, 57). There is also a suggestion of the oscillating Rousseau in Gustave Lanson's (1912, 29) description of Rousseau's "sentimental barometer...whose variations are abrupt, incessant, enormous."
39. David Wootton (1996, 403) has called Tracy Strong's reading of Rousseau "post-modern." Morton Schoolman (1994, xv–xvi), in his introduction to Strong's book on Rousseau, observes that Strong's Rousseau "anticipates some of the most radical indictments of modernity by our contemporary postmodern and poststructuralist theorists" and thus has an "affinity for post-modern and post-structuralist critique." Strong (1994, 3) himself emphasizes Rousseau's *modernity*, but in a way not inconsistent with the observations of Wootton and Schoolman.
40. For another description of the relationship between Rousseau's oscillations and his thought that, like Starobinski's, tends to put Rousseau's psychology before his philosophy, see Wahl (1955, 54–5).

Chapter 2: The Savage Pattern

1. Starobinski (1988, 252), Sandel (1996, 320), Babbitt (1968, 149–50). Babbitt admits that he presents an exaggerated account of Rousseau that a more balanced account would qualify. My purpose in this study is to present such a balanced account, though I doubt the results are what Babbitt would have expected.
2. See Derathé (1950, 103–104) for a discussion of Rousseau's reading of Hobbes. Derathé believes that Rousseau was directly acquainted not only with *De Cive* but also with *Leviathan* in the Latin edition. In any event, "it is certain that he studied Hobbes' theories closely" (Ibid., 104).
3. Plattner and Scott stick most closely to the view I have outlined, though Plattner thinks that Rousseau may have consciously exaggerated man's natural asociality (Plattner 1979, 75). Strauss and especially Melzer doubt the importance of Rousseau's "anthropological" description of original man but otherwise reconcile the individualist and collectivist arguments in Rousseau along those same lines.
4. For a discussion of the influence of Cassirer's interpretation, see Gay (1989, 24–6). See also Pippin (1991, 1992). He stresses Rousseau's "idealist" side with regard, at any rate, to morality and politics. For valuable discussions of Rousseau's influence on and relation to Kant, see Velkley (1989) and Galston (1975). For Kant's own reading, see the "Conjectural Beginning of Human History" in Kant (1963).
5. From the "Idea of a Universal History in the Interest of World Citizenship," quoted in Cassirer (1963, 23).
6. Cf. Melzer (1990, 90): "If the contradiction of society...is what divides man against himself and others, then he can be restored to unity and justice by inducing him to embrace totally either side of the contradiction: complete selfishness or complete sociability. To eliminate divisive personal dependence, men must be either totally separated or wholly united."

7. The Hobbesian reading allows that unity may also be restored by removing oneself from society, but this individualistic attempt to recapture the goodness of nature can succeed only for "a few isolated and rare human beings" (Melzer, 1990, 93). In keeping with his view that original, natural individuality is not true individuality, Cassirer denies that the mature Rousseau held his own life up as any kind of alternative to citizenship: "[I]t is completely mistaken to make Rousseau's ethics responsible for the weaknesses of his character" (Cassirer, 1989, 95).

8. For Judith Shklar, the Spartan citizen and the peasant of the "golden age" are two utopian models between which no compromise is possible, and "because they are incompatible, the attempt to pursue both enhances the strain under which men actually labor" (Shklar, 1969, 6).

9. Melzer (1990, 92), for example, describes the solution of *Emile* as "a less extreme, if also less perfect form of the individualistic solution."

10. Melzer (1990, 70) argues that some middling states are acceptable to Rousseau because what they lack in unity they make up for in "extent" or the capacity to feel life more. This explanation is an important elaboration of the Hobbesian interpretation and a powerful alternative to my reading. I will take it up toward the end of this chapter.

11. I have altered Gourevitch's translation, substituting "sweetness of independent commerce" for "gentleness of independent dealings." The French is "des douceurs d'un commerce independant."

12. Rousseau, as he notes, is quoting from the fifth volume of the *Histoire Générale des Voyages* (Paris: Didot, 1748, 175).

13. I have altered Gourevitch's translation, substituting "manners and morals" for "morals." The French is "moeurs." In translating *moeurs* this way, I follow Allan Bloom's practice in his translation of the *Letter to D'Alembert*.

14. For a different treatment of the savage nation, which, however, recognizes its importance in Rousseau's thought, see Lovejoy (1948, 29–30). One difference in Lovejoy's account is that he does not think Rousseau's thought is a unity at all; by the time he writes the *Social Contract*, Rousseau, Lovejoy thinks, has abandoned the most important claims of the *Second Discourse* (Ibid., 33–37).

15. Société.

16. George Armstrong Kelly develops some of the implications of this passage in an essay recently reprinted in the *Cambridge Companion to Rousseau* (Kelly, 2001, see especially pp. 25–26). Consider also Todorov (2001, 55–56) and Strong (1994, 104–38).

17. I will limit myself to discussing the *Dialogues*, the *Reveries*, and the *Letters to Malesherbes*, all of which have the advantage of concentrating on Rousseau's life in solitude.

18. Cf. *D* (I, 820; 124, I, 869; 162).

19. Cf. *D* (I, 854; 150).

20. See also *Letter to d'Alembert* (V, 24–42; 37–45), in which Rousseau treats misanthropy at length.

21. Cf. *D* (I, 814–815; 119, I, 858; 153, *M*, I, 1131).

22. Similarly, the *Letters to Malesherbes*, which proclaim Rousseau's happiness in retreat, end with the hope for a new, intimate society with the Luxembourgs.

23. It is worth noting, however, that his imagination is inflamed once again by the end of the First Walk.

24. Cf. *R* (I, 1074; 123).

25. *Commerce.*

26. Cf. *R* (I, 1013; 50). For a very helpful discussion of the interdependence of independence and sociality, see Melzer (1990, 77–78).

27. It may not be too farfetched to compare this manipulative and distanced role to that of the legislator of the *Social Contract* or the tutor in *Emile*. Todorov, who is careful to draw attention to the sociality of the autobiographical writings, argues that the sociality found there is debased, insofar as it depends on dehumanizing those with whom Rousseau socializes (Todorov, 2001, 38). That seems to me to go too far, especially with respect to Mme. De Warens, who is "a friend after [Rousseau's] own heart" (*R*, I, 1099; 154).

28. N. J. H. Dent has drawn attention to this important point (Dent, 1997, 25–7).

29. Miller, emphasizing above all Rousseau's idealized image of Geneva, makes a similar but more extreme claim about Rousseau's political writings (Miller, 1984, 26–28, 59–75). Indeed, I think that Miller overestimates the place for individualism (and individuality) in Rousseau's politics. Moreover, I think that he is mistaken in his claim that Geneva is superior to the ancient republics in Rousseau's eyes. The Roman republic remains "the model of all free peoples" (*SD*, III, 113, Dedicatory, 6). Finally, while I certainly agree with Miller that the incommensurablility of Rousseau's exemplary types has been exaggerated, I think that he goes rather too far in the opposite direction when he claims that Geneva unifies the "image[s] of Rousseau's desire" (Miller, 1984, 42) from the Spartan to the great legislator to the solitary walker. While Rousseau thinks that the human good requires a fortunate or contrived arrangement of apparent opposites, such as individual and social goods, he is too much the republican and too much the realist to think that individualism is not greatly compromised by the demands of politics, even in the best of circumstances.

30. George Armstrong Kelly's essay is an important dissent from the position that the civil society described in the *Social Contract* is the antithesis of nature. On the contrary, Rousseau sought, even in his political writings, to "assimilate the independence of nature to the mutuality of common life" (Kelly, 2001, 37). Kelly also has the advantage over James Miller in fully recognizing Rousseau's pessimism or realism (Ibid., 45). The argument of this chapter can be regarded as an expansion and elaboration of the position Kelly advances briefly in the course of his main effort to understand Rousseau's stance toward history.

31. Lester G. Crocker thinks the *Corsica* in some ways even more important than *the Social Contract*, though he also views it as the best evidence of Rousseau's totalitarian intention. I take up here his implicit challenge: "One searches in vain for a trace of personal liberty in [Rousseau's] *Constitutional Project for Corsica*" (Crocker, 1995, 258).

32. Indeed, in at least one way, the Swiss may be even more independent than the savage: Isolated from his fellows for half the year, he may be less concerned with the esteem of his fellows than the savage. In any event, frequent feuds over recognition are not part of the Swiss tableau.

33. *Particuliers.*

34. I have altered Watkins's translation, substituting "savage" for "wild." The French is "sauvages." By making this change, I draw attention, as the French does, to the connection between Corsicans and "savages."

35. Judith Shklar notes this element but views it as anomalous. She writes that the rustic golden age is fundamentally "anti-political" (Shklar, 1969, 27), and the goods of the rustic and Spartan utopias are simply not compatible. I disagree. Bertrand De Jouvenel, on the other hand, makes a convincing case for the close connection between the "Arcadian dream" and Rousseau's politics (De Jouvenel, 1961–62, 87–90).

36. Because Rousseau makes Rome above all his model, I do not take up the case of Sparta. While Sparta was surely still more collectivistic than Rome, Rousseau does not regard it as the peak of republicanism. One reason for Sparta's lesser status may be that the Spartan maintains his independence and self-sufficiency much less than the Roman does. For a superb and much more detailed treatment of this matter, see Kelly (2003, 123–24).

37. For an old, qualified defense of Rousseau as liberal, see Cobban (1934).

38. Gay summarizes and gives references to this tendency in the literature in the Introduction and Postscript to Cassirer (1989, 7–8, 137–38).

39. *Amour-propre* is the term translated as vanity.

40. For a useful discussion of unity over time, see Melzer (1990, 65–6).

41. Quoted in Chapman (1956, 74).

42. It is remarkable that Chapman, who is generally a defender of the proposition that Rousseau is a liberal, thinks Rousseau's argument for a civil religion evidence of a totalitarian strain in his thought (Chapman, 1956, 86).

43. While I focus on Talmon, here, his appraisal of Rousseau shares more than one premise with the more psychologically acute and more sympathetic analysis of Jean Starobinski's *Transparency and Obstruction*. That work argues that Rousseau "dreams of total transparency and immediate communication" (Starobinski, 1988, 41). Moreover, it looks beneath both Rousseau's conduct and work to "discover the images, obsessions and nostalgic desires that more or less constantly governed them" (Ibid., xi). While Starobinski steers clear of simple reductionism, the philosophical and political are closely linked to the personal in his interpretation of Rousseau. Rousseau's impatience with mediation, including speech, finds expression both in his retreat from society and in his vision of a society constituted legally by the general will and emotionally by the festival. Both the general will and the festival are fulfillments of Rousseau's longing for transparency (Ibid., 44, 96–97, 99); the purpose of Rousseau's politics is to "preserve or restore a compromised state of transparency" (Ibid., 13). That transparency is, for him, not merely or primarily a theoretical vision of happiness but a psychological, personal *need*. For Starobinski that need is related to an inability to "confront the uncertainty of life" (Ibid., 252). See also Crocker (1995, 261); Crocker's treatment

interestingly combines the thesis that Rousseau's paranoia drives his work with the thesis that Rousseau was a deep and in some sense practical thinker concerning political power. Thus Rousseau, while a utopian, is hardly naïve (Ibid., 254–55).

Chapter 3: Rousseau's Rhetorical Strategy

1. Needless to say, there are degrees of taking Rousseau's artistry seriously, so that Starobinski's work remains within what Ann Hartle calls the "psychological orientation" to Rousseau's thought, whereas Hartle's own work regards even Rousseau's *Confessions*, right down to its insistence that people are plotting against him, as a "philosophical work of art" and is uncommonly attentive to Rousseau's deliberate intention, at the deepest level, in the *Confessions*, as well as his use of rhetoric in that work (Hartle, 1983, 7, 9–37, 118–25, 176 n.39). Christopher Kelly's *Rousseau's Exemplary Life: The Confessions as Political Philosophy* takes a similar approach still further (Kelly, 1987).

2. On Enlightenment polemics, including Rousseau's, and the danger of disregarding them, see Hulliung (1994, for example: 4, 6, 20–21, 48, 78–94, 106, 143, 189, 198–99, 202–20, 229, 237, 240–241). See also Rahe (1994b, 12–13); Rahe's volume contains numerous examples of dissimulation on the part of modern political thinkers.

3. For another non-Straussian treatment of Rousseau that gives Rousseau credit for composing his works with great care and for deliberately using characters after the fashion of a novelist or dramatist, see Spink (1980).

4. Lester G. Crocker, who has treated Rousseau's duplicity in several places, Penny A. Weiss, and Elizabeth Wingrove are additional examples of non-Straussian authors alive to the rhetoric of Rousseau's work, especially with respect to his presentation of nature (Crocker, 1995, 248, 252; Weiss, 1993, 50–51; Wingrove, 2000, 10, 59, 67–68).

5. Lovejoy uses the phrase "state of nature," which Rousseau uses to cover not only the original state but also the precivil state altogether. We are justified in substituting "original state" for "state of nature" here because Lovejoy argues that the latter term, in Rousseau's writings, usually refers to the first phase of human history, in which human beings are such as they must have left the hands of nature; he uses the phrase accordingly (Lovejoy, 1948, 16).

6. As Nannerl Keohane observes, Montaigne is also a source for a praise of the savage state; while many took up Montaigne's "historical pessimism," his praise of antiquity at modernity's expense, few took up his "anthropological pessimism," his praise of savages at modernity's expense (Keohane, 1978, 463–64).

7. See Rahe (1994a, 205–207).

8. This argument also explains why Rousseau claims that even good social institutions "denature" man (*E*, IV, 249; 40). Insisting that natural man is asocial requires insisting also that everything social is unnatural. That is not to deny,

of course, that the kind of thorougoing socialization that takes place in a Sparta does violence to nature.

9. For more detailed discussions of the rhetoric of the *First Discourse*, see Strauss (1947), Plattner (1979, 5–10), Masters (1968, 7–14), and Orwin (1998). My argument is indebted to their accounts. See also Marshall (1980).

10. See Wokler (1995, 22–24).

11. In subsequent paragraphs, Rousseau blames "a taste for letters" (twice, *PN*, II, 965; 19, 20) and "a taste for letters, philosophy, and the fine arts" (twice, *PN*, II, 966; 21, 23).

12. For a provocative argument that Rousseau's Emile is a kind of philosopher, see Cooper (2002).

13. One should add to the example of Emile that of men in provincial towns who are said to provide "most of the useful discoveries and new inventions" admired in Paris, though, in their comparative inactivity and "tranquil solitude" they suffer much less than Parisians do from civilized corruption (*LA*, V, 55; 59–60). Their originality and inventiveness seem to do them no harm. More specifically, the farmers of Neufchatel "have useful books and are tolerably well educated. They reason sensibly about everything and about many things with brilliance. They make syphons, magnets, spectacles, pumps, barometers, and cameras obscura . . . [so that] you would take a farmer's living room for a mechanic's workshop and for a laboratory in experimental physics" (*LA*, V, 56; 61). These "mountain men" are also inventive, and at least one has been honored by the Academy of Science; but they are apparently protected from corruption by their independence and good sense and, perhaps, by their attachment to tradition (*LA*, V, 55–57; 60–62).

14. For the argument that "Hobbes' teaching is not as egalitarian as it first may seem," see Rahe (1994b, 150–51).

15. For a rich and detailed treatment of the rhetoric of Rousseau's religious teaching, including his teaching on conscience, see Melzer (1996).

16. Cassirer cannot mean that Rousseau always championed the natural goodness of man in the same sense. He thinks that the embrace of "real freedom" in favor of natural independence is an abandonment of the thesis the *Second Discourse* "seems to defend." (The remainder of this passage, in which Cassirer attributes the change to an insight Rousseau has "now achieved," shows that Cassirer has in mind not merely a change in rhetorical emphasis but the emergence of an argument that was, at best, not fully worked out by Rousseau when he wrote the *Second Discourse*.)

17. Rousseau does say, however, that he might take on a companion, if necessary, to satisfy his sexual desires (*E*, IV, 685; 350).

Chapter 4: Rousseau and Charles Taylor

1. It is an odd feature of communitarianism that many of the most prominent figures in it are uncomfortable with the label. For one of the main reasons, the label's "checkered history," see Etzioni (2003, 205–206). For two other important reasons, see Abbey (2000, 124–26). The label has stuck, and I will use it, for want of a better one.

2. Taylor is the most obvious example, and this chapter centers on him and Rousseau. Michael Sandel is another prominent defender of community whose defense of community seems not only consistent with but even for the sake of a defense of authentic identity. See Sandel (1982, 175–83). Nancy Rosenblum argues that this characteristic is widely shared among communitarians: "The communitarian purpose in opposing community to atomistic individualism is not the traditional one of transcending the self through identification with a group or nation. On the contrary, the object is to recover strong, expressive selves, to make "thin" selves "thick" (Rosenblum, 1989, 218).

3. As I noted in the Introduction, Kautz's interpretation of Rousseau, following Arthur Melzer's, emphasizes the bipolarity of Rousseau's thought and its almost complete abandonment of nature, the main theses I argue against in Chapters 1 and 2 (Kautz, 1997, 251, 267).

4. Elizabeth Frazer has identified this observation as a "key theme in philosophical communitarianism." Frazer's roster includes Alisdair MacIntyre, Michael Sandel, Taylor, and Michael Walzer (Frazer, 1999, 4, 78). See also Avineri and De Shalit (1992, 2–8). Amitai Etzioni, a leading "political communitarian" to adopt Frazer's distinction, has distanced himself from what he sees as the radical and unwarranted conclusions that have been drawn from this observation (Etzioni, 2000, 221).

5. I am aware that the term "community" is also controversial. It is somewhat arbitrary but, I think, not inconsistent with Rousseau's or Taylor's usage, to understand community as a group united by language, "manners and morals," a common way of life, and a (perhaps quite limited) common good. Admittedly, Rousseau usually uses "community" in a stronger sense, to refer to the association that is formed by the social pact ("Each member of the community gives himself to it at the moment of its formation" (*SC*, III, 365; 56)). But he also uses it nonpolitically to refer to the "little community" at Clarens (*J*, II, 619; 507). I will most often use "community" in a political sense, and so will be considering its coercive power. This usage is somewhat narrower than but not inconsistent with Taylor's usage. It is both broader, because it includes political associations that hardly meet the exacting standards of the *Social Contract*, and narrower than Rousseau's. For a discussion of the range of meanings of "community," see Frazer (1999, 47–85).

6. Ferrara's work on Rousseau and authenticity consistently dodges this crucial issue as well. Like Taylor, Ferrara is eager to show that the ideal of authenticity can take into account the "norms, roles and institutions" that "*sustain* subjectivity" and so that the ideal of authenticity need not be simply antisocial (Ferrara, 1993, 122). But although Ferrara sometimes writes about an "internal nature" that Rousseau thinks ought to be expressed, that internal nature is not human nature or even "natural genius" as Rousseau understands it but the individual's adapatation to unique circumstances (Ibid., 84–5, 106, 109).

7. See Karl Weintraub's treatment of Rousseau's autobiographical work (1978, 319–20, 331–32). This point is, however, certainly in dispute among Rousseau

scholars. See, for example, Mason (1997), Morgenstern (1996, xii–xiii), and Hartle (1983, 152, 157).

8. "The feeling of existence as Rousseau experienced and described it has a rich articulation which must have been lacking in the feeling of existence as it was experienced by man in the state of nature" (Strauss, 1953, 292).

9. For an argument that Rousseau overstates it, see Masters (1997). Masters argues that recent scientific research has invalidated Rousseau's understanding of human beings as naturally asocial. Melzer also finds Rousseau's theoretical individualism indefensible (Melzer, 1990, 51, 291). My argument does not insist that Rousseau's portrait of a perfectly solitary original man is scientifically accurate, though it does suppose that Rousseau's account of our ineradicable and sometimes very sweet separateness from others is plausible.

10. Cf. Taylor (1985, 259; 1991, 34).

11. Steven Kautz has pointed out a similar tendency in the work of Michael Sandel (Kautz, 1995, 34). It is true that Taylor, in other contexts, draws attention to our "embodiment," but he deploys our embodiment only to refute what he takes to be the Cartesian–Lockean argument that the self or consciousness can be perfectly detached from its circumstances, the body being one circumstance among others, including traditions, habits, and temporality (Kautz, 1991, 105–106; 1989, 172, 175). Taylor's embodiment works, then, to draw the individual, who may seem disengaged on account of his consciousness, into engagement with his particular circumstances, among which are his social circumstances; it points in a communitarian rather than a liberal direction.

12. "Profession of Faith of the Savoyard Vicar" is a more literal rendering of the title, but "vicar" has a Church of England connotation that does not suit the (admittedly unorthodox) Catholic star of this piece. I thank Tracy Strong for alerting this Jew to that connotation.

13. Cooper (1999, 84–85). Christopher Kelly, though, cautions us about taking even apparently private letters to be unequivocal expressions of Rousseau's own view. Rousseau was well aware that his letters would be "circulated and probably published." "What seem to be private communications are written with publication in mind" (Kelly, 2003, 7).

14. I am aware that Rousseau sometimes gives conscience a broader meaning (Cooper, 1999, 91–93), but the narrower meaning, which he uses more often, is a safe enough point of departure.

15. This is, admittedly, the Savoyard priest and not Rousseau. Also, admittedly, the priest's understanding of conscience is more conventional than Rousseau's. In particular, the priest sharply distinguishes self-regarding sentiments and conscience in a way that Rousseau ultimately does not. Finally, Rousseau at times writes as if conscience and sentiment can be distinguished (*E*, IV, 523; 235). I do not think the difference matters for the argument here. Compare Rousseau in his own voice: "[I]f this were the place for it, I would try to show how the first voices of conscience arise out of the first movements of the heart" (Ibid.). Even if conscience is not precisely a sentiment, it is so closely connected to sentiment that there seems good reason to take the child's outburst to be its primitive manifestation.

16. Those selfish passions appear to include *amour-propre*, that love of self which concerns one's status. It is not, after all, the pain of being struck that angers the child but the "manifest intention of offending him." The turning of Emile's pride to the support rather than the overturning of morality is an important part of the story of Emile's moral development. For a general account of the redirection of *amour-propre* in Emile's moral development that can also be applied to the development of conscience in particular, see Orwin (2000b, 74–77).

17. See for example, Taylor (1989, 393, 512). For a different version of the complaint that Taylor is too quick to equate the views of progressive intellectuals and "our" views, see Skinner (1994).

18. It is debatable even among communitarians – consider Amitai Etzioni's recent evocation of the idea of self-evident truths (Etzioni, 2003, 398–400). Consider, too, Bellah et al. (1996, 28–30, 50) on the continued strength of the Biblical tradition, however transformed, in America.

19. See also Hartle (1983, 41–48).

20. For the existentialist roots of Taylor's religion, see Morgan (1994, 58–61). Taylor's language, it is only fair to note, is guarded in the part of the book I quote – "one *may* face a crisis of affirmation; one *may* be compelled to meet it through a transfiguration of one's own vision." Yet everything else Taylor says leads one to believe that taking post-Romantic developments seriously means facing a crisis of affirmation and recognizing that a simple affirmation of an objective order is an impossibility.

21. That seems to me to be the case, even if one supposes that Rousseau was himself an out-and-out atheist. That an argument is true does not imply that it has won historically.

22. For Rousseau's attack on the Enlightenment on its own, humanistic, grounds, see Melzer (1996, 361).

23. Wilson Carey McWilliams, without slighting the new problems that modernity poses, makes a convincing argument for the permanence of the problems of "assurance of identity" and recognition. This argument is closely related to his "essentialistic" understanding of fraternity and his assumption that there is a "nature of man" (McWilliams, 1973, 1–63, quotations from 5 and 8).

24. Taylor frequently draws our attention to this problem in a qualified way in *Sources of the Self*. But he wavers between a strong formulation – "the dissipation of our sense of the cosmos as a meaningful order" – and a much weaker one – "the sense that no framework is shared by everyone" (Taylor, 1989, 17). While the first formulation may be too strong, the second one, which applies to any number of, if not all, historical periods, is much too weak to support Taylor's description of the problem as "essentially modern" (Ibid., 10).

25. Taylor (1994, 36). Cf. Steven Kautz's argument in *Liberalism and Community* that communitarianism is an attack on a certain, respectable, individualist way of life (Kautz, 1995, 217–18). Taylor does wish to claim, of course, that his argument is able to support some kind of independence (see, for example, Taylor, 1989, 39–40).

26. Ibid., 48–49. H. D. Forbes notes that Taylor also maintains, inconsistently, that Rousseau thought only the virtuous should share equally in the light of public esteem. "Nothing is said about the crucial difference between these contrasting formulations" (Forbes, 1997, 230). Forbes's essay offers other telling criticisms of Taylor. Finally, one could add that it is simply untrue that Rousseau's account has society taking a turn for the worse when preferential esteem comes to matter – in fact, that stage coincides with the "savage nation," which is, as I observed in Chapter 2, "best for man."

27. Julie, Wolmar, and Saint Preux all speak in this section, but I think I have said enough about "natural genius" in the first chapter to demonstrate that Rousseau advances this idea in his own name.

28. Ronald Beiner makes a similar criticism of Taylor: he is good when it comes to describing the importance of identity in modern culture but unhelpful when it comes to assessing the merits of different identities (Beiner, 1997, 164–65).

29. Abbey elaborates on the necessary and historical preconditions of selfhood as Taylor understands them. They remain insufficiently robust to help us distinguish between recognition and misrecognition.

30. It is true that Rorty calls the social creative imagination a "hypergood," not *the* hypergood, but he plainly means it to stand in for the various moral sources Taylor wishes to put us in touch with. For an account of Rorty's attempt to make his radical elevation of community consistent with an equally radical endorsement of private poetry, and for an account of the difficulties to which this attempt is subject, see Kautz (1997).

31. K. Anthony Appiah argues that this idea of Rousseau's – that "there is a real self buried in there, the self one has to dig out and express" (Appiah, 1994, 155) – is essentialist and consequently implausible. But to attempt to understand the development of character in complete abstraction from innate differences of intelligence and temperament seems still more implausible. Appiah has some of the same concerns as I do about the threat to the individual posed by Taylor's argument but, in order to avoid what he regards as the essentialist pitfall, avoids the issue of distortion and sticks to that of autonomy.

32. I owe this observation to Ruth Abbey.

33. In this context, it is very difficult to make sense of Taylor's claim that "we are now in an age in which a publicly accessible cosmic order of meanings is an impossibility" and in which "personal resonance" is the only means by which to explore "the order in which we are set" (Taylor, 1989, 512); this may be the view of certain philosophers, but it is not obviously a defining characteristic of the age.

34. On the considerable moral agreement that persists in American society in spite of differences see Wolfe (2001). Allan Bloom suggests that such moral agreement is more fundamental than the acknowledgement of pluralism regarding what Taylor calls moral sources. Bloom deals with relativism, from which Taylor wishes to distance himself, but there is no question that he would also understand the claim that there are irreconcilable differences regarding the good as a dogma behind which is an agreement about equality and tolerance (Taylor, 1987, 25–43).

35. Shlomo Avineri and Avner de Shalit consider this premise to be a premise of communitarian thinking and find it also in Alisdair Macintyre and Sandel (Avineri and De-Shalit, 1992, 2–4).

36. These particular prescriptions are drawn from "Atomism" (Taylor, 1985, 187–210) and "The Politics of Recognition" (Taylor, 1994). My list is not meant to be exhaustive. In a confessedly polemical part of *Sources of the Self*, Taylor gets more specific and blames "the atomist outlook" for blinding people to the defects of "the recent rash of neo-conservative measures in Britain and the United States, which cut welfare programs and regressively redistribute income, thus eroding the basis of community identification" (Taylor, 1989, 505)

37. Taylor, in "Atomism," arguably commits the reverse error, drawing conclusions about an author's ontological stance from his poltical stance. See Holmes (1989, 237–39). See Tuck (1994, 163–67) for the related argument that Taylor neglects the extent to which seventeenth-century natural rights theorists introduced natural rights not as the foundation of a philosophical system but as a means of negotiating a *modus vivendi* between different cultures and religions.

38. However, Patrick Cullen, in comparing Rousseau to certain defenders of community, including Taylor, rightly draws our attention to the context of this claim. The legislator must impose a dependence where no dependence existed before. Whereas the relation of community to identity is a point of departure for some prominent contemporary defenders of community, that relation, for Rousseau, is the product of elaborate artifice (Taylor, 1993, 144–45). That is the case, even if, as I argue, the legislator merely substitutes a healthy form of dependence for an unhealthy form.

39. As I argued in Chapter 2, however, this description is somewhat inaccurate. We know from the *Second Discourse* that human beings are not animals governed by instinct but dependent and moral beings who prefer each other's company to peace. Political society cannot be credited for the formation of our intelligence or capacity for morality. It is true that, as we will see when we turn to *Emile*, it may be possible to credit political community for the invention of law and of the notion of submitting to it, and thereby to credit it, even in its least attractive forms, for offering a model of virtue. While morality and even duty arise before political society does, one could argue, the idea of virtue could not arise as long as "the terror of vengeance had to take the place of the Laws' restraint" and submission to duty could not be distinguished from submission to the arbitrary will of another (*SD*, III, 170–71; II, 17–18). But we will also see how limited the obligations are, if any, that flow from this benefit political communities, usually in spite of themselves, offer.

40. In making this argument, I do not mean to go back on my earlier claim that even Rousseau's political writings aim to leave individuals independent within the sphere not covered by legislation. As we saw in Chapter 2, the limited sense in which a human being becomes nothing without the others in political society, or in which Caius and Lucius dissolve into Rome, does not do away with the private person. Indeed, even, the Romans – especially the Romans – "stood out over all the peoples of the earth for the deference of the

government toward private individuals" (*PE*, III, 221, 257). The justification of polities is multilayered, so that it is not just by educating men to be virtuous citizens but also by protecting them as private individuals that political life imposes obligations on them.

41. I set aside the important question of whether Rousseau points to Kant by raising morality above considerations of happiness or instead upholds virtue for the sake of happiness. The classic Kantian interpetation is Cassirer (1989. For a convincing rebuttal, see Melzer (1990, 61–3). Although I am inclined toward Melzer's view, it compels us, in his view, to think Rousseau's enthusiasm for virtue ultimately inconsistent with Rousseau's arguments (Ibid., 256–61).

42. But see Taylor's "Atomism" for an argument that draws our obligation to society from its capacity to support a particular kind of identity, namely of a free autonomous moral agent (Taylor, 1985, 205). This argument, however, appears to be no more than an application of the broader argument in question; in other words, Taylor's argument is pitched to the proponent of individual rights and says to him: "[E]ven your identity, like all identities, is incoherent outside of a particular social matrix."

43. Dennis Wrong has chided communitarians for "deploying fairly commonplace sociological considerations" about the constitution of the self to demonstrate obligations that do not follow from them (Wrong, 2000, 25); see also Holmes (1989, 232–33).

44. Cf. (1989, 37) on philosophers like Socrates who remain in a "web of interlocution" but not that of the "given historical community."

45. Rousseau here leaves open the possibility that there are some moral notions not connected with taste. But in the next sentence he includes honesty and decency among the moral notions so connected. And in the *Dialogues*, Rousseau is said to love virtue as an idolator "du beau dans tous les genres" (*D*, I, 824; 127), the same phrase translated by "of the beautiful of every sort" in the passage to which this note is appended.

46. Christopher Kelly sees Emile's bonds to the community as stronger than I have suggested they might be but still, it seems to me, looser than the ties communitarians tend to favor (Kelly, 2003, 95–98).

47. That is not to say that he will fail to abide by the laws of whatever country in which he happens to find himself. He will be a kind of resident alien wherever he lives and a citizen of the world: "I shall not be free in this land, in this or that region; I shall be free everywhere in Earth" (*E*, 471–2; IV, 856).

Conclusion: Rousseau's Challenge to Classical Liberals

I do not consider here Rousseau's challenge to Rawlsian liberals, but Joseph Reisert has done so recently (Reisert, 2003, 5–9, 185–96).

1. As Clifford Orwin notes, this "thinker whose fertile mind hatched so many attacks on liberalism had no personal experience of it. Living under the ancien regime in France, he knew liberalism at first hand only as a project, not as a political reality." The direct object of Rousseau's assault was the Enlightenment (Orwin, 2000, 54). While I will be discussing Rousseau's

attack on liberalism in the next several pages, it is always with this qualification in mind.

2. For two recent, relatively mild versions of this attack, see Schor (1998) and Etzioni (2001).

3. Liberalism and capitalism are, of course, analytically distinct, but both are related to a more realistic understanding of the passions that can be traced all the way to Machiavelli, in whom a new politics and a new embrace of acquisitiveness are already bound together. For the Machiavelli link as seen by two very different commentators, see Hirschman (1977, 12–14) and Strauss (1953, 60–61). See also Machiavelli (1998, 14, 91).

4. *Fureur.*

5. See Steven Kautz (1995, 42–47, 179). Kautz, drawing on Montesquieu, argues that "liberal politics is no more, but also no less, than a quest for 'that tranquillity of spirit which comes from the opinion each one has of his security,' where 'one citizen' cannot fear another citizen" (Ibid., 30). See also Shklar (1989). For a statement that captures simultaneously the insistence that Lockean liberalism promotes certain virtues and the insistence that it must hold passion and imagination and, in general, the aspiration to a more colorful and expressive way of life at arm's length, see Tarcov (1984, 210–11).

6. What Barber calls strong democracy remains a form of liberal democracy. See, for example, Barber (1989).

7. As I observed in Chapter 4, Taylor also thinks that liberalism is defective with respect to authenticity and his communitarianism intends to remedy this defect. For the capacity of liberalism to accommodate romantic aspirations, see Rosenblum (1989).

8. For a good, brief discussion of Rousseau's prudence and openness to political compromise, see Grant (1997, 104–10).

9. For discussions of Rousseau's at least partial success in advancing new virtues and the complex relationship between his intent and the way in which his thought has been appropriated, see, in the same volume, Melzer, "Rousseau and the Modern Cult of Sincerity" and Orwin, "Rousseau and the Discovery of Political Compassion."

10. Bloom (1997, 165–66). See also Bloom (1990, 312–13) and Reisert (2003, 189). For an argument that Rousseau is in important respects *more* hopeful than Tocqueville, though not for liberalism, see Strong (2000, 114–17).

11. Quoted in Richter (1995). The Richter essay discusses the influence of Rousseau on Tocqueville, especially with respect to the meaning of legitimacy. On the Rousseau–Tocqueville connection, see also Jardin (1988, 243–44, 269) and Koritansky (1986). Peter Augustine Lawler, in a book that emphasizes Tocqueville's debt to Pascal, argues that Tocqueville is more starkly opposed to Rousseau than most interpreters think. However, Lawler's interpretation assumes that Rousseau locates perfection in an utterly simple prehistoric man: "For Rousseau, human beings are well-ordered, or perfect, to the extent that they are not human. To be human, or not a brute, is to be corrupt" (Lawler, 1993, 76). That interpretation, which is closest to Babbitt's, is among those I have been contesting in this book. Perhaps Tocqueville did so interpret Rousseau, but Lawler offers no evidence that he did. Boesche, in

fact, has Tocqueville overlapping with Rousseau in almost precisely the opposite way: For Rousseau, as for Tocqueville, "people approach a perfection only in a healthy culture" (Boesche, 1987, 167). Again, until new evidence emerges, we cannot know the precise character of Rousseau's influence on Tocqueville; we can argue only, as Boesche does, about how their understandings do and don't overlap.

12. While Tocqueville writes about democratic man, he unmistakably describes a man who is the outcome of liberal theory. See Manent (1996, 55).

References

Abbey, R. 2000. *Charles Taylor.* Princeton: Princeton University Press.

Appiah, K.A. 1994. "Identity, Authenticity, Survival: Multicultural Societies and Social Reproduction." In *Multiculturalism: The Politics of Recognition.* See Taylor, 1994.

Aristotle. 1958. *The Politics of Aristotle.* London: Oxford University Press.

Avineri, S. and A. De-Shalit. 1992. *Communitarianism and Individualism.* Oxford: Oxford University Press.

Babbitt, I. 1968. *Rousseau and Romanticism.* Cleveland, OH: Meridian Books.

Barber, B. 1989. "Liberal Democracy and the Costs of Consent." In *Liberalism and the Moral Life.* See Rosenblum, 1989.

Beiner, R. 1997. "Hermeneutical Generosity and Social Criticism." In *Philosophy in a Time of Lost Spirit: Essays on Contemporary Theory.* Toronto: University of Toronto Press.

Bellah, R.N., R. Madsen, W.M. Sullivan, A. Swidler, and S.M. Tipton. 1996. *Habits of the Heart: Individualism and Commitment in American Life.* Updated ed. Berkeley: University of California Press.

Berman, M. 1970. *The Politics of Authenticity: Radical Individualism and the Emergence of Modern Society.* New York: Atheneum.

Bloom, A. 1979. Introduction to *Emile, or On Education.* New York: Basic Books.

———. 1987a. "Jean-Jacques Rousseau." In *The History of Political Philosophy,* 3d edition. Edited by Leo Strauss and Joseph Cropsey. Chicago: The University of Chicago Press.

———. 1987b. *The Closing of the American Mind: How Higher Education Has Failed Democracy and Impoverished the Souls of Today's Students.* New York: Simon and Schuster.

———. 1990. "The Study of Texts." *In Giants and Dwarfs: Essays 1960–1990.* New York: Simon and Schuster.

———. 1997. "Rousseau's Critique of Liberal Constitutionalism." In *The Legacy of Rousseau.* See Orwin and Tarcov, 1997.

Boesche, R. 1987. *The Strange Liberalism of Alexis de Tocqueville*. Ithaca: Cornell University Press.

Cassirer, E. 1963. *Rousseau, Kant, and Goethe*. Translated by J. Gutmann, P. Kristeller, and J. Randall Jr. New York: Harper & Row.

———. 1979. *The Philosophy of the Enlightenment*. Boston: Beacon Press.

———. 1989. *The Question of Jean-Jacques Rousseau*. 2d. ed. Translated and edited by P. Gay. New Haven, CT: Yale University Press.

Chapman, J.W. 1956. *Rousseau: Totalitarian or Liberal?* New York: AMS Press.

Cobban, A. 1934. *Rousseau and the Modern State*. London: Allen & Unwinj.

Cooper, L. 1999. *Rousseau, Nature, and the Problem of the Good Life*. University Park: The Pennsylvania State University Press.

———. 2002. "Human Nature and the Love of Wisdom. Rousseau's Hidden (and Modified) Platonism." *Journal of Politics* 64(1): 108–25.

Crocker, L.G. 1995. "Rousseau's Soi-Disant Liberty." In *Rousseau and Liberty*. See Wokler, 1995b.

Cullen, P. 1993. *Freedom in Rousseau's Political Philosophy*. De Kalb: Northern Illinois University Press.

Dannhauser, W.J. 1997. "The Problem of the Bourgeois." In *The Legacy of Rousseau*. See Orwin and Tarcov, 1997.

Dent, N.J.H. 1988. *Rousseau: An Introduction to his Psychological, Social, and Political Theory*. Oxford: Basil Blackwell.

———. 1997. "'An Integral Part of His Species...'?" In *Jean-Jacques Rousseau and the Sources of the Self*. See O'Hagan, 1997.

Derathé, R. 1950. *Jean-Jacques Rousseau et la science politique de son temps*. Paris: Presses Universitaires de France.

Derrida, J. 1998. *Of Grammatology*. Reprint edition. Translated by G. Chakravurti Spivak. Baltimore: Johns Hopkins University Press.

Etzioni, A. 2000. "Epilogue." In *Autonomy and Order: A Communitarian Anthology*. See Lehman, 2000.

———. 2001. "The Post Affluent Society." In *The Monochrome Society*. Princeton: Princeton University Press.

———. 2003. *My Brother's Keeper: A Memoir and a Message*. New York: Rowman and Littlefield.

Ferrara, A. 1993. *Modernity and Authenticity: A Study of the Social and Ethical Thought of Jean-Jacques Rousseau*. Albany: State University of New York Press.

Forbes, H.D. 1997. "Rousseau, Ethnicity and Difference." In *The Legacy of Rousseau*. See Orwin and Tarcov, 1997.

Frazer, E. 1999. *The Problems of Communitarian Politics: Unity and Conflict*. Oxford: Oxford University Press.

Galston, W. 1975. *Kant and the Problem of History*. Chicago: University of Chicago Press.

Gay, P. 1989. "Introduction." *The Question of Jean-Jacques Rousseau*. See Cassirer, 1989.

Gourevitch, V. 1988. "Rousseau's Pure State of Nature." *Interpretation* 16(1): 23–59.

———. 1993. "The Political Argument of Rousseau's Essay on the Origin of Languages. In *Pursuits of Reason: Essays in Honor of Stanley Cavell*. Edited by T. Cohen, P. Guyer, and H. Putnam. Lubbock: Texas Tech University Press.

———. 2001. "The Religious Thought." In *The Cambridge Companion to Rousseau.* See Riley, 2001.

Grant, R. 1997. *Hypocrisy and Integrity: Machiavelli, Rousseau, and the Ethics of Politics.* Chicago: The University of Chicago Press.

Grimsley, R. 1968. *Rousseau and the Religious Quest.* London: Oxford University Press.

Hampsher-Monk, I. 1995. "Rousseau and Totalitarianism – with Hindsight?" In *Rousseau and Liberty.* See Wokler, 1995.

Hartle, A. 1983. *The Modern Self in Rousseau's Confessions: A Reply to St. Augustine.* Notre Dame, IN: University of Notre Dame Press.

Hirschman, A.O. 1977. *The Passions and the Interests: Political Arguments for Capitalism before Its Triumph.* Princeton, NJ: Princeton University Press.

Hobbes, T. 1985. *Leviathan.* Edited by C.B. Macpherson. New York: Penguin Books.

———. 1993. "The Citizen: Philosophical Rudiments Concerning Government and Society." In *Man and Citizen* (*De Homine and De Cive*). Edited by B. Gert. Indianapolis: Hackett.

Holmes, S. 1989. "The Permanent Structure of Antiliberal Thought." In *Liberalism and the Moral Life.* See Rosenblum, 1989.

Horowitz, A. 1987. *Rousseau, Nature, and History.* Toronto: University of Toronto Press.

Hulliung, M. 1994. *The Autocritique of Enlightenment: Rousseau and the Philosophes.* Cambridge, MA: Harvard University Press.

Jardin, A. 1988. *Tocqueville: A Biography.* Translated by L. Davis with R. Hemenway. Baltimore, MD: Johns Hopkins University Press.

Jouvenel, B. de. 1961–62. "Rousseau the Pessimistic Evolutionist." *Yale French Studies* 28: 83–96.

Kant, I. 1963. "Conjectural Beginnings of Human History." Translated by E.L. Fackenheim. In *On History.* Edited by L.W. Beck. New York: Macmillan.

Kautz, Steven. 1995. *Liberalism and Community.* Ithaca, NY: Cornell University Press.

———. 1997. "Privacy and Community." In *The Legacy of Rousseau.* See Orwin and Tarcov, ed. 1997.

Kelly, C. 1987. *Rousseau's Exemplary Life: The Confessions as Political Philosophy.* Ithaca, NY: Cornell University Press.

———. 2003. *Rousseau as Author: Consecrating One's Life to Truth.* Chicago: The University of Chicago Press.

Kelly, G.A. 2001. "A General Overview." In *The Cambridge Companion to Rousseau.* See Riley, 2001.

Keohane, N. 1978. "The 'Masterpiece of Policy in Our Century': Rousseau on the Morality of the Enlightenment." *Political Theory* 6(4): 457–84.

Koritansky, J.C. 1986. *Alexis de Tocqueville and the New Science of Politics.* Durham, NC: Carolina Academic Press.

Lanson, G. 1912. "L'unité de la pensee de Jean-Jacques Rousseau." *Annales de la Société Jean-Jacques Rousseau* 8: 1–32.

Lawler, P.A. 1993. *The Restless Mind: Alexis de Tocqueville on the Origin and Perpetuation of Human Liberty.* Lanham, MD: Rowman and Littlefield.

Lehman, E.W., ed. 2000. *Autonomy and Order: A Communitarian Anthology.* Lanham, MD: Rowman and Littlefield.

Lovejoy, A. 1959. "Buffon and the Problem of Species." In *Forerunners of Darwin.* Edited by B. Glass, O. Temkin, and W.L. Strauss, Jr. Baltimore, MD: Johns Hopkins University Press.

———. 1948. "The Supposed Primitivism of Rousseau's *Discourse on Inequality.*" In *Essays in the History of Ideas.* Baltimore, MD: Johns Hopkins University Press.

Machiavelli, N. 1998. *The Prince.* 2nd ed. Translated by H.C. Mansfield. Chicago: The University of Chicago Press.

Manent, Pierre. 1996. *Tocqueville and the Nature of Democracy.* Translated by J. Waggoner. Lanham, MD: Rowman and Littlefield.

Marks, J. 2002. "Who Lost Nature? Rousseau and Rousseauism." *Polity* 35: 479–502.

Marshall, T. 1980. "Rousseau and the Enlightenment." In *Trent Rousseau Papers/ Études Rousseau-Trente.* Edited by J. MacAdam, M. Neumann, and G. LaFrance. Ottawa: University of Ottawa Press.

Mason, J.H. 1997. "Originality: Moral Good, Private Vice, Or Self-Enchantment." In *Jean-Jacques Rousseau and the Sources of the Self.* See O'Hagan, 1997.

Masters, R. 1968. *The Political Philosophy of Rousseau.* Princeton, NJ: Princeton University Press.

———. 1997. "Rousseau and the Rediscovery of Human Nature." In *The Legacy of Rousseau.* See Orwin and Tarcov, 1997.

McWilliams, W.C. 1973. *The Idea of Fraternity in America.* Berkeley: University of California Press.

Meier, H. 1988–9. "The *Discourse on the Origin and the Foundation of Inequality Among Men*: On the Intention of Rousseau's Most Philosophical Work." *Interpretation* 16: 211–27.

Melzer, Arthur. 1990. *The Natural Goodness of Man: On the System of Rousseau's Thought.* Chicago: The University of Chicago Press.

———. 1996. "The Origin of the Counter-Enlightenment: Rousseau and the New Religion of Sincerity," *American Political Science Review* 90: 1018–33.

———. 1997. "Rousseau and the Modern Cult of Sincerity." In *The Legacy of Rousseau.* See Orwin and Tarcov, 1997.

Miller, J. 1984. *Rousseau: Dreamer of Democracy.* New Haven, CT: Yale University Press.

Moran, F. III. 1995. "Of Pongos and Men: *Orangs-Outang* in Rousseau's *Discourse on Inequality.*" *The Review of Politics* 57: 641–64.

Morgan, M.L. 1994. "Religion, History and Moral Discourse." In *Philosophy in an Age of Pluralism: The Philosophy of Charles Taylor in Question.* See Tully, 1994.

Morgenstern, M. 1996. *Rousseau and the Politics of Ambiguity: Self, Culture, and Society.* University Park: The Pennsylvania State University Press.

O'Hagan, T., ed. 1997. *Jean-Jacques Rousseau and the Sources of the Self.* Aldershot: Avebury.

Olafson, F.A. 1994. "Comments on *Sources of the Self* by Charles Taylor." *Philosophy and Phenomenological Research,* 54(1): 191–96.

Orwin, C. 1997. "Rousseau and the Discovery of Political Compassion." In *The Legacy of Rousseau.* See Orwin and Tarcov, 1997.

———. 1998. "Rousseau's Socratism." *Journal of Politics* 60(1).

———. 2000a. "Rousseau Between Two Liberalisms: His Critique of the Older Liberalism and His Contribution to the Newer One." In *The Liberal Tradition in Focus.* Edited by J.C. Espada, M.F. Plattner, and A. Wolfson. Lanham, MD: Lexington Books.

———. 2000b. "Rousseau on the Sources of Ethics." In *Instilling Ethics.* Edited by Norma Thompson. Lanham: Rowman and Littlefield.

Orwin, C. and N. Tarcov, eds. 1997. *The Legacy of Rousseau.* Chicago: The University of Chicago Press.

Parry, G. 1995. "Thinking One's Own Thoughts: Autonomy and the Citizen." In *Rousseau and Liberty.* See Wokler, 1995.

Pippin, Robert. 1991. "Hegel, Ethical Reasons, Kantian Rejoinders." *Philosophical Topics* 19(2): 99–132.

———. 1992. "The Modern World of Leo Strauss." *Political Theory* 20(3): 448–72.

Plattner, M. 1979. *Rousseau's State of Nature: An Interpretation of the Discourse on Inequality.* De Kalb: Northern Illinois University Press.

Rahe, P. 1994a. *Republics Ancient & Modern, Volume I: The Ancien Régime in Classical Greece.* Chapel Hill: University of North Carolina Press.

———. 1994. *Republics Ancient & Modern, Volume II: New Modes Orders in Early Modern Political Thought.* Chapel Hill: University of North Carolina Press.

Rapaczynski, A. 1987. *Nature and Politics. Liberalism in the Philosophies of Hobbes, Locke, and Rousseau.* Ithaca, NY: Cornell University Press.

Reisert, J.R. 2000. "Authenticity, Justice, and Virtue in Taylor and Rousseau." *Polity* 33(2): 305–30.

———. 2003. *Jean-Jacques Rousseau: A Friend of Virtue.* Ithaca, NY: Cornell University Press.

Richter, M. 1995. "Rousseau and Tocqueville on Democratic Legitimacy and Illegitimacy." In *Rousseau and Liberty.* See Wokler, 1995.

Riley, P., ed. 2001. *The Cambridge Companion to Rousseau.* Cambridge: Cambridge University Press.

Rorty, R. 1994. "Taylor on Self-Celebration and Gratitude." *Philosophy and Phenomenological Research* 54(1): 197–201.

Rosenberg, A. 1992. "Eighteenth century theories of generation and the birth and development of Rousseau's natural man." In *Rousseau and the Eighteenth Century: Essays in Memory of R. A. Leigh.* Edited by M. Hobson, J.T.A. Leigh, and R. Wokler. Oxford: The Voltaire Foundation.

Rosenblum, Nancy L., ed. 1989a. *Liberalism and the Moral Life.* Cambridge, MA: Harvard University Press.

———. 1989b. "Pluralism and Self-Defense." In *Liberalism and the Moral Life.* See Rosenblum, 1989a.

Rousseau, J.-J. 1953. *Constitutional Project for Corsica.* In *Political Writings.* Translated and Edited by F. Watkins. Madison: University of Wisconsin Press.

———. 1959–95. *Oeuvres Complètes.* Volumes 1–5. Edited by B. Gagnebin and M. Raymond. Gallimard: Bibliothèque de la Pléiade.

———. 1960. *Politics and the Arts: Letter to M. D'Alembert on the Theatre.* Translated by A. Bloom. Ithaca, NY: Cornell University Press.

———. 1978. *On the Social Contract with Geneva Manuscript and Political Economy.* Edited by R.D. Masters. Translated by J.R. Masters. New York: St. Martin's Press.

———. 1979. *Emile, or on Education.* Translated by A. Bloom. New York: Basic Books.

———. 1986. *The First and Second Discourses Together with the Replies to Critics and Essay on the Origin of Languages.* Translated by V. Gourevitch. New York: Harper & Row.

———. 1990. *Rousseau, Judge of Jean-Jacques.* Translated by J. Bush, R.D. Masters, and C. Kelly. Volume 1 of the *Collected Writings of Rousseau.* Edited by C. Kelly and R.D. Masters. Hanover: University Press of New England.

———. 1992. *Discourse on the Origins of Inequality (Second Discourse), Polemics, and Political Economy.* Translated by J.R. Bush, R.D. Masters, C. Kelly, and T. Marshall, Volume 3 of the *Collected Writings of Rousseau.* Edited by R.D. Masters and C. Kelly. Hanover: University Press of New England.

———. 1997a. *Julie, or the New Heloise: Letters of Two Lovers Who Live in a Small Town at the Foot of the Alps.* Translated and Annotated by P. Stewart and J. Vaché. Volume 6 of the *Collected Writings of Rousseau.* Edited by C. Kelly and R.D. Masters. Hanover: University Press of New England.

———. 1997b. *The Social Contract and Other Later Political Writings.* Translated and Edited by V. Gourevitch. Cambridge: Cambridge University Press.

Sandel, M. 1982. *Liberalism and the Limits of Justice.* Cambridge: Cambridge University Press.

———. 1996. *Democracy's Discontent: America in Search of a Public Philosophy.* Cambridge, MA: Harvard University Press.

Schoolman, M. 1994. Series Introduction to *Jean-Jacques Rousseau: The Politics of the Ordinary.* See Strong, 1994.

Schor, J.B. 1998. *The Overspent American: Upscaling, Downshifting, and the New Consumer.* New York: Basic Books.

Scott, J. 1992. "The Theodicy of the *Second Discourse*: the "Pure State of Nature" and Rousseau's Political Thought." *American Political Science Review* 86(3): 696–711.

Schwartz, J. 1984. *The Sexual Politics of Jean-Jacques Rousseau.* Chicago: The University of Chicago Press.

Shklar, J. 1969. *Men and Citizens: A Study of Rousseau's Social Theory.* Cambridge: Cambridge University Press.

———. 1989. "The Liberalism of Fear." In *Liberalism and the Moral Life.* See Rosenblum, 1989a.

Skinner, Q. 1994. "Modernity and Disenchantment: Some Historical Reflections." In *Philosophy in an Age of Pluralism: The Philosophy of Charles Taylor in Question.* See Tully, 1994.

Smith, J.A. 2002. "Natural Happiness, Sensation, and Infancy in Rousseau's *Emile.*" *Polity* (25):1: 94–122.

Spink, J. 1980. "Rousseau and the problems of composition." In *Reappraisals of Rousseau: Studies in Honor of R.A. Leigh.* Edited by S. Harvey, M. Hobson, D. Kelley, and S.S.B. Taylor. Manchester: Manchester University Press.

Starobinski, J. 1988. *Jean Jacques Rousseau: Transparency and Obstruction.* Translated by A. Goldhammer. Chicago: The University of Chicago Press.

Strauss, L. 1947. "On the Intention of Rousseau." *Social Research* 14 (4): 455–87.

———. 1953. *Natural Right and History*. Chicago: The University of Chicago Press.

Strong, T. 1994. *Jean-Jacques Rousseau: The Politics of the Ordinary*. Thousand Oaks, CA: Sage Publications.

———. 2000. "Seeing Differently and Seeing Further: Rousseau and Tocqueville." In *Friends and Citizens: Essays in Honor of Wilson Carey McWilliams*. Edited by P.D. Bathory and N.L. Schwartz. Lanham, MD: Rowman and Littlefield.

Talmon, J.L. 1952. *The Rise of Totalitarian Democracy*. Boston: Beacon Press.

Tarcov, N. 1984. *Locke's Education for Liberty*. Chicago: The University of Chicago Press.

Taylor, C. 1985. *Philosophy and the Human Sciences: Philosophical Papers, Volume 2*. Cambridge: Cambridge University Press

———. 1989a. *Sources of the Self: The Making of the Modern Identity*. Cambridge, MA: Harvard University Press.

———. 1989b. "Cross-Purposes: The Liberal-Communitarian Debate." In *Liberalism and the Moral Life*. See Rosenblum, 1989a.

———. 1991. *The Ethics of Authenticity*. Cambridge, MA: Harvard University Press.

———. 1994a. *Multiculturalism: Examining the Politics of Recognition*. Edited by A. Gutmann. Princeton, NJ: Princeton University Press.

———. 1994b. "Reply and Rearticulation." In *Philosophy in an Age of Pluralism: The Philosophy of Charles Taylor in Question*. See Tully, 1994.

———. 1994c. "Reply to Commentators." *Philosophy and Phenomenological Research* 54(1): 203–13.

———. 1995. "Lichtung or Lebensform: Parallels between Heidegger and Wittgenstein." In *Philosophical Arguments*. Edited by C. Taylor. Cambridge, MA: Harvard University Press.

Tocqueville, A. de. 1969. *Democracy in America*. Translated by George Lawrence. Edited by J.P. Mayer. Garden City, NY: Doubleday & Co.

Todorov, T. 2001. *Frail Happiness: An Essay on Rousseau*. Translated by J.T. Scott and R.D. Zaretsky. University Park: The Pennsylvania State University Press.

Tuck, R. 1994. "Rights and Pluralism." In *Philosophy in an Age of Pluralism: The Philosophy of Charles Taylor in Question*. See Tully, 1994.

Tully, J., ed. 1994. *Philosophy in an Age of Pluralism: The Philosophy of Charles Taylor in Question*. Cambridge: Cambridge University Press.

Velkley, R. 1989. *Freedom and the End of Reason*. Chicago: The University of Chicago Press.

——— 2002. *Being After Rousseau: Philosophy and Culture in Question*. Chicago: The University of Chicago Press.

Wahl, J. 1955. "La bipolarité de Rousseau." In *Annales de la société de Jean-Jacques Rousseau* 33. Geneva: Juillian.

Weil, E. 1952. "Jean-Jacques Rousseau et sa Politique." *Critique* 56: 4–28.

Weintraub, K.J. 1978. *The Value of the Individual: Self and Circumstance in Autobiography*. Chicago: The University of Chicago Press.

Weiss, P.A. 1993. *Gendered Community: Rousseau, Sex, and Politics*. New York: New York University Press.

Wingrove, E. 2000. *Rousseau's Republican Romance*. Princeton, NJ: Princeton University Press.

Wokler, R. 1995a. *Rousseau.* Oxford: Oxford University Press.

———, ed. 1995b. *Rousseau and Liberty.* Manchester: Manchester University Press.

Wolfe, A. 2001. *Moral Freedom: The Search for Virtue in a World of Choice.* New York: W.W. Norton & Company.

Wootton, D., ed. 1996. *Modern Political Thought: Readings from Machiavelli to Nietzsche.* Indianapolis: Hackett.

Wright, E. 1929. *The Meaning of Rousseau.* London: Oxford University Press.

Wrong, D. 2000. "Communitarianism, Nature, and the Spirit of the Times." In *Autonomy and Order: A Communitarian Anthology.* See Lehman, 2000.

Index